MULTINATIONAL MANAGERS

AND

HOST GOVERNMENT INTERACTIONS

MULTINATIONAL MANAGERS AND
DEVELOPING COUNTRY CONCERNS

Lee A. Tavis, series editor

*Multinational Managers and Poverty
in the Third World*, 1982

Multinational Managers
and
Host Government Interactions

LEE A. TAVIS, Editor

University of Notre Dame Press
Notre Dame, Indiana

Library of Congress Cataloging-in-Publication Data

Multinational managers and host government
interactions.

1. International business enterprises — Social
aspects — Developing countries.   I. Tavis, Lee A.
HD2932.M847   1987   658.4'08'091724   86-40590
ISBN 0-268-01364-0

TO TOM AND TIM

Contents

Foreword

In the eight years since this seminar first convened, I have been confirmed in the original idea that led me to cheer its inception. I am still more than convinced that the multinational corporation, properly run and properly oriented, can be a greater engine of development than most governments. Multinational corporations can provide capital, which every developing country needs, and they have the flexibility to direct it toward specific projects. They are adept at judging the economic potential of an area to decide what can or cannot be produced successfully there. Once something is produced, they can identify and reach the appropriate market anywhere in the world. Moreover, multinationals are great educators. In this country they spend $40 billion on the education of their people and many of them spend additional sums abroad. Finally, these corporations have an extraordinary capacity for transferring the science and technology needed for development.

It is easier to club multinationals than to encourage and praise them or to even analyze them from a fair and honest perspective. It is foolish to automatically say that they are evil or corrupt or exploitative — a terribly bad influence in this world. I would much rather say that if they can be encouraged to bring their unique qualities and potentialities to developmental tasks, we might be able to create a better world.

I like to think that a multinational company could come into a country with many unemployed people — in Latin America or Africa or the Orient — and do what its government cannot: create jobs by the thousands, create the conditions for doing something successfully, create a world market for the product. The company could do this on a ten- or twenty-year contract for a reasonably good fee, with the contract renewal subject to the judgment that its behavior in the country was responsible. Of course, such success would depend totally on the company's positive relationship with the government. That interaction between the multinational corporation and host government in all its contexts—religious, cultural, and legal—is explored in this volume.

There are no simple answers. We are in a very messy, very difficult world where the little people are ground down and too often overwhelmed with military power, where violence and torture are taken as normal procedure for getting something done. For this world to become more just, we have to use every mechanism we possess that will help the Third World improve its situation. There is hope for the Third World, and indeed for ourselves, if somehow we are creative enough to realize that peace is the work of justice and justice is a thing to which multinationals as well as governments can dedicate themselves.

If there is anything that characterizes the participants of this seminar, coming as they do from different countries, different cultures, with different languages, philosophies, and theologies, it is that they all share a hunger for justice.

A university's greatest glory is that it is one of the few places left on earth where people can disagree without being disagreeable. A group like this is replete with ideas. Some may contradict others, but that doesn't matter. Universities are built on this attrition of competing ideas; truth emerges from the clash. I thank God for these differences. From such disagreement, we can discover a truth than can sustain the differences and move forward. Through the interaction of various ideas of world development, we will come up with the right ones.

I have seen, over the past several years, the wonderful people who have come to this university, the great ideas that have been circulated and discussed. I have been really grateful for the publications that have emerged—publications that I think have given heart to people by letting them know that somewhere on earth some people are talking for their good, for their future, and ultimately for justice.

Rev. Theodore M. Hesburgh, C.S.C.
The University of Notre Dame

Preface

This volume addresses the question of how the involvement of multinational firms in Latin American, Asian, and African societies can be worked out in conjunction with host governments. The potential contributions of multinationals are especially needed at the present time. The human skills, technology, and capital provided by these firms are essential as we attempt to work our way out of the debt crisis in a period of sluggish economic recovery, agricultural famine, and persistent population growth.

While enhancing development is primarily the responsibility of host governments, multinationals play a central role in the process. Their presence enhances productivity and spurs economic growth. Enhanced productivity serves the wealth-related goals of the multinational as well as the economic needs—tax revenues, employment, and potential balance of payments effects—for the host government. Alternatively, national governments have a much broader range of social and developmental objectives and find the multinational with its size and sophistication to be a delimiting factor on their freedom to pursue many of these broader goals. There are thus areas of goal congruence as well as divergence of interest between the purpose of the firm and those of the host country. The local multinational subsidiary, as a component of the local private business sector and citizen of the host country while simultaneously an element of the multinational organization, can be pulled in conflicting directions.

There are many examples where multinational subsidiaries and host governments have worked together to their mutual advantage. There are others, however, where multinationals and nation-states have clashed to their joint disadvantage. In others, a close association between multinational managers and governmental officials has led to extortion and bribery. The local employees, suppliers, and the poor are too often the big losers in these negative sum games. Thus, collaboration must be approached with great care.

We need to think through, and know more about, this interaction. How does the process work? Does it result in discrimination?
Under what conditions is the potential gain high enough to warrant
the risk undertaken by both the private sector and the nation-state
in collaborative efforts? When should it be avoided? These are questions to which this volume is addressed.

This is the second volume reporting on the work of the "Notre
Dame Program on Multinational Corporations and Third World
Development." The first volume analyzed the impact of multinationals
in the Third World from different perspectives. The papers and discussions reported in both volumes are taken from the workshops and field
research sponsored by the program. In existence since 1978, the program annually brings together diverse groups of multinational managers, religious activists, faculty from across the university, governmental
officials, and others involved in development to discuss some dimension of the multinational presence in the poorer countries of Africa,
Asia, and Latin America. The analytical process is initiated with a planning workshop where the issues are analyzed on a conceptual basis
and field research is planned. The field research is then commissioned
among seminar participants and outside experts. The third step is an
evaluation, in which the seminar participants reassemble to analyze
results of the field research.

The planning workshop for our study of the multinational corporate interaction with host governments was held in the Republic of
Panama in January 1985. During the following year, field research teams
interviewed multinational executives, host country entrepreneurs, and
governmental officials in Korea and Mexico. The evaluation workshop
was held at Notre Dame in March 1986. The materials in this volume
are drawn from the workshop papers and discussions, the reports of
the field research teams, and the evaluation of research findings.

The nature of our seminar discussion and potential contribution
has changed since the initiation of the program in 1978. In the early
years, discussion was focused on the controversy over the multinational
corporate presence in the Third World. The diversity of worldviews
represented among the seminar participants, and their willingness to
listen to one another, led to enhanced insight into that debate as
reported in volume 1. The present volume represents a shift in focus.
At this time, the concern is how to rekindle development in those coun-

tries given the constraint of the debt overhang, and how multinationals can best fit into that process.

Development will not be rekindled without the participation of multinational corporations. The effectiveness of their participation will, of course, be vastly enhanced if they can work in collaboration, rather than conflict, with host governments. This volume analyzes the factors that influence the interaction between multinational managers and their host government counterparts, within the confines of the many other groups involved in issues of multinational presence. Our purpose is to aid the managers of multinational corporations and banks in assessing the nature of this interaction. Also, we trust that host government officials might reevaluate their process of regulating the multinationals in light of our findings.

The book is divided into six parts:

Part 1 describes the role of multinational firms in the Third World. Drawing from the first volume in this series, as well as the work reported here, it discusses the involvement of multinationals in host societies and how that involvement is shaped by host governments.

In Part 2, the economic role of the multinational and how it is regulated is overviewed. A Third World governmental official outlines what host governments want from multinationals; the unique economic structure of Latin America and how multinationals fit these stuctures is outlined; the contribution of multinationals to economic development and how it should be regulated is debated.

Part 3 shifts to the cultural context of the interaction. Our workshop discussions and field research continually reinforced the need to better understand the cultural components which influence the objectives of the institutions as well as the behavior of the managers and officials. The social doctrine of the Catholic Church is compared to the non-institutionalized ancient Confucian tradition. The important differences between the common law of the United States and the civil law tradition of most Third World countries are analyzed. The religious and legal roots of bribery as they have evolved in the United States and been extended globally through the Foreign Corrupt Practices Act are explored.

Part 4 presents the results of our field research in Korea and Mexico. Given the close interaction of the many factors that impinge upon the multinational–host government relationship, it is necessary to analyze all of the factors in confluence.

Mexico and Korea were selected as two countries in similar circumstances that have gone about the regulation of multinationals in different ways. One panel compares and contrasts the two studies while a second addresses bribery in these specific contexts.

Part 5 presents a unique dimension of our discussions. Whereas virtually all of the concern about the multinational presence in the Third World is based on how the self-interest of the institutions is worked out, Part 5 addresses the moral responsibilities and requirements for collaboration.

In the concluding Part 6, the different ways of viewing the multinational–host government interface are analyzed and alternative multinational strategies evaluated.

Acknowledgments

A great many people and organizations have contributed to this volume. Credit for the insight shared in the following pages is due to the participants in the work sponsored by the Program on Multinational Corporations and Third World Development. A list of the participants is included at the end of this volume. Each has committed his or her time and effort to involve multinational corporations in helping ameliorate the conditions under which Third World peoples live. Participants have shared their views freely in the workshop discussions, presented papers, served as panelists and, when possible, participated in the field research. Given the diversity of the participant backgrounds and their involvement in so many different kinds of activities, few dimensions of the multinational corporate–host government interaction have gone unexamined.

Funding for the program activities and the publication of this volume have been provided by a grant from the Rockefeller Foundation and seventeen multinational corporations.

Aluminum Company of America
Caron International
Castle & Cooke, Inc.
Caterpillar Tractor Company
The Coca-Cola Company
Continental Illinois National
  Bank
CPC International, Inc.
General Mills, Inc.
W. R. Grace and Company

H. J. Heinz
Johnson & Johnson
Mobil Oil Corporation
Mine Safety Appliances
  International Company
Pfizer International, Inc.
Ralston Purina Company
Smith Kline Beckman
  Corporation
Texaco, Inc.

These organizations have funded the program with no attempt to influence the direction of the research or the workshop evaluation of the field findings. Neither the Rockefeller Foundation nor the supporting multinational corporations necessarily endorse the material presented here.

Others have contributed by editing papers, panel comments, and discussion summaries: Diane Wilson, Tom Tavis, and Carol Roos. Driss Maachouk was very helpful in tracking down elusive data. Special credit and thanks go to Jule Poirier. She coordinated the workshops, demonstrated great patience and skill in typing and retyping the manuscript, and participated in the editing.

PART I

The Role of Multinational Corporations in the Third World

LEE A. TAVIS*

The past decade has been a tumultuous time for countries in Africa, Asia, and Latin America, particularly for those in the process of rapid industrialization, as well as for the multinational corporations operating there.[1] The progress in the 1960s and 1970s toward sustained economic development in the Third World has, for most of these countries, given way to austerity and stagnation. As integral components of those national systems and the key economic link between the First and Third Worlds, multinationals are part of the present circumstances and must be a major component of any long-term solution. In this process, the multinational interaction with host governments will be the critical nexus which determines the future patterns of corporate involvement in those countries and the resulting benefits or penalties for both.

The changes in Third World conditions are reflected in the nature of the discussion about the developmental role of multinational firms. An increasing number of observers are recognizing the potential contribution of multinationals to the development process, especially in producing and marketing nontraditional exports and in facilitating the growth of a national research and development capacity. The shrillness of the challenge to the presence of multinationals and the calls from

*Lee A. Tavis is the C. R. Smith Professor of Business Administration and director of the Program on Multinational Corporations and Third World Development at the University of Notre Dame.

1

religious activists, host governments, and the United Nations to contain the perceived power of multinationals vis-à-vis host countries has diminished — in part, paradoxically, because host governments have gained confidence in their ability to defend national interests through more calibrated systems of monitoring and control, and, in part, because multinationals have begun more explicitly to recognize their role as good corporate citizens.

The determination on the part of Third World governments to control for the sake of control is thus, albeit slowly, giving way to a determination to use multinationals as a means of dealing with their present development cusp. The international financial community, too, is attempting to incorporate multinational manufacturing corporations as a central component of plans to ameliorate the debt crisis.

At the same time, from the firms' viewpoint, the pressures for withdrawal from the Third World are mounting. Host country domestic markets are not growing at the rate they were, the price of entering or staying in a domestic market is increasing as host governments push for the export of local production. Local financial resources are gone. Economic and political risks have increased. With the projection of a decade of low returns and high risks, Third World countries are far less interesting than they were five years ago. Multinational managers are reassessing their Third World exposure, their corporate strategies, and their ability to direct these global organizations in desired new directions.

From a global perspective it is imperative that the contribution of multinational corporations to Third World host countries be enhanced. This can only occur in a favorable investment climate.

The renewed role of the multinational in development will be worked out on a case-by-case basis between many firms and many governments. We need to think about the ways that the corporations and governments can interact to reach their objectives simultaneously. The goal of this volume is to help in better understanding how that interaction takes place — how the role of the multinational is defined through the interaction with institutions and individuals in the Third World.

As background for that discussion, this introductory paper will consider the position of the multinational firm as a key link between the First and Third Worlds, and analyze how the actions of the firm in those countries are shaped by host governments.

The Multinational Spanning Function

The global span of the multinational corporation contrasts with the geographic and political limits of nation-states. While each country is economically, politically, and socially discrete, the multinational is organizationally a single system, directly tying diverse national units one to the other, within and between countries.

The spanning function of the multinational corporation is diagramed in chart 1.

CHART I
The National Spanning Function
of Multinational Corporations

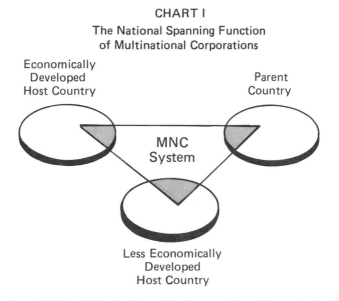

Source: Lee A. Tavis and Roy L. Crum, "Performance-Based Strategies for MNC Portfolio Balancing," *Columbia Journal of World Business*, 19 (no. 2, Summer 1984): pp. 85–94.

The triangle represents a multinational organization; the circles, nation-states. The shaded intersection between the triangle and each circle represents the activities of the multinational in that country or, organizationally, its subsidiary. Technically, each local subsidiary is a resident of the nation-state, subject to its sovereign power, and bearing the responsibility of a legal citizen in that society. Each subsidiary is, simultaneously, a component of the multinational system. It is an integral part of the multinational's global financial, production, and marketing systems. No matter how decentralized the organization, each subsidiary is linked to the firm through its planning, information, and control networks.

The multinational subsidiary is thus unique as an integral element of a specific national system and, at the same time, as an element of the multinational organization. Both the nation-state and the multinational organization make demands on their common element, demands that depend on the objectives pursued by each system and the ability of each to control its elements. Sometimes the objectives of the multinational and the nation-state coincide, sometimes they pull in opposite directions. When systemic objectives diverge, the subsidiary is stretched between the sovereign power of the nation-state and the economic power of the multinational.

Nation-states differ on all conceivable measures. Each is at a different stage in its economic development with its unique political structure and govermental bureaucracy. The sophistication of local institutions (the ability to process information and represent the best interests of its members) varies greatly among countries. The role of the private sector is unique as is the efficiency of the markets. Interactions between institutions and individuals are dominated by national cultures. Within each host country, the multinational subsidiary must somehow find the economic opportunities, live within the constraints of that society, and meet complex sets of objectives.

That this interaction yield efficient and effective results is especially important in the Third World. It is in those countries where the needs are so great and where the skills and resources available through the multinational system can have the greatest incremental effect. It is also in those countries where product and financial markets are grossly inefficient; where governmentally owned parastatals represent large shares of the productive assets; where the determination, if not the capability, of local governments to control the private business sector is great; where governments see the interdependence caused by the multinational linkage as dependency; and where culturally based barriers to communications between host governments and multinationals can be almost insurmountable.

The multinational manager must somehow manage the firm's spanning function between the First and Third World in a way that serves both the multinational corporation and Third World countries. Individual subsidiaries must fit the characteristics of each country. Still, a multinational subsidiary that fits imperceptibly into the local community, isolated from the multinational organization and not drawing on the global resources of the firm, does not introduce skills and resources locally to the benefit of either the firm or the host country. Alternatively, a foreign enclave isolated from the local community does not draw on local resources for the benefit of the firm nor does it optimize its contributions to the local society. Multinational managers must strike a delicate balance between uniform policies, programs, and patterns of management that apply across the organization set against the need to conform to the specific conditions of each country and culture.

The role of the firm in each country will be worked out in conjunction with host governments. To better understand the multinational corporate–host government interaction, this introductory paper will first remind us of the differences among countries, particularly those in the First and Third World, and how the multinational presence can affect the less-developed parts of our globe, before turning to the demands and constraints imposed on the firm's activities by the various groups that shape its environment — its stakeholders. We conclude with the most critical Third World stakeholder, the host government.

North-South Economic Disparity

There are glaring economic disparities among the peoples of our world. All statistics reveal a chasm in standards of living between high-income and low-income countries. Table 1 compares population and

TABLE 1

Population and Gross National Product, 1980

COUNTRY CLASSIFICATION	POPULATION		GROSS NATIONAL PRODUCT			
	Millions	Percent of Total	Billions of Dollars	Percent of Total	Dollars Per Capita	Percent of High Income
High-Income	733	19	7,766	79	10,595	100
Middle-Income						
oil importers	580	15	963	9.8	1,660	16
oil exporters	441	11	551	5.6	1,250	12
Low-Income	2,102	55	550	5.6	260	2.5
Total	3,856		9,830	100		

Source: The World Bank, *World Development Report, 1986* (Oxford University Press), p. 154.
See note 2 for enumeration of countries and classifications.

gross national product (GNP) for countries classified into four groups.[2] High-income countries (Group I) represent the developed countries of Europe, North America, and Asia plus high-income oil exporters. Middle-income countries are divided into oil importers (Group II) and oil exporters (Group III). Finally, the low-income countries are listed as Group IV at the bottom of the table.

The differences are striking. One fifth of the world's population is using four fifths of its resources as measured by the gross national product. Over half of the people on our globe, more than two billion, living in the low-income countries represent only 5.6 percent of the global GNP.

Are the people in the less-affluent countries making headway? The pattern of growth rates is mixed. Table 2 presents the GNP growth for the four income groups from 1965 through the first oil crisis in 1973, from then to the beginning of the austerity pressures in 1980, and to the most recent data available, 1985.

The period 1965–1973 was a good one for economic growth across the globe. In spite of continuing increases in population, per capita growth rates in the middle- and low-income countries were quite favorable, although less than the United Nations' targets. Following the first oil price shock in 1973, these countries held their own in spite of the slowdown that was triggered in the industrialized countries. The pattern in the last period, 1981–1985, demonstrates the vulnerability of middle-income countries and shows how oil prices, debt, interest rates, and high-income country recession began to take effect, especially for oil importers. The encouraging news is the recent growth among the mass of people in the low-income countries. As a group, these coun-

TABLE 2

Average Annual Growth Rates of Per Capita GNP

Country Classification	Annual Growth of GNP Per Capita (%)		
	1965–73	1973–80	1981–85
High-Income	3.9	1.2	.4
Middle-Income			
oil importers	4.6	3.1	− .3
oil exporters	4.6	3.4	−1.0
Low-Income	3.0	2.7	5.2

Source: The World Bank, *World Development Report, 1986* (Oxford University Press), p. 154.

tries achieved the highest GNP per capita growth rate for any classification in any period measured. With favorable agricultural conditions and a low population growth, China dominates the group with an average annual growth between 1981–85 of 8.2 percent. India managed a positive growth of 2.6 percent, its highest for the three periods measured, while the poor countries of Africa experienced their lowest with an average annual loss of 1.9 percent from 1981 through 1985. These favorable growth rates, however, are based on low starting points—an average GNP per capita in 1980 of $260 for all low-income countries with $290 for China and $240 for India.

In considering the quality of people's lives, other measures may be more meaningful. Indicators such as life expectancy, infant mortality, or literacy rates tell us much about how people live. These indicators have been combined by the Overseas Development Council into a Physical Quality of Life Index (PQLI).[3] PQLI figures are presented in table 3 for the same country groupings. Literacy rates and life expectancy are sharply different. While major strides have been made in infant mortality, it is staggering to comprehend that the chance of death under age one is almost six times greater in the low-income countries than in the high-income ones.

The poor in these countries are truly destitute. Robert McNamara described their plight as follows:

The word [poverty] itself has become almost incapable of communicating the harshness of the reality. Poverty at the absolute level—which

TABLE 3

Physical Quality of Life (PQLI) Statistics

Country Classification	PQLI (1981)	Infant Mortality Per 1,000 Live Births	Life Expectancy at Birth	Literacy Rate (%)
High-Income	95	17	74	97
Middle-Income				
oil importers	70	56	61	65
oil exporters	59	86	58	56
Low-Income	58	99	58	51

Source: Data taken from John W. Sewell, Richard E. Feinberg, and Valeriana Kallab, editors, *U.S. Foreign Policy and the Third World: Agenda 1985–86* (New Brunswick, New Jersey: Transaction Books, 1985). See note 3 for definition of terms.

is what literally hundreds of millions of men, women, and most particularly, children are suffering from in these countries—is life at the very margin of physical existence. The absolute poor are severely deprived human beings struggling to survive in a set of squalid and degraded circumstances almost beyond the power of our sophisticated imaginations and privileged circumstances to conceive.[4]

There are more hungry and malnourished people in the world today than ever before in history, and the number is growing. It is estimated that in 1980 as many as 800 million people in Africa, Latin America, and Asia (excluding China) were living in absolute poverty. For most of them, the economic growth of the 1960s and 1970s did not improve their circumstances.[5] As many as 70 pecent of the children in the Third World suffer from malnourishment and as many as 300 million people suffer from mental or physical retardation due to inadequate diets.[6]

At the same time, there is some basis for hope that significant improvement in the quality of life of the majority of the population can occur among low-income countries. China again stands out. In addition to its recent economic growth, China's PQLI has increased from an index of 71 measured in 1976 to an index of 75 in 1981. The Chinese experience attests to the importance of a social redeployment of resources in raising the well-being of a population.

In addition to the observed variation in living conditions, there are fundamental differences among people in the way they structure their societies. Culture lies at the core of these differences. There is a vast array of political and governmental structures, stability, and legitimacy. Economic structures exhibit the same variability. The distributions of income within Third World countries reflect the same pattern of severe discrepancy as that observed between the high-income and low-income countries.

Again, multinationals forge links between these very different countries and among the people within a country. Within Third World countries, multinationals have direct linkages through the products they produce, many flowing to consumers who cannot read; through their workers who are often drawn from urban slums or rural poverty; through the purchase of materials, components, and services from local suppliers. The secondary effects are great. Communities in short supply of physical and social infrastructure and managerial capability call upon the local multinational subsidiaries.[7]

The Developmental Influence of Multinationals

Due to organizational efficiency combined with global product sourcing and marketing structures, the multinational linkages are strong. Human, material, and financial resources flow across these linkages between the affluent North and the poor South, exerting a significant influence on host country development. This impact can be analyzed in three ways: (1) the local economic impact of a subsidiary in the host country, (2) the social results of the firm's presence in local communities, and (3) the net effect of the international economic structure of which multinationals are an inextricable component.[8]

The positive contributions have been well-documented. As Baer points out: "Rapid industrialization would have been almost impossible without the appearance of multinationals."[9] McGrath and de Avila support this view, "In large measure, it is the multinationals which have brought about the industrial growth of Latin America."[10]

The contribution most agreed upon by supporters and critics alike is the enhancement of local skills. In a study analyzing diverse sources ranging from capitalist to neo-Marxist, Francis and Manrique found that the diffusion of skills in Third World societies through the activities of multinational corporations was the single area of agreement.[11]

The view that multinationals increase local employment is generally, but not universally, supported.[12] The value of technology is still a contentious issue. There is no question that technology is transferred. The issue is whether the technology transferred is appropriate to the needs of the developing countries, whether research and development should be located in Third World countries, and whether the price for technology is too high.[13]

The net balance of payments effect is also the subject of a good deal of disagreement. At issue is whether the balance of payments can be set apart from the internal sector impact and how the international flows themselves would be measured.[14] One point is clear. The present debt situation in the Third World is leading to a flow of capital from the South to the North, including no little amount of capital flight from Third World investors. Given the imbalance outlined in the previous section, that flow is in the wrong direction.

The net influence of the multinational on local entrepreneurs is in an area where generalization is practically impossible. In the milieu of many multinationals interacting with many local entrepreneurs, within the unique private sectors in each country, one can find examples across the whole range, from the multinational destruction of indigenous entrepreneurs to the enhancement of their prosperity.

An area where the multinational linkages between First and Third World countries have become increasingly important is the access to developed country markets. Multinationals have the information and the marketing channels through which Third World host governments can push exports. As development strategies turn to a greater concern for foreign exchange and a stronger emphasis on exports, this dimension of the multinational spanning function becomes more critical.

On balance, most observers believe that the multinationals contribute to local economic development. The most stinging criticism of these firms is directed toward their participation in the international economic system and their involvement with the process of host country development.

The international economic system has not worked to diminish significantly the gap between the North and the South. Moreover, the quality of life for those at the bottom is just not improving at an acceptable rate. Multinationals are an inextricable component of the international economic system and, as a group, share the responsibility for its results. McGrath and de Avila state, "In the effort to evaluate multinationals operating in the Third World in general, or Latin America in particular, one must consider whether or not these corporations have helped increase the growing gap between the rich and the poor nations, and between the rich and the poor in the poorer nations. It is this increasing gap that leads to the accusation prevalent throughout much of Latin America, and so often expressed by religious leaders, that multinationals operate as part of an international system which exploits the dependence of the poor for the benefit of the rich."[15] Disagreement over the international economic structure and the function of multinationals as a component of that system is perhaps the least amenable to dialogue, and surely the most difficult to change.[16]

The third area of concern is the change in local societies associated with the presence of multinationals. The Western model of economic development in which U.S. multinationals participate is productivity- and market-driven. This approach to development often runs counter to traditional values.

The market focus raises the issues of basic values. It is charged that multinationals distort local patterns of consumption. They produce to meet the demands of the wealthy, thus serving and enhancing a materialistic consumerism while diverting resources from products that would serve the broader segments of society. A related charge is that multinationals, through their advertising message, manipulate the poor to switch their expenditures from essential products to status symbols.[17] An extension of this argument is that multinational corporations reinforce class structures.

The class structure criticism is an example of a charge against multinationals that is never joined. In this case, all of the discussion is on one side of the issue. Managers are seldom versed in class arguments and fail to see the connection between their activities and local class structures, or the importance of the issues.

Another "social" criticism is that multinationals contribute to the maldistribution of income in these countries. Francis argues that this is one of only two propositions of dependency theory that are easily defensible. He states the proposition as follows: "The current economic growth in less-developed countries is unevenly distributed among the sectors of the society. Because income distribution is so badly skewed, the poorer half of most societies is left relatively untouched by economic growth."[18] That income is maldistributed in these countries is clear; the participation of multinationals in that imbalance is less so.

Finally, the process of development itself is destructive of local cultures. Workers are specialized, regimentation is imposed in the workplace, promotion is based on achievement rather than ascriptive norms, women are employed, concentration of employment opportunities creates rural and urban slums.[19] Some multinationals are particularly sensitive to and capable of modifying local operations to fit the specific characteristics of different operating locations. Still, to fully conform would be to give up the economic contribution that the firm can bring to these communities.

In summary, multinational corporations are capable of great economic contributions to the Third World. One set of concerns is whether these local contributions in practice have been sufficient or whether the market-driven international economic order offsets these local advances. A more basic issue, from the host government's view, is whether the associated social change, the loss of national independence, and the destruction of local cultures are worth it.

The difference among countries and peoples, as well as the

strength of the multinational influence (positive or negative) provides leaven for the multinational manager's bread. Over the long term, the multinational corporate presence in Third World countries must contribute effectively and efficiently to those countries while, at the same time, meeting the firm's responsibility to First World, parent country constituents. The vast economic, political, and social differences among these countries lead to an unparalleled managerial challenge. There is a strategic question of how local subsidiaries can best fit the unique local environments on the one hand, offset against the need for the global standardization of managerial policies and practices on the other. How does the firm balance the resource flows between the affluent North and the poor South? Each corporate decision is subject to the constraints imposed by markets and governments and the pressures from others with a stake in the outcome of the firm's activities.

MULTINATIONAL STAKEHOLDERS: CONSTRAINTS, PRESSURES, POWER, AND RESPONSIBILITIES

The role of the multinational firm is worked out within the relative power of the many groups within each society who have a stake in the firm's activities. These groups can be diagramed as in chart 2. Each is demanding something of the firm, demands that cannot all be met. Constituents in relatively efficient markets are represented by that market power. Governments have the power of the sovereign. Some groups have been mandated responsibilities with inadequate capabilities or insufficient power to exercise, while others bind together to enhance their bargaining power. Some stakeholders are very effective in using the strength of the multinational linkages to create change in other countries.

Direct Constituents in the First and Third Worlds

The direct constituents of the multinational firm are diagramed at the top of chart 2. Firms with investments in the Third World deal in the financial, product, and labor markets of those countries as well as in the United States.

The corporate interface with those constituents who are market participants is dominated by the characteristics of the market. In the industrialized countries, owners and creditors trade in efficient financial markets. Equity and credit markets are competitive in structure and information flows freely. In the product markets, suppliers have alternative customers, and consumers have alternative products from which to choose. While not as efficient as the financial markets, most product markets exhibit competitive characteristics. This is not the case in the Third World. National markets are too often small and protected, particularly for countries pursuing a development policy of import substitution. Governmental technocrats take over market mechanisms thus further spreading already thin regulatory staffs and politicizing the marketplace. Governments invest heavily in productive assets, the so-called parastatals, which then pursue social as well as economic goals.

Constituents who participate in relatively competitive product or efficient financial markets are represented well in the power workings of the marketplace. There is, therefore, a vast difference between the

CHART 2
MNC Stakeholders

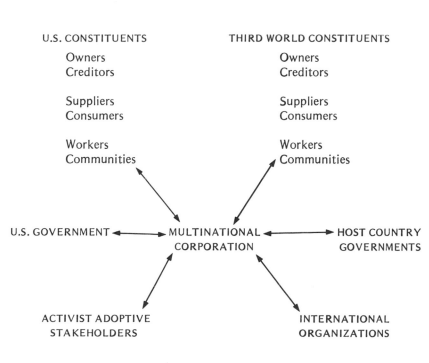

U.S. CONSTITUENTS

Owners
Creditors

Suppliers
Consumers

Workers
Communities

THIRD WORLD CONSTITUENTS

Owners
Creditors

Suppliers
Consumers

Workers
Communities

U.S. GOVERNMENT ⟷ MULTINATIONAL CORPORATION ⟷ HOST COUNTRY GOVERNMENTS

ACTIVIST ADOPTIVE STAKEHOLDERS

INTERNATIONAL ORGANIZATIONS

representation of constituents in the United States compared to those in the Third World. On a global basis, the efficiency of Northern markets pushes against the inefficiency of those in the South through the international economic system.

Labor markets are typically noncompetitive by social design. Unions are formed to enhance the relative bargaining power of the laborers. Under ideal circumstances, labor unions represent the best interest of their members and lead to optimal wages and working conditions. While U.S. unions may not meet this ideal, they are far more effective in serving their membership than are their counterparts in most Third World countries. In locations such as Chile or Korea, national governments legislate against unions and minimize their power. As with financial and product markets, effective organizations enhance the power of the stakeholders.

Partially as a result of this labor power imbalance, Third World laborers are, in some instances, paid less than their marginal product. Even though multinationals tend to pay at the top end of the local wage scales, wages there for the same contribution are less than in the developed countries, though, to be sure, the opportunity costs of labor tend to differ no less widely. The net result is a flow of resources from the Third to the First World.[20]

Local communities are examples of groups with vast differences in the capability or willingness to represent their members to the multinational corporation. Some are well-represented by municipal governments and other consumer organizations. Here again, there is a major difference between the relatively well-represented communities of the U.S. and those in the Third World. This is not to say that life in Third World communities is not well-structured. In a cultural sense, it is. Tight local interrelationships can be observed across rural villages and metropolitan slums. In the interaction with multinationals, however, local communities do not reflect their tight social organization.

U.S. Government

Our government extends the reach of United States regulation to the foreign operations of multinational firms. The United States has legislated its anti-trust laws to apply to multinationals operating in other countries. The Foreign Corrupt Practices Act is a dramatic example of this extraterritoriality. Beyond the extension of these regulatory requirements, the U.S. government has not missed the importance of multinational corporate linkages to other countries and uses multi-nationals as instruments of foreign policy. Caterpillar Tractor paid a heavy price when the executive branch required it to withdraw from intended participation in the Trans-Siberian Pipeline Project.

Adoptive Stakeholders

Adoptive stakeholders are those who choose to represent other stakeholders who are unable to represent themselves. These activists recognize the strength of the multinational linkages between the de-veloped and less-developed world, as well as the corporate vulnerabil-ity to U.S. public opinion. Activists use multinational corporations as levers to influence conditions in the poorer countries.[21] For exam-ple, a number of shareholder resolutions have been brought against multinational banks as a result of the debt crisis. Attempts to protect small indigenous farmers from cash-crop agriculture has led to con-tinuing pressure on multinational agribusinesses. A loose coalition of many religious and medical groups called INFACT mounted a boycott against Nestlé over its infant formula marketing in the Third World. In South Africa, the great clamor for divestment (the selling of shares) of U.S. companies doing business there, the existing boycott of Shell and the threat of other boycotts, the pressure on banks holding South African debt, and the calls for economic sanctions, all come from an attempt to represent black South Africans, whose rights are bounded by the laws of apartheid and who have no voice in their own future.

Activists can be viewed positively as sincerely trying to represent those who cannot represent themselves, to represent groups who are marginalized and defenseless against the pressure of international markets or unjust governments.[22] Surely these are the most worthy of motives. Alternatively, adoptive stakeholders can be seen as ideologues who see themselves as "defending the good and the poor against the evil and unscrupulous," and bringing them to "justice before the court of public opinion."[23]

However one views activists' motives, however unrealistic their demands may seem, or whether they appear to be acting from a general antagonism toward multinational corporations, their actions are based on an understanding of the close multinational ties between the pressure points in the United States and the desired result in the Third World.

Conflict between activists and managers is unfortunate. Issues too quickly become polarized and views entrenched. The ultimate goal on both sides as it relates to the Third World is the same — to improve the conditions under which those people live. Too often, the commitment and insight of managers who have worked in less-developed countries is overlooked. When early interaction or dialogue on issues between the groups who can do something about the issue ceases, the most fruitful time to approach the best solution is lost. Once politicized, those with knowledge of the circumstances as well as commitment to principle are too seldom heard.[24]

International Institutions

There are a host of international institutions concerned with the activities of the multinational firm. Given the position of multinationals in the international economy, almost any issue addressed by an international institution will involve these firms.

The activities of institutions such as the World Bank or the International Monetary Fund influence the economic conditions across the world within which the multinationals must operate. A major thrust of the United Nations and other international institutions has been directed toward codes of conduct for multinational corporations.

Pressure for codes began in the United Nations in the mid-1960s over the concern with multinational corporate power and the potential or reality of its misuse. Multinationals were viewed as the new sovereigns with the capability of dominating host governments. Early consideration of codes occurred in the United Nations Commission on Trade and Development and led to the United Nations Commission on Transnational Corporations. Topics included in the discussion were technology transfer, employment issues, transfer prices, and corrupt practices. At issue was whether the codes should be mandatory or voluntary, whether they should include state-owned enterprises, and what requirements should be placed on host governments.

Code initiators undertook an enormous task. They were trying to bring uniform guidelines to bear across vastly different cultures and to apply them to many different kinds of business firms. Early progress was made on voluntary guidelines for technology transfer and employment policies. There has been much less progress, or even activity, in the last decade. Recent inactivity may be a result of the dramatic increase in the capability of Third World governmental officials to regulate the multinational presence. It surely is a reflection of the changing conditions in the Third World.

In contrast to the United Nations, the International Chamber of Commerce (ICC) and the Organization for Economic Cooperation and Development (OECD) moved rapidly to adopt voluntary codes on multinational operations. These efforts were in response to the negative discussion in the U.N. and the possibility of very restrictive covenants in their codes. The ICC adopted "Guidelines for International Industry" in 1974. The OECD adopted "Guidelines for Multinational Enterprises" in 1976.[25]

These codes can serve a purpose. They provide a basis for specific discussion between governments, business, labor, and other groups. As they are thrashed out, they tend to create a uniformity of expectations. They can provide helpful guidelines to which multinational corporate management can point in their Third World activities. Alternatively, there is a natural evolution of these codes from discussions, to voluntary standards, to binding, although still vague, requirements.

Effective codes are still at some distance. In the meantime, the role of multinationals in the Third World will continue to be worked out between multinationals and host governments within the boundaries imposed by markets, other governments, and pressure groups.

HOST GOVERNMENT REGULATION OF MULTINATIONAL PRESENCE

Governments are unique in their stakeholder relationship with the multinational firms. Governments have the sovereign right and responsibility to regulate the private sector and its multinational component. In this process, the government regulates competitors and other stakeholders of the multinational firm. Governments are thus involved in the tradeoffs the multinational manager must make among the various stakeholders.

Goal Conflict and Balance of Power

Problems that arise as a result of the multinational subsidiary being a common element of the host country and of the multinational organization come to rest at this interface. When the goals of these two systems coincide, mutual efforts can enhance the outcome. In the case of goal conflict, resolution must be worked out.[26] In this interaction, the multinational has the power of an organization spreading beyond the geographic limits of the nation-state set against national sovereignty.

As the representative of the local society, the government has a range of economic, security, and social goals. Except for a few closed societies, governments pursue sustained economic growth. This serves the best interests of the people and helps to maintain the governments in power. For the internal sector, governments want economic advancement in terms of productivity, employment, and tax revenues. Some, but surely not all, seek a more equitable distribution of the fruits of that productivity. Most act to protect some sectors of societies, such as labor, from the unfettered workings of the marketplace. Externally, the host government wants foreign exchange and the independence to pursue its own developmental objectives.

The goals and objectives of the multinational organization are wealth-related. They are more uniform than those of the nation-state. The overarching goal is the optimization of the present value of future cash flows. Nested within this goal are market, production, and labor objectives. Although frequently accused of pursuing short-term results, normative corporate objectives are long-term.

The multinational corporation and the nation-state share a uniform subset of objectives. Local markets and the related multinational wealth grow with sustained economic development. Stable economic advancement increases multinational wealth by reducing risk while simultaneously enhancing the existing government's political position.

Other objectives conflict. Nation-states want the capability of locally developed technology. Multinationals want to centralize this activity globally. Host governments use political power to press for multinational exports from their country which may take the place of lower-cost sourcing from other countries. The relative importance of near-term and long-term will always be an issue. From the multinational perception, Third World countries tend to be high-risk investments, thus requiring high-discount rates with the resulting deemphasis on downstream cash flows. Nation-states see themselves as responsible and in control of the private sector, thus envisioning much lower discount rates and a greater sacrifice of near-term for long-term returns. Many multinational–host government conflicts can be traced to the difference in the time weighting of results.

There will always be a range of goal congruence to goal conflict between the host government and the multinational. These will be worked out between governmental officials and multinational managers within the contraints imposed by their many common stakeholders.

Given the differences in market efficiency and the push of efficient First World and international markets across multinational linkages against the less-efficient markets of the Third World, the existence of conflicting goals between the multinational and host governments, and the differences in geographic span, the outcome of the regulatory process is strongly influenced by the balance of negotiating power. The power balance between multinationals and host governments has been cycling over the past three decades. Initially it was young, inexperienced governmental officials facing a few sophisticated U.S. multinationals. By the early 1970s that had changed. Surging nationalism was matched by the negotiating skills of governmental officials, facing multinational ranks swelled by Japanese, Western Europeans, and many more U.S. firms seeking sources of supply and markets in the Third World. The present debt crisis is changing the power balance back to the multinational, but not necessarily the attitudes of host regulators.

Regulatory Issues

There are three basic issues in governmental regulation of multinational firms: the right to regulate, the ideal amount of regulation, and the ability to regulate. The right of the host government to regulate the private sector and the activities of the multinational is generally well-supported.[27] The extent of the controls that should optimally be imposed on the private sector is a matter of continuing political debate in all societies—capitalist, socialist, and even most of the communist countries. The balance resolved in each society is a structure within which the multinational must fit. The degree to which host governments are able to impose their wills on multinationals, although recognized as increasing, is still a matter of controversy.

Whatever the answer to the most desired amount and kind of regulatory control of the private sector, the manner and extent to which national wills are imposed on the multinational presence are worked out in the trenches. They are formed within the economic, bureaucratic, and legal structures of the host country as influenced by their religious and legal traditions interfacing with the multinational organization spanning more than one country, representing the Western culture, and often involving managers from those foreign cultures.

As background for our discussion of how the multinational presence in the Third World is worked out with host governments, we should consider the many regulatory approaches of Third World governments and the factors that influence their implementation.

On their side, host governments rely on a wide array of methods to shape the role of the private sector and of the multinational participation in that sector. Internal private sectors tend to be heavily regulated. As noted earlier, local product and financial markets are far from efficient.[28] Governments contribute to this inefficiency through policies such as tariff protection or reserving markets for local entrepreneurs. Then, having disrupted the market structure, these governments find it necessary to directly intervene in market mechanisms with techniques such as price controls to prevent firms from taking advantage of the inefficiencies. In labor legislation, many countries impose the full cost of unemployment benefits on the private sector in terms of high severance pay requirements. In attempts to limit urbanization, most Third World countries impose locational restrictions or incentives. In many sectors, governments enter directly into investment in productive assets, areas that would be reserved for private investment in the United States. This "state capitalism" is an especially important factor in Latin America.[29]

In addition to controls on the private sector, there are requirements directed specifically to multinationals. The United Nations Centre on Transnational Corporations monitors the experience of nation-states in applying these controls.[30] Host governments are particularly alert to investment requirements, since this is where they can exert influence on the multinational linkage that ties them to the international economic systems. Most countries have foreign direct investment laws, requiring the application and approval of new foreign direct investment as well as local expansions. Once in place, periodic reports enhance governmental monitoring. Increasingly, the same type of screening is placed on technology transfers.

A whole range of regulations controls the behavior of multinationals. In the internal sector, local content requirements or employment targets for nationals are commonplace. In the external sector, limits on profit and royalty remittances and control of transfer prices are an integral component of regulation as Third World countries struggle for foreign exchange. Many countries require a component or majority of local ownership. These policies vary considerably among countries as do their implementation among multinationals within a country.

Host governments thus have a wide range of legislative and regulatory controls upon which they can rely in defining the role of their private sectors and directing the activities of the multinational subsidiaries. And governmental officials, particularly in the newly developing countries, are getting better and better at it. As will be demonstrated in the Korean and Mexican field reports, however, the process of interaction itself is not easy to discern, and there are more exceptions than consistency in the way this regulation is carried out.[31]

Factors Influencing the Interaction

As this discussion suggests, the nature of the interaction between each multinational subsidiary and each country is the result of a complex set of factors. It takes place within the host country's unique economic, bureaucratic, and legal structures; it involves institutions that have many common stakeholders locally and internationally; it takes place among individuals from different cultures with different value systems.

Of the factors that impinge on the multinational–host government interaction, five are particularly important.

1. The attitudes of host governments toward foreign direct investment evolve from a nation's historical experience and the traditions of its people. Especially difficult for an outsider to understand, these attitudes are reflected in national objectives and what is demanded from the multinational. At base, religious traditions explain a great deal of a country's unique character over the long term, overarching the shorter term economic and political ebbs and flows.

    In Latin America, the religious tradition is institutionalized in the Catholic Church. The continuing evolution of Catholic social doctrine is of fundamental importance to multinationals. It reflects, and is reflected in, all segments of those societies. Of particular importance is its role in shaping governmental attitudes. Over time, one can expect a growing influence of this changing doctrine on political structures and governmental demands.[32]

In a country such as Korea, the Confucian tradition dominates the overall structure of society as well as personal interactions. Confucianism goes a long way toward explaining the sense of hierarchy and rigidity or orthodoxy throughout these societies and the tendency to centralize power.[33]

2. The role of law and judicial systems differ among countries. Many Third World countries, particularly those in Latin America, follow the Roman law tradition rather than our common law. In those countries, legal precedent is not worked out in the courts as in the United States.

   In Latin America, the gap between the law on the books and the law in practice can be vast. Legal standards tend to be ideals, not necessarily achievable. The role of judges, legal structures, and court practices are quite different. In those countries, it is particularly difficult to anticipate the legal constraints on corporate activities.[34]

   Confucian societies are based on the idea of nonconfrontation. The notion of law as a means of neutral confrontation between individual disputants, or between individuals and the state, is not well-developed. There are few lawyers in these countries and they tend to have a relatively low status among professional groups.[35] In Korea, the strength of the Confucian tradition dominates its legal system. Formal laws tend to be overridden by the moral force of interpersonal relationships. Litigation is socially unacceptable. When parties go to court, they both are perceived as having lost.[36]

3. The control of multinationals by Third World governments tends to be individualistic, on a case-by-case basis. The legislation and regulation of foreign direct investment formally allow for exceptions. From the Western view, "everything is negotiable." Moreover, the process of screening and approval is not clearly specified or uniform. These bureaucratic processes operate in mysterious ways. While they may seem inscrutable to us, there is logic within the host country cultural context.

   There is a benefit to analyzing the kaleidoscope of factors as they interact with one another in an individual country. The reports of the field work in Mexico and Korea trace through this process, suggesting why it is as it is, against the cultural backdrop of those countries.[37]

4. As the specific requirements of the multinational are worked out, the interaction takes place among people from different cultures. Culturally based communication barriers are in evidence when a manager from the United States represents his or her firm to Third World host government officials. Barriers can also be observed when the manager is a national of the host country. Since the ethos of U.S. multinationals is Western, local managers reflect this corporate culture.

5. In an environment where specific requirements are worked out through negotiations on a case-by-base basis among individuals from different cultures, there are many opportunities for extortion and bribery. Attitudes, legal treatment, and the reality of bribery differ across countries. The position on bribery in the United States at the present time reflects a point of evolution in our Judeo-Christian and common law traditions. Other countries are at different points in their religious and legal traditions. Through the Foreign Corrupt Practices Act, the United States has extended its position on bribery extraterritoriality throughout the world.[38]

The following papers, responses, and discussion summaries are intended to enhance our understanding of host government goals, local economic structures, and how the above factors influence the interaction between the multinational manager and host government officials. The concluding paper of the volume analyzes the implications of this environment for corporate strategy.

Notes

Kenneth Jameson and William Glade provided valuable comments on an earlier version of this paper.

1. Terminology relative to multinational firms and the Third World is not standardized. Terms such as "multinational firms, multinational corporations, multinational enterprises, transnational corporations, or transnational enterprises" tend to be used interchangeably. In the papers presented in this volume, the terminology used by the author-presenters has been maintained.

While the terms "multinational" and "transnational" are commonly interchanged, there is a subtle difference. "Transnational" as used in the United Nations Commission and Centre on Transnational Corporations focuses on the interaction between the parent and the subsidiary. It does not incorporate fully the important aspect of the multinational as a component of host countries. The term "multinational" is thus technically more appropriate for the subject of this volume.

As for the distinction between corporation and enterprises the term "corporation" is the most commonly used and one that fits with the idea of corporate management and governance. "Enterprise" technically recognizes the labyrinth of corporate and non-corporate entities that can form a legal structure that is viewed and managed as a single corporation. For a good discussion of these terminological differences, see Werner J. Feld, *Multinational Corporations and U.N. Politics: The Quest for Codes of Conduct* (New York: Pergamon Press, 1980), p.1, or Cynthia Day Wallace, *Legal Control of the Multinational Enterprise: National Regulatory Techniques and the Prospects for International Controls* (The Hague: Martinus Nijhoff, 1983).

"Third World" is a term used here in its broadest sense. The distinction between the First and Third Worlds is between the industrialized countries of Europe and North America plus Japan as distinct from the other nations of Africa, Asia, and Latin America. "The Second World" is a term reserved for Eastern Bloc Countries. Among the countries in Africa, Asia (excluding Japan), and Latin America, there is a further distinction between those that are treated as newly industrializing and the others. In our discussion of living standards, we will distinguish between middle-income countries and low-income countries. The use of "Third-World" in this volume, however, is intended to cover both middle-income and low-income countries.

2. Data for table 1 were prepared from the The World Bank, *World Development Report, 1986*. Countries were classified according to 1980 Gross National Product (GNP) per person as follows:

High-Income: $3,700 and greater (e.g., Australia, Democratic Republic of Germany, Federal Republic of Germany, France, Hong Kong, Israel, Japan, Libya, Saudi Arabia, United States, U.S.S.R.)

Middle-Income: $400 or more. These countries are also divided into oil exporters and oil importers, identified below:

— Middle-Income oil exporters comprise Algeria, Angola, Cameroon, People's Republic of the Congo, Ecuador, Egypt, Gabon, Indonesia, Iran, Iraq, Malaysia, Mexico, Nigeria, Peru, Syria, Trinidad and Tobago, Tunisia, and Venezuela.

— Middle-Income oil importers comprise all other middle-income developing nations not classified as oil exporters such as Brazil, South Africa, Argentina, and Colombia.

Low-Income: $400 and less (e.g., Afghanistan, Bangladesh, Chad, Ethiopia, Gambia, Haiti, India, Kenya, Laos, Niger, Sri Lanka, Vietnam)

3. The Physical Quality of Life Index is based on an average of life expectancy at age one, infant mortality, and literacy. This index was developed by the Overseas Development Council as a non-income measure of well-being. The scale is defined as "0" (the least favorable performance in 1950) to 100 (the best performance expected by the year 2000). For life expectancy at age one, the most favorable experience anticipated to be achieved by any one country by the year 2000 is 77 years. This would thus be set at 100 for the index. The most unfavorable performance registered in 1950 was 38 years in Guinea-Bissau. This becomes the zero index point. For infant mortality, the best performance expected by the year 2000 is 7 deaths per 1,000 live births (index of 100), and the poorest performance in 1950 was 229 deaths per 1,000 live births in Gabon (index base or zero). The literacy index is the percentage of the population over 15 years of age who can read and write. The three indexes are averaged

together giving equal weight to each. The PQLI numbers presented in table 3 measure the physical quality of life as of 1981.

4. Robert S. McNamara, *Address to the Board of Governors 1976* (Washington, D. C.: World Bank, 1976).

5. For data on poverty, see *Poverty and Hunger: Issues and Options for Food Security in Developing Countries* (Washington, D. C.: World Bank, 1986). Also see the International Labour Office report, *Employment, Growth, and Basic Needs: A One-World Problem* (New York: Praeger Publishers, 1977). A third source for data on poverty is the World Bank report by David Morawetz, *Twenty-Five Years of Economic Development, 1950–1975* (Baltimore: Johns Hopkins University Press, 1978).

6. *North-South: A Program for Survival*, Report of the Independent Commission on International Development Issues, Willie Brandt, Chairman (Cambridge, Massachusetts, MIT Press, 1980), pp. 90–104.

7. For a further examination of these ties, see Lee A. Tavis, "The Editor's Chair: Multinationals as Foreign Agents of Change in the Third World," *Business Horizons* (September-October 1983).

8. The impact of multinationals in Third World host countries and how it is viewed by supporters and detractors is the subject of volume 1 in this series, *Multinational Managers and Poverty in the Third World*, ed. Lee A. Tavis (Notre Dame, In.: University of Notre Dame Press, 1982). Reference to statements in the first volume of the series will hereafter be cited as volume 1.

9. In his paper on "Industrial Structure of Latin America and Multinationals" in this volume, Baer succinctly presents the positive, as well as the negative, dimensions of the multinational corporate contribution. The panel and discussion summary following the paper present alternative views.

10. Archbishop Marcos McGrath, C.S.C., and Fernando Bastos de Avila, S.J., "Multinationals and Catholic Social Teaching in Latin America" in this volume.

11. Michael J. Francis and Cecilia G. Manrique, "Clarifying the Debate," in volume 1, p. 79.

12. See Francis and Manrique in volume 1, p. 74, as well as Baer, and McGrath and de Avila in this volume.

13. See for example, Baer or McGrath and de Avila in this volume; Francis and Manrique, volume 1, p. 75, and Bourgin, Grimsely, and Henriot, "The United Nations Conference on Science and Technology for Development," volume 1, pp. 59–67.

14. See Baer and the discussion following his paper in this volume; Francis and Manrique, volume 1, pp. 84–85.

15. McGrath and de Avila in this volume.

16. Rev. Donald McNeill, C.S.C., and Lee A. Tavis, "The Nature of the Debate," in volume 1, pp. 257–260.

17. See Baer, Francis and Manrique, volume 1, pp. 76, 80.

18. Michael J. Francis, "Dependency: Ideology, Fad, and Fact," in *Latin America: Dependency or Interdependency?* ed. Michael Novak and Michael P. Jackson (Washington, D.C.: American Enterprise Institute for Public Policy Research, 1985), p. 95.

19. Lee A. Tavis, "Stewardship Across National Borders," in *Stewardship: The Corporation and the Individual*, ed. T. R. Martin (New York: KCG Productions, Inc., 1984), pp. 74–88.

20. John W. Houck and Oliver F. Williams, C.S.C., editors, *Catholic Social Teaching and the U.S. Economy: Working Papers for a Bishops' Pastoral* (Washington, D.C.: University Press of America, 1984), p. 225.

21. For excellent, objective coverage of activist shareholder activities and the response of the multinational firms, see *Investor Responsibility Research Center* publications.

22. For a good discussion of the various views on church activists, see S. Prakash Sethi, "The Righteous and the Powerful: Differing Paths To Social Goals," *Business and Society Review* 54 (Summer 1985): pp. 37–44.

23. Ibid., p. 41.

24. A study group of the "Program on Multinational Corporations and Third World Development" is analyzing the activists-multinational interaction. They have considered two issues, South Africa and the marketing of pharmaceuticals in the Third World. After an initial meeting, the group concluded that the South African issue had become too politicized and that added insight would have little effect. For Third World pharmaceutical marketing, however, the goal congruence between religious activists and pharmaceutical companies offers the possibility of constructive interaction. The results of these meetings and research will be reported in a later volume of this series.

25. Volumes of material have been written about the codes of conduct of international organizations. For a recent and insightful analysis, see Feld, *Multinational Corporations and U.N. Politics.*

26. Jaime Laya outlines the aspirations of less-developed host governments relative to multinationals and points out how these can conflict with corporate objectives. See "Economic Development Issues" in this volume.

27. Throughout all of the meetings of the "Program on Multinational Corporations and Third World Development," the right of host governments to control the activities of multinationals has always been affirmed.

28. For a discussion of the same issue in the context of a Production–Social separation principle, see Lee A. Tavis, "Multinational Corporate Responsibility for Third World Development," *Review of Social Economy* 40 (no. 3, December 1982): p. 18.

29. For a review of state ownership in Latin America, see Werner Baer in this volume. For a discussion of the nature of state capitalism, see Howard J. Wiarda, "Economic and Political Statism in Latin America," in *Latin America: Dependency or Interpendence?* ed. Michael Novak and Michael P. Jackson (Washington, D. C.: American Enterprise Institute for Public Policy Research, 1985), pp. 4–5.

30. *National Legislation and Regulations Relating to Transnational Corporations* (New York: United Nations Centre on Transnational Corporations, 1983).

31. See Kwan S. Kim, "The Korean Case: Culturally Dominated Interactions" and Kenneth P. Jameson and Juan M. Rivera, "The Mexican Case: Communications Under State Capitalism" in this volume.

32. In this volume, McGrath and de Avila present the Catholic tradition in Latin America. Discussion of how that tradition can be reflected in host country policies is included in Chapman, "An Application of Doctrine to Economic, Political, and Social Policy," and Bartell, "The Tensions in Applying a Moral Standard in Today's World."

33. In this volume, David I. Steinberg plumbs the inscrutability of the Confucian tradition in "The Confucian Backdrop: Setting the Stage for Economic Development."

34. See Keith R. Rosenn, "A Comparison of Latin American and North American Legal Traditions" and the responses by Trai Le and Ricardo Arias in this volume. The Latin traditions can be observed in Jameson and Rivera, "The Mexican Case."

35. See David Steinberg, "The Confucian Backdrop."

36. Kwan Kim, "The Korean Case."

37. In addition to the case studies, Ernesto Marcos, William P. Glade, and George Suter examine the similarities and differences of the process as it occurs in each country. See "Patterns of Similarity and Difference" in this volume.

38. In this volume, John T. Noonan follows the evolution of the U.S. position on bribery from the Hebrew Bible through the Foreign Corrupt Practices Act in "Bribery in the Judeo-Christian Tradition and the Common Law." The opportunities for extortion and bribery can be seen in the report of the field work in Korea and Mexico. A panel then contrasts the process in Korea and Mexico with the U.S. tradition and law from a managerial, legal, accounting, and Third World government perspective in the section on "Coping with Extortion and Bribery."

PART II

The Economic Regulatory Context

Part 2 is directed toward the role of the multinational corporation in the development strategies of host countries. This is the starting point for discussion of how multinational managers interact with host country governmental officials within the economic and political constituencies of each.

Two papers are presented. Both comment on the positive and negative aspects of multinational involvement in Third World countries from their own perspectives and on how host governments attempt to control that involvement. Jaime Laya speaks from the perspective of an Asian government official, Werner Baer ties his analysis to the state capitalism of Latin America.

Following the papers, we expand our worldview. A number of panelists share their reaction to the issue of host government control of multinationals. Panelists include multinational executives, Tony de la Reza, John Ryan, III, and George Suter; a Mexican lawyer, Raymundo Enríquez; and a member of the United Nations Economic Commission for Latin America, Joseph Ramos.

Economic Development Issues

JAIME C. LAYA*

Transnational corporations (TNCs) now constitute a powerful presence in the world economy. Their activities cover the entire range of finance, commerce, service, and industrial undertakings. Sales, debts, and resources of the largest of the TNCs exceed the Gross National Product, public and private debt, and possibly the resources, respectively, of some nations. The legal framework of each grouping of TNCs often represents a complex and unique web of branches, subsidiaries, holding companies, and other ownership, management, and operating arrangements. The nationality of the TNCs is no longer exclusive to the developed nations; many are from the less-developed countries (LDCs), competing not only in other LDCs but also in developed countries. The nationality of some is indeterminate, materializing as they do out of certain tax havens.

Defining the size and shape of TNCs is not easy. Particularizing their effects on LDCs is even harder. More difficult is reaching agreement at corporate and international levels on a common approach, on a common standard of behavior, which will help accelerate world development and thus alleviate poverty in the Third World.

ASPIRATIONS

The viewpoint of the LDC vis-à-vis an incoming TNC varies with the country's philosophy. At one extreme, some countries allow un-

*Jaime C. Laya is managing partner of J. C. Laya & Co. Ltd., Manila, Philippines. He was formerly the governor of the Central Bank of the Philippines and chairman of the United Nations Intergovernmental Working Group of Experts on International Standards of Accounting and Reporting.

limited entry, following a traditional pattern whereby raw materials are exported and finished goods are imported. At the other extreme, some countries refuse foreign investment as a matter of policy, preferring self reliance as an approach, financing investment purely from domestic savings. There are special cases such as Hong Kong and Singapore, which for historical and geographical reasons are centers of offshore operations and specialized manufacturing. Most LDCs, however, would be somewhere between the two extremes.

It is difficult to generalize on the LDC viewpoint with respect to TNCs and I would ask to speak in the context of Philippine experience and the United Nations group of experts on accounting standards. National policies affecting business investment and development apply to all corporations, both domestic and foreign. The following review therefore applies to corporations in the LDC in general, those pertaining solely to foreign-based profit-oriented TNCs alone being those concerned with areas of investment and foreign exchange transactions:

1. *Growth*. The entry of TNCs is welcome as it represents an inflow of foreign savings into the country, supplementing domestic savings and directly increasing the level of investment. This results in growth of production and employment, which, after all, is what development is about.

2. *Areas of investment*. Not all types of investment are fully open to foreign interests. The Philippine Constitution and law limits to a certain percentage foreign investment in natural resources, public utilities, and banking institutions. Tax and other incentives apply, however, to investment in the preferred areas identified as such in the Industrial and Export Priorities Plans.

3. *Employment*. The maximum domestic processing of indigenous raw materials and labor intensive industries in general are encouraged in order to create the maximum number of new job openings.

4. *Export expansion*. National development programs call for expanding investment, mainly imported capital equipment and other commodities. This calls for increasing export receipts to cover the cost of capital imports and the amortization of any debts incurred as a consequence of the development process.

5. *Industrial location*. Dispersal of industry is a basic policy, consistent with the objective of regionally balanced development and of a systematic infrastructure program covering power, utilities, transport, and other services.

6. *Foreign exchange*. Free convertibility of currency is not to be taken for granted, as most LDCs have to carefully monitor and program foreign exchange flows in trade, invisibles, and capital. Foreign financed investments preferably should generate sufficient incremental foreign exchange receipts or savings so as to at least cover incremental foreign exchange payments for debt servicing, dividends, and any capital repatriation.

7. *Repatriation of investments*. Capital and earnings are freely remittable at prevailing exchange rates. Debt payments may be made in accordance with the terms approved upon negotiation of the debt. Payments for current transactions of imported materials and the like are made routinely. The only requirements would be the registration of inward remittances of equity investments as basis of eventual repatriation.

8. *Domestic credit*. The idea of foreign investment is to bring in foreign savings. Accordingly, certain restrictions are in force which limit domestic borrowings to some specific multiple of foreign funds inflows.

9. *Transfer of technology*. To improve investment and domestic labor capability, work force training, and the importation of advanced technology is part of general policy, balanced with policies for encouraging labor-intensive industries.

10. *Transfer pricing*. The valuation of commodities and services imported and exported is not always made at arms-length, particularly when transacted among units of the same TNC grouping. Policy calls for such transfer payments to be at market rates.

APPROACHES TO POVERTY

The objective of the exercise, as far as the LDC is concerned, is improvement in general welfare. Increased production and employment, better distribution of income, and the alleviation of poverty are all basic considerations in determining not only policy toward TNCs but development policy in general.

Many companies on their own volition invest, do business, and initiate projects that are directly addressed to LDCs and to pockets of poverty in the countries within which they do business. They have sometimes deliberately supported marginally profitable lines for the social benefits provided. They have been known to market products of sponsored neighborhoods or associations. They have contributed to worthy causes, sometimes as cooperative undertakings. Executives of TNCs comprise a major portion of high-level organizational and managerial skills in some countries. Their personal time has been used in many cases to support poverty-related and livelihood projects undertaken by extra-government groups. Church organizations have been particularly active as catalysts for a focus of human and financial resources from government, private sector, and other groups.

The main contribution of TNCs, and industry in general, toward poverty alleviation, however, is in the fulfillment of their basic task of creating employment and productivity. In the final analysis, the elimination of poverty, be it in the depths of an LDC countryside or in its urban ghettos, lies in the employment of the population, in the full employment of their skills in productive undertakings, and in their ability to market their products, locally or abroad. Creating employment opportunities and ensuring fair wages is the challenge. The solution often forwarded is the maximum play of free market mechanisms, supported wherever necessary by appropriate government policy and infrastructure. This would, so the thinking goes, succeed in channeling available savings and investment funds to those projects that will result in maximum results to investor, consumer, and employee alike.

The concept applies domestically as well as internationally. In the latter case, this calls for the free flow of capital funds and trade goods, to result in (1) maximum investment yields as profitable projects are identified and put into operation regardless of national boundaries, (2) employment where labor supply is at a maximum and where, consequently, wage rates are least, (3) increased worldwide productivity with the identification of a country's comparative advantages in production and trade, (4) reduced consumer goods prices everywhere as production increases and the results of international competitive advantages are felt.

Uncertainties and discontinuities inevitably reduce the scope of free market possibilities. Other things being equal, TNCs would understandably tend to keep in their home or other preferred country the capital intensive stages of the manufacturing process and limit funds placed at risk in the LDC. Differences in tax laws would tend to encourage the booking of transactions and the shifting and recognition of profits where tax advantages are at a maximum. Country limits tend to be imposed on funds invested, independent of project opportunities.

More than these, there is sometimes a conflict between company objectives and national goals. For business reasons, technology transfers could be delayed or hampered. A desire to quickly repatriate earnings sometimes finds expression in ingenious ways. TNCs sometime speculate against the foreign exchange rate of the host country, aggravating what may otherwise be a controllable situation. National export programs may be in conflict with TNC worldwide production and marketing strategy.

Finding a reasonable balance between company and host country objectives would seem to be a promising area for contributing to the resolution of the poverty problem in LDCs. In the final analysis, any long term and continuing relationship would have to be based on mutual benefit: profitability on the side of the TNC and employment, taxes, production, and growth on the part of the LDC.

WORLD ECONOMIC STRUCTURE

Any specific company action or decision will of course have immediate impact, but the full effectiveness of concerted action can only be possible if this is in harmony with what securities analysts like to call "fundamentals" of the international situation. We have to see, to be exact, if individual company action will make significant headway in the current of international policies and thinking.

There is perhaps a lingering and unexpressed feeling that the poor countries can lift themselves to prosperity by their own efforts and through hard work. There are numerous success stories, of course, and still much room for such application, but looking at aggregates and particularly among the non-oil producing developing countries, it does seem sometimes that the cards are stacked against them. The ground rules are such that no amount of effort would lift certain countries from penury.

The usual prescriptions are well known: reduce imports, increase exports, improve foreign investment climate, conserve energy, reduce government expenditures, currency devaluation, and so on. Unfortunately, many of these simply will not work. The poor nations can hardly further conserve energy. Their present per capita energy consumption definitely cannot be considered prodigal. The bulk of government expenditures are for capital projects, for infrastructure and utilities needed for development. Export drives are hampered by protectionist attitudes among some advanced countries, notably in fiber and garments and in agricultural commodities, both mainstays of many LDC economies.

World economic and trade conditions have not been felicitous to LDCs, particularly the non-oil producing countries. During the 1970s, energy costs more than quadrupled, terms of trade turned against most LDCs as their export markets softened, interest payments on foreign debts went up, growth rates were down. The real growth rates of middle-income oil importing countries averaged 7.0 percent in 1965–73, 5.5 percent in 1973–80, and 2.2 percent in 1981–85. These contrast with UNCTAD estimates that a minimum average growth rate of 7 percent is needed just to maintain the employment rate. The effect of all these is ironically a transfer of resources from the poor to the advanced nations, keeping in mind that some of the advanced countries are able to ignore balance of payments deficits in the light of the international acceptability of their currencies as international reserve assets.

The International Monetary Fund (IMF) and the World Bank have taken the lead in addressing these and related concerns affecting the international economy. Oil prices have receded from their highs and interest rates likewise have declined, both welcome developments among LDCs. World economic growth still has to respond adequately.

Originally formed as a means of ensuring stable international monetary conditions, the IMF helps finance countries encountering temporary balance of payments deficits. In particular, the IMF seeks to make funds available for payments deficits while the countries concerned are in process of adjusting their internal economies and exchange rates so as to ultimately achieve a balance in international payments. The mechanism of the gold standard which achieved automatic balance among exchange rates, money supply, and domestic prices among countries has been replaced by the theoretically more sensitive IMF mechanism.

The world economic situation has been dislocated by a series of oil price changes, requiring structural adjustments in all countries. These structural adjustments take time and need to be made not only by the deficit countries but also by the surplus countries. In the Philippines, for example, we have decided to accelerate energy exploration and development, to free interest rates, reduce tariffs, embark on industrial and financial reforms, make exchange rates more flexible, and encourage exports, all intended to result in a greater play of the free market mechanism and to allow the economy to better function in the new environment of high-cost energy. The same approach is being adopted by many other countries.

The structural adjustment process has to be two-way, as the oil shocks have affected surplus and deficit countries alike. There will be no progress if the deficit countries are unable to finance their deficits while in the process of structural adjustment. Neither will there be any progress if, even after achieving structural adjustment, they are unable to export due to protectionist barriers erected by developed nations. Among the solutions proposed by the IMF staff itself and by the LDCs are proposals to increase world liquidity through an increase in the supply of Special Drawing Rights (SDRs) and the reduction of protectionist trade barriers in all countries. Failure to find a solution to these difficulties will mean failure in attaining the objectives of world development and poverty elimination.

The performance of the United States economy is closely watched by other countries in view of its status as the biggest player in the field. Any slowdowns in the U.S. economy will inevitably affect the volume of world trade and the world prices of commodity exports of LDCs. The level of its interest rates will influence the flow of capital funds, the domestic currency cost of international debt, and thus the level of new foreign investment. The success, therefore, of the economic policies of the Reagan administration will also mean the success of other countries' own objectives.

These are difficult times, but particularly so for the non-oil developing nations. Some countries are better placed than others, but the general trends are discernible. The LDCs feel that the solutions lie in the improvement of international liquidity mechanism through improved regulation and distribution of SDRs, the removal of protectionist barriers to trade, flexible exchange rates in all countries, and other related measures. Without these, it would seem that attempts of nations and of individual TNCs to reduce poverty can meet only with limited success.

INFORMATION

TNCs have been formally acknowledged by the United Nations, which has initiated various TNC-related activities through its Economic and Social Council and the Commission on Transnational Corporations. The Commission has started a data bank of TNCs and various activities including work leading to the formulation of a Code of TNC ethics and of international standards of accounting and reporting. Much of the work would have the effect of improving the availability of information for decision-making purposes, guiding action on the part of TNCs themselves and of UN-member governments, and in general improving the capability of LDCs in coping with the presence of such enterprises.

The Commission has observed the need for usable financial and non-financial information on the activities of TNCs and for improved comparability of corporate reports. The current thinking among some experts is that an international and comparable system of standardized accounting and reporting will fill these needs. With greater information, it is thought that LDCs can be better able to look after their interests and thus exert somewhat more countervailing power.

To be sure, work is going on within professional groups of accountants and within country groups, notably the European Economic Community. However, Commission thinking is that U.N. involvement may be appropriate as LDCs are not fully represented in the ongoing professional efforts.

The thrust is to initially improve the availability and comparability of information presented in the general purpose reports of TNCs, with emphasis on the identification of the minimum items of both financial and non-financial information to be disclosed in general purpose reports. The objective is for such reports to meet the basic information needs not only of shareholders and creditors but also of other interested parties and the international community as a whole. To this end, the Commission is studying the need for general purpose reports on the enterprise as a whole and on member companies of the TNC grouping.

In general, the reports proposed to be made universally available include balance sheets, profit and loss statements, and statements of sources and uses of funds. Adequate details are envisioned to be presented so as to disaggregate certain information by geographic area, by line of business, and by individual member company. These are to be supplemented by a list of identified non-financial information on employment, technology transfer, organizational structure, and the like. Discussions are also underway on the asset or other criteria to be used in determining the applicability of the proposed standards.

There is as yet no consensus on the proposed Code of Ethics or on the proposed accounting and reporting standards. Perhaps more enlightened TNCs can help forward the work which will, among other things, achieve the purpose of providing better information and thus help LDCs and the TNCs themselves in day-to-day dealings.

SUMMARY

The concerns in this volume touch upon the very heart of the world development process and the very purpose of national development efforts. The elimination of poverty and the increase in the welfare of their population is in fact the announced goal of developing nations. The resources and skills at the command of multinational corporations are of such scope and magnitude that these can either accelerate or hamper the development process in many countries. Multinational company participation in poverty alleviation can be undertaken in several levels:

1. Individual company programs addressed to specific circumstances in the countries in which they operate would be useful. Many enterprises have begun such programs, in many cases successfully incorporating them into their basic operating strategy.
2. The interests of TNCs and of host countries could in many instances be divergent. More TNCs could explicitly consider the proper balance between corporate objectives and national objectives as a basis of a long-term presence. The benefit from such an approach would be the continuing productivity, employment, tax payments, and other contributions to the local economy—all, in the final analysis, accruing to the reduction of poverty.
3. The full impact of TNC efforts against poverty cannot be realized if institutional restrictions exist and if the international monetary and economic system hamstring private sector efforts. It is therefore important that the context of international discussions in the

monetary, information, and other fields be properly considered and that such discussions benefit from the experience of individual TNCs.

The problems of LDCs are many but are manageable. They hold much of the world's resources. Many of them are blessed with a climate that allows year-round agriculture. They hold much of the world's population and as such, much of the world's markets and labor force. Their relationships with developed nations are not one-sided, and cooperative efforts will result in the improvement of well-being all around. It is in this spirit of one world and of goodwill that the world can be truly transformed.

Industrial Structure of Latin America and Multinationals

*WERNER BAER**

Foreign capital has played an important role in Latin America's economies since the early nineteenth century. Until almost the middle of the twentieth century its main thrust was to cement the region's integration into a rapidly growing world trading system as a supplier of food and primary materials. Foreign investments (at first mainly British, then also French, German, and U.S.) were to be found mainly in commerce, finance, public infrastructure, plantations, and mines.[1]

The presence of foreign capital in these sectors gradually declined as the twentieth century wore on. Installations were either bought out or nationalized, usually by state entities.[2] After World War II most of the new foreign investment went into the industrial sector—having been attracted by host governments' incentives to participate in the process of import substitution industrialization (ISI).[3]

In this paper some of the positive contributions of multinationals and some of the frictions their presence has created will be analyzed. This will be done against a background discussion of the industrialization strategy of major Latin American countries and of the evolution of the other ownership sectors—private domestic firms and state enterprises.

*Werner Baer is professor of economics and director of the Center for Latin American and Caribbean Studies at the University of Illinois. He has been associated with a number of Latin American research institutes and has taught at the University of Sao Paulo, the Vargas Foundation in Rio de Janeiro, and the Catholic University of Rio de Janeiro.

THE INDUSTRIALIZATION STRATEGY

Since the Second World War the major countries of Latin America have followed a strategy of industrialization in their efforts to modernize their economies and societies. Until the 1960s the emphasis was on import substitution, and since the second half of the 1960s and throughout the 1970s there has also been a stress on export diversification—involving the promotion of industrial exports.

The policy tools used to promote industrialization consisted of protection (usually a combination of protective tariffs, exchange controls, and/or direct import restrictions), special incentives for firms locating in favored sectors (e.g., imports without foreign exchange cover for multinationals or imports at favored exchange rates), financing from government development banks, and the creation of state firms in sectors where neither private nor multinational firms were prepared to enter (e.g., public utilities, steel, some areas of petrochemicals, etc.).[4] Large government investments in sectors where state enterprises were located insured adequate (and often subsidized) inputs into various sectors where domestic private and multinational enterprises were dominant.

The net result of industrial policies in Latin America's largest countries was a major transformation of their economies as the industrial sector came to surpass agriculture as a contributor to Gross Domestic Product. For the region as a whole the industrial sector accounted for about 40 percent of GDP in the early 1980s (manufacturing 24 percent), while agriculture and mining was less than 14 percent.[5] After a period of intensive import substitution, many countries began to emphasize export diversification, creating special incentives for nontraditional exports for both agricultural and industrial products. As a result, there has been a notable expansion of their share in total exports. In Brazil, in the early 1980s, industrial products accounted for over 50 percent of total exports, 32 percent in Colombia, and 23 percent in Argentina.

INSTITUTIONAL SETTING

From an institutional point of view, the rapid industrialization process resulted in the emergence of a mixed ownership system of the industrial park. Domestic private capital usually became dominant in such sectors as cement, furniture, wood products, clothing, shoes, etc. State enterprises were dominant in steel, mining, petroleum and petrochemicals, and public utilities. Multinationals dominated in transport equipment, pharmaceuticals, electrical equipment, and other specialized types of capital goods and consumer durables. Strong representation of both domestic and multinational private capital is to be found in beverages, food products, hygienic products, etc.

One comparison of ownership sectors for Mexico and Brazil in the 1970s, based on assets shares, shows the following distribution among the largest 200 firms:[6]

Percentage Distribution

	FOREIGN	PRIVATE	STATE	TOTAL
Mexico	34	45	21	100
Brazil	35	33	32	100

It is interesting to note that the relative importance of foreign enterprises was the same in both countries, while the share of state enterprises was larger in Brazil than in Mexico. Asset distribution, however, can be misleading, since often state enterprises are engaged in sectors with very high output/capital ratios. Thus the picture changes considerably when comparing asset with sales distribution. A much larger sample of Brazilian firms shows that although state firms had a 50.5 percent share of assets, their share of sales was only 26.4 percent, while multinationals' share of assets was only 9 percent, and their share of sales was 20.2 percent; private firms had 40.5 percent share of assets and 53.4 percent share of sales.[7]

The average size of the private domestic firm is smaller than the average multinational subsidiary. The latter, in turn, is smaller than the average size of state firms. In the 1960s the average foreign subsidiary in Argentina sold 1.8 times as much as the average domestic firm.[8] In the 1970s similar differences in relative sizes were found in Brazil and Mexico. Taking the average domestic firm (state and private) size as 100, the average size of foreign firms in Brazil was 105, domestic private firms 77, and state enterprises 366; in Mexico the average foreign firm's size was 108, domestic private 81, and state enterprises 192.[9] Another study of Brazil found that in the late 1970s foreign firms' sales were 2.4 times as large as those of domestic private firms, assets 1.6 times as large, and employment 1.6 times as large.[10]

THE DOMESTIC PRIVATE SECTOR

The relative importance of this ownership sector in industry was much greater prior to the intensive industrialization process. The reason for its proportional (although not absolute) decline was the small financial and technical resources of private domestic firms and also their traditional organizational structure. In other words, the domestic private sector did not have the capacity to rapidly establish many of the import substitution industries desired by policy-makers.

With few exceptions, private Latin American firms are small and family-owned and have traditionally relied on retained earnings for their investment activities. Until the import-substitution period there were no significant capital markets to make long-term investment loans or to obtain substantial outside funds through stock sales.[11]

In most Latin American countries, however, the import-substitution process resulted in both a substantial expansion of existing firms and in the appearance of new private enterprises. This occurred in a number of ways: 1) Government development banks made long-term financing available to domestic private firms which were located in or entering into priority sectors. Financing was either through long-term loans (often at subsidized interest rates) or through minority stock participation. Government development bank financing was usually not available to foreign firms, which were expected to furnish their own capital (though this was not the case with short-term credit needs). 2) Those countries which emphasized rapid vertical integration of the industrial structure forced multinationals and state firms to purchase substantial amounts of components domestically. This meant new opportunities for private domestic firms, which often received technical aid from multinationals to be able to produce the appropriate intermediary product. This type of relationship also forced such enterprises to improve their performance as multinationals placed a premium on quality controls. 3) The growth of state enterprises also had beneficial effects on the private domestic sector, both as purchasers of goods (in Brazil over 70 percent of private capital goods firms' sales go to state enterprises) and suppliers of crucial inputs, such as power, special steel, etc.

Despite substantial absolute growth of the private domestic sector and its impressive performance in some cases as an aggressive exporter of industrial products (such as the shoe industry of some countries, which is dominated by domestic firms, or some enterprises in the Argentinian and Brazilian capital goods sectors), it still retains a number of structural weaknesses: 1) The closed family firm continues to prevail, and thus major investment financing still comes mainly from retained earnings and/or loans from development banks. Though stock markets have grown, trading takes place either in minority shares or in non-voting preferred shares. 2) Most of the benefits from protection and special incentive programs have gone primarily to a small group of large firms, thus increasing the oligopolistic nature of Latin American industry. Some countries have tried to develop special programs to support small and medium-sized firms, but these have had only marginal effects.[12] 3) With some notable exceptions, Latin America's domestic private firms remain technologically behind multinationals, both due to their lack of adequate funds and due to their more antiquated organizational structure, which makes research and development efforts relatively small. Most therefore remain concentrated in the less dynamic sectors of the economy.[13]

STATE ENTERPRISES

State enterprises are dominant in a number of basic fields: public utilities, steel, mining, petroleum and petrochemicals.[14] These firms are usually very large and their performance has varied among countries, between sectors in the same country, and also in the same sector over different periods of time.

In most countries state enterprises have accomplished the tasks which were set for them when they were created — e.g., providing adequate (and often cheap) power, telecommunication, steel, etc. Beyond being suppliers of essential inputs for rapidly growing industries, they also provided employment, trained large cadres of efficient technicians and administrators, and engaged in technological developments.

Their performance and their impact on other sectors has been the subject of considerable controversy.[15] The major points of contention are:

1. Since one of the major justifications for the existence of state

enterprises is their "social" impact on the economy — i.e. the decision-maker of a state firm takes into account social rather than just "private" returns in making investment or pricing decisions — traditional efficiency criteria for judging the performance of private firms become inapplicable. Public firms providing cheap steel, power, transportation, or locating in economically depressed areas will have lower returns than if they had acted only in their own immediate interests. The positive secondary and tertiary impacts of public firms do not show up in their accounts and may give an erroneous picture of their efficiency (or inefficiency).

2. Once a public firm becomes well-established, its economic and political power may make it relatively independent of the central government. Such power may be used to maximize its own (private) returns, which means that its investment, pricing, employment, and other decisions will no longer be made with a view toward their general social impact. That is, the firm becomes more "capitalistic" than "social" in its behavior pattern.

3. Public firms often have monopolistic powers as either suppliers of inputs or monopsonistic powers as purchasers from the private sector. These can often be abused.

Privatization is not always the best remedy for such problems, since the private domestic sector usually does not have the resources to purchase large public firms, and multinationals have either little interest in tying up funds in large public utility operations or heavy industrial undertakings. Also with reference to multinationals, most governments would be unwilling to pay the political price for selling large and highly visible public firms to foreign interests. The solution for effectively checking public enterprise operations without demoralizing them remains to be worked out.[16]

The Multinationals: Their Benefits and Costs

Rapid industrialization would have been almost impossible without the appearance of multinationals. The specific benefits they brought along were:

1. During their initial entrance in the days of intensive import substitution, they brought along substantial amounts of foreign exchange (which complemented the domestic savings efforts). One should

note that multinationals did not have access to local savings for long-term investment purposes. Capital markets were still underdeveloped and thus long-term private borrowing was limited, expansion through equity offering was also institutionally or legally limited, and access to long-term government credit was not possible for foreign-controlled firms. Of course, once a subsidiary is established, a substantial amount of its investment will be financed from retained earnings. Even the latter, however, are usually not sufficient for major expansion programs, and thus additional foreign exchange inflows are needed.

2. Multinationals made possible the rapid transfer of advanced technology, enabling Latin American countries to develop new industrial sectors in a relatively short period of time. Given the limited domestic technical and financial capacity of local firms prior to the import substitution process, the growth of new industrial sectors without multinationals would have required a much longer period of time than was in fact the case.

3. In addition to the physical know-how, multinationals also brought along new organizational or administrative technology. Complex industrial operations required a type of organization, both from the productive and bureaucratic aspect, which did not previously exist in the countries of the region.

4. Multinationals also had an influence on the technology and organization of locally owned firms. This was especially the case in countries which followed policies of vertical integration, forcing firms to maximize domestic value added by either producing most of the products themselves or purchasing components domestically. The latter increased opportunities for domestic private firms not only to produce inputs for multinationals, but also to incorporate new technology in the process.

5. Multinational investments have directly and indirectly created a substantial amount of employment. In addition, given the nature of their product and organization, they have upgraded the quality of the labor force through training both their line workers and administrative staff, which nowadays is drawn entirely from the local manpower supply. Most multinationals' subsidiaries are almost entirely staffed by Latin Americans.

6. In a number of countries (especially Brazil) multinationals have been very useful in programs of export diversification, i.e. the export of nontraditional products. With an established production and market-

ing network throughout the world, the multinationals were in an excellent position to facilitate government programs to promote the export of manufactured products. Some multinationals also were using their Latin American production facilities to participate in a worldwide vertical division of labor, in which subsidiaries produce components for assembly in other parts of the world.

In the 1970s the share of multinational firms in manufactured exports for some of the region's principal countries was: 42 percent in Argentina; 40 percent in Brazil; 50 percent in Colombia and Mexico.[17] Throughout the 1970s, however, exports made up less than 10 percent of these firms' sales.[18] Multinational exports in Brazil and Mexico were concentrated in chemicals, non-electric and electric machinery, and transport equipment; in Colombia they were found mainly in chemicals, metal products, paper, and cement.[19]

There is little hard evidence available about the degree of sourcing engaged in by multinationals. It is of interest to note that almost 15 percent of Brazil's exports of transport equipment in 1983 consisted of components.[20] In a more qualitative vein Jenkins reports that

> Some TNCs have gone beyond regional specialization to integrate Latin America into their global operations. . . . Latin American countries may either be allocated the production of particular product lines or models for international markets, or produce certain parts and components. In the early 1970s, Volkswagen sourced its Safari model in Mexico for worldwide distribution, and since stopping production of the Beetle in West Germany, it has also been sourced from Brazil and Mexico. IBM follows a similar strategy, exporting electric typewriters from Mexico and printers, card sorters, and copiers from Argentina. A number of car firms have sourced parts and components from Latin America. General Motors in Mexico for instance, exports engines not only to the United States but also to affiliates in Canada, Australia, South Africa, and the United Kingdom. Fiat exports engines from Brazil to Italy, and Mercedes Benz exports parts from its Brazilian subsidiary to the United States.[21]

Ever since Latin America policy makers have encouraged the influx of multinationals to develop import substitution industries, there has grown a polemical and academic literature dealing with the problems and negative impact of a significant multinational presence in the dynamic sectors of Latin America's economies.[22] The following are some of the major problems which have and still are being debated in Latin America:

1. The presence of multinationals will sooner or later be a drain on the balance of payments of host countries. Since the principal motive of multinationals in opening facilities abroad is to make a profit, sooner or later a large proportion of these profits will be repatriated to the parent firm and thus cause a drain on the foreign exchange earnings of the host country.

Not only do multinationals operate abroad to make profits, but since investments in the Third World are viewed to be riskier than investments at home or in other advanced industrial countries, the rate of return from such investments is usually expected to be higher in order to compensate for such risks. The latter include the political instability of many countries in the area, the possibility of nationalization without adequate compensation, tight controls over operations by a nationalist government, or inconvertability of earnings due to the host country's balance of payments problems. Such a perception on the part of multinationals is quite understandable. It may clash, however, with the view of many groups within the host countries, who will perceive the multinationals as desiring a higher rate of return from poor countries than from their own country of origin where per capita income is very high.

Since most Latin American countries have some types of limits on profit remittances, many multinationals are suspected of secretly transferring profits to the parent company by engaging in transfer pricing—i.e., the parent company overcharges the subsidiary inputs, or the subsidiary underinvoices exports to the parent company or other affiliates.[23]

In some areas the practice of transfer pricing has been decreasing due to nationalizations, co-production agreements, and state marketing boards, which have reduced intrafirm transactions. This is especially the case in the primary sectors and related products. The problem has become increasingly confined to high technology sectors, especially where there is substantial product differentiation. An EEC survey found that "prices between different brands of the same product could vary by as much as 79% for small transistor radios, 56% for tape recorders, 52% for washing machines, and 27% for coffee grinders— all in the absence of tariff barriers and import restrictions. This makes it almost impossible for an external agency to prove that, say, an intentional 2% intra-firm price change constitutes a manipulated transfer price."[24]

2. Although multinationals have been crucial in transferring modern technology to newly industrializing countries, there are many critics who feel that either the wrong type of technology has been transferred, or that new technological development in the host country is usually neglected, or that technology payments are a cover for secret profit remittances.

One set of critics fault multinationals for not contributing to the solution of one of the major socioeconomic problems of Latin America — the creation of employment. It is claimed that capital-intensive technology is imported which is not adapted to local conditions, and thus the employment impact of multinationals has been relatively weak. Multinationals are not eager to spend substantial sums in trying to adapt technology to local factor availability, since that would not have much of a payoff. One of the principal attractions of Latin American markets has been the possibility of getting an extra return on R&D expenditures that were previously undertaken for the home market.

There are other critics who are less concerned about the employment impact of multinationals. In fact, they believe that worrying excessively about employment and prodding firms to adopt relatively backward technology will result in an industrial structure which is permanently a few generations behind that of advanced industrial countries. This will cement the dependency relationship from which some of the leaders of developing countries would like to escape. This school of thought is critical of multinationals because of their unwillingness to engage in basic R&D work in the host country. Although many multinationals have laboratories of some kind as part of their operations in the host countries, these are usually part of quality control activities rather than part of an effort to engage in fundamental technological research. Since technology is the most potent bargaining weapon a multinational has, it will be extremely reluctant to transfer the capacity to develop new advanced technology to the host nation. This is increasingly resented by many groups within the host country. They feel that without the involvement of engineers and scientists in basic R&D, there will be a permanent dependency on foreign technology and thus no possibility to increase the bargaining position of the host country in negotiating for better technology transfer terms.[25]

With R&D concentrated in the country of the parent company, subsidiaries are usually charged in one form or another for technology payments. Although this is justified on the ground that all consumers of the company's product benefit from technological innovations resulting from R&D expenditures and should thus contribute to reimburse the company for its expenses, there exists to date no fair formula for distributing the burden of this reimbursement. In fact, some observers have claimed that technology payments from subsidiary to parent company provides an opportunity for hidden profit remittances.

In an informative study, Daniel Chudnovsky found that around 1970, 52 percent of Brazil's technology payments were of an intrafirm variety and in 1972 Argentina's were 42 percent. He also found that royalty rates were lower in interfirm transactions than in payments between subsidiaries and parent companies and that "the average share of sales under license in total sales was 40% for national firms and 93% for foreign subsidiaries. Subsidiaries tend to produce almost everything under license from the parent." Finally, "if instead of calculating royalty rates, average royalty payments per contract for all sectors are taken into account, we found that average royalties charged on intra-firm transactions were 4.4 times higher than in inter-firm ones."[26]

Chudnovsky also calls attention to a U.S. study which showed that "royalties from abroad contributed 47% of that portion of global expenditure allocable to the overseas activities [of multinationals]. This suggests that royalties do play an important part in the financing of centralized R&D activities." But since "94% of the sales of multinationals were made in industrialized countries . . . R&D expenditures favor the corporation's activities in those markets. Subsidiaries located in developing countries may be receiving less in terms of technological output than they have actually contributed to finance."[27]

3. Although the multinationals have had a positive impact on the growth of some private domestic firms which supply components, their presence has also in some cases acted to inhibit the development of local enterprises in the same field. These do not have the financial or technological means to compete. In some sectors, formerly dominant local firms may be squeezed out and/or taken over by incoming multinationals. In the pharmaceutical sector, domestic firms were once dominant in the major countries of the region, but in the last thirty years the market has been lost to multinationals (in Brazil, for instance the share of domestic firms has fallen from about 80 percent to 20 percent).[28]

Denationalization of various sectors of the Latin American economies has often occurred during periods of stabilization. After severe bouts of inflation, some countries adopted (or were forced to adopt) stabilization measures which included severe credit restraints and very high real interest rates. Such policies have usually placed domestic firms in precarious circumstances. Multinational firms, with ready access to funds from the parent firm, have often taken advantage of this situation and bought out domestic firms at relatively low prices. Such occurrences have left a feeling of inequity and resentment among many citizens of the host country.

Multinationals are also associated with monopoly power, as they tend to locate in sectors where most of the output is produced by a smaller number of firms. In Argentina, for instance, "foreign firms accounted for 39.3 percent of production in sectors of high concentration . . . compared to only 3.5 percent in those sectors where the share of the largest eight firms was less than 25 percent. Similarly in Mexico, foreign firms accounted for 53.1 percent of output in the most concentrated sectors . . . and only 12.8 percent in the least concentrated sectors."[29] Similar findings were made in Chile and Brazil.[30]

Reviewing various case studies, Newfarmer found that underlying the association between multinationals and oligopoly was "a blend of behavioral and technological causes. Technologies of many modern [multinational] products play a dual role: Patented technology forms part of the unique package of assets that is the monopolistic advantage of [multinationals] in the market, and thus accords [multinationals] an absolute cost advantage over potential competitors. Also, production technologies generate economies of scale which create a scale barrier to entry and limit the number of producers a market can efficiently support. Economies stemming from the internalization of international flows of information may also act as a scale barrier."[31]

The denationalization and concentration issues can also be examined from a more aggregative point of view. As the most dynamic sectors of the host economy are often dominated by multinationals, there will be a trend to transfer an increasing proportion of the decision-making locus concerning levels of investment, of production, etc., abroad. Multinationals are known to centralize decisions in the parent company. The latter usually formulates policies with a view to optimize its world activities, and the resulting decisions are not necessarily optimal from the point of view of the individual host countries. This type of conflict of interest might be sharpened to the extent that multinationals increasingly engage in exports of finished and semi-finished products from their subsidiaries. For instance, though it may be optimal during a world recession for a multinational to drastically curtail its activities in a specific Latin American country rather than in its home plants, few citizens of the host country would sympathize with such actions.

4. Multinationals (and to some extent private domestic firms) have contributed, according to some analysts, to the distortion in the consumption pattern of the population. Import substitution represented a move to produce domestically goods which were formerly imported. Since the demand profile is based on the distribution of income, which was already concentrated at the beginning of the import substitution process, the industrialization resulted in a production capacity profile which mirrored the demand profile. As multinationals were a key element in import substitution, they acquired a stake in the newly established production profile and thus a vested interest in the status quo. They feared that a drastic change in the distribution of income would reduce their domestic markets. A complementary argument is that multinationals have an interest in increasing markets by influencing lower income groups to consume their products (especially consumer durables) through advertising and credit schemes, thus "distorting" their consumption patterns.[32]

What is meant by "distortion" is a situation where lower income groups are induced to switch their expenditures from essential products (like food, clothing, housing) to such status symbols as cars, color television sets, etc. Although most critics who take this position are well-intentioned, the policy implications raise some troubling questions. Under the present system, lower income consumers are not forced into their consumption patterns, but only persuaded. If through the control of multinationals (and other firms) the production of goods is limited to what the current group in power thinks is essential for the population, this group, in fact, sets itself up as the sole judge about what is good for the people at the present stage of development. Both points of view can be defended or attacked on legitimate moral grounds.

5. It would be naive to assume that the presence of multinationals can be politically neutral. One does not have to cite such extreme cases as that of Chile in the early 1970s, where multinationals were involved

in direct political actions, or Chile and Peru in the same decade, when multinationals placed direct pressure on their home governments to obtain favorable action on compensation for nationalization. In a much less dramatic fashion, it will only be natural for multinationals to use their political influence through their home country's diplomatic channels to influence the host countries' policies—for example, with respect to relaxing rules on import controls, price controls, labor policies, profit remittance laws, etc. Resistance by host governments to such pressures will depend on various circumstances, such as the policy-makers' attitude to foreign capital in general, or impending international loans, or the status of debt renegotiations, etc.[33]

These political side effects should be considered as one of the costs of relying on multinationals in the process of industrialization and general development. If these costs are too high due to the sensitivity of the host country's population to anything seeming to interfere with the sovereignty of the country, a policy of less reliance on foreign investments would be in order, even if that would diminish the rate of industrialization and the various benefits which multinationals bring along.

GOVERNMENT POLICIES TOWARD MULTINATIONALS AND THE OTHER OWNERSHIP SECTORS

There is evidence that many of the problems which multinationals brought with them are being handled by host governments with an increasing amount of sophistication. It is generally realized that a nationalistic backlash resulting in the outright nationalization of foreign subsidiaries would be damaging to economic growth. Since industrialization has also involved the rapid growth of other ownership sectors—state firms and domestic private firms—a number of countries have developed policies which use these sectors as counterweights to the foreign presence.

Some Latin American governments have developed special programs to strengthen the domestic private sector by giving it special advantages. Government development banks' financing facilities have been reserved for domestic firms. In the case of Brazil, this has resulted in a rapid expansion of the domestically owned capital goods industry in the 1970s.[34] Exclusive access to government credit has also given domestic firms an important bargaining tool in setting up joint ventures with multinationals.

Another technique to strengthen domestic firms vis-à-vis multinationals has been to use the monopsonistic power of state firms. For instance, in the case of Brazil, ownership of supplying firms was the principal criterion for "a massive contract for telecommunications equipment. Telebras announced that none of the three competing [multinationals] could win the contract unless they presented immediate plans for 'Brazilianization', that is, evidence that 51 percent of their equity would be locally owned."[35] Currently the Brazilian government is also using a policy called "reserva de mercado" to check the relative growth of multinationals and to give an incentive to local firms to enter new technologically advanced fields. One of the best examples is the attempt to restrict the market for minicomputers to a reduced number of firms that would be predominantly domestic in character, that is, more than 50 percent controlled by local firms.

The rapid growth of state enterprises in some of the economy's key public utility and basic industry and mining sectors has also acted as a countervailing measure. In the case of Brazil this is becoming increasingly evident since the mid-1970s as the government has been following a strategy to develop its raw material resources and related industries. The development of the bauxite mining and aluminum industries, of the Carajas resources, and of some new petrochemical and steel complexes is based on joint ventures between state enterprises and multinationals, with the former holding the dominant shares in each of the projects. The state enterprises are large, technologically sophisticated, and financially backed by the government, and are thus in a good position to face multinationals on a fairly even level in bargaining about technology and profit sharing.

Over the last decade Latin American governments have also increased their capacity to negotiate with and control the behavior of multinationals. They used both various techniques of control and incentives to have multinationals conform to what is considered to be the national interest. Their capacity has also been helped by the fact that there has been a growing diversification of national origin of foreign companies operating in the large Latin American economies and also of the number of sectors in which they are active.[36]

Although many key sectors of Latin American economies are dominated by multinationals and decisions about their policies are made abroad, it is not clear to date whether, on balance, decisions have been favorable to multinational world strategy but harmful to the interests of Latin America. Multinationals have collaborated with policies of export diversification. Of course, this was not done out of altruism since multinationals were amply rewarded for this collaboration through export-incentive programs. It is also noteworthy that in the recession which hit many countries in the region in the early 1980s, many multinationals substantially increased their exports to compensate for local market declines.

These favorable trends, however, have to be counterbalanced by the consideration that once again (in the 1980s) a rising share of multinational trade consists of intracompany transactions, which bring along a growing opportunity for transfer price manipulations and other dangers involved in excessive international interdependence.[37]

NOTES

1. For more detailed analyses of the traditional role of foreign capital in Latin America, see: William P. Glade, *The Latin American Economies* (New York: American Book, Van Nostrand, Reinhold, 1969), chaps, 7–9; Werner Baer, "Latin America and Western Europe: Economic Relations Through World War II," in *A New Triangle: Latin America, Western Europe, and the United States*, ed. R. Roett and W. Grabendorf (New York: Praeger, 1985).

2. For the case of Brazil's railroads, for instance, see Annibal V. Villela and Wilson Suzigan, *Política do Governo e Crescimento da Economia Brasileira*, 1889–1945 (Rio de Janeiro: IPEA/INPES, 1973). The basic motivation for nationalization was that public utilities' tariffs were controlled by governments and set in such a manner that the rate of return on invested capital was too low to have private foreign firms make new investments. Nationalization of mines and petroleum was motivated by the urge to have domestic control over non-renewable resources.

3. For a general review of ISI in Latin America, see Werner Baer, "Industrialization in Latin America: Successes and Failures," *The Journal of Economic Education* 15 (no. 2 Spring 1984): pp. 124–135.

4. In some of these sectors private firms were present (like steel), but in insufficient quantities relative to the needs of the growing industrial park.

5. In Brazil and Mexico agriculture's share of GDP had fallen to about 10 and 9 percent respectively.

6. Douglas H. Graham, "Mexican and Brazilian Economic Development: Legacies, Patterns and Performance," in *Brazil and Mexico: Patterns in Late Development*, ed. S. A. Hewlett and R. S. Weinert (Philadelphia, Penn.: ISHI, 1982), p. 32.

7. "Quem é Quem Na Economia Brasileira," *Visão* (Agosto 1984): p. 22.

8. Alfredo Eric Calcagno, *Informe Sobre las Inversiones Directas en América Latina* (Santiago: Naciones Unidas, Cuadernos de la CEPAL, 1980), p. 49.

9. Ibid., p. 100.

10. Annibal V. Villela and Werner Baer, *O Setor Privado Nacional: Problemas e Políticas Para Seu Fortalecimento* (Rio de Janeiro: IPEA/INPES, 1980), pp. 34–35.

11. Ibid., ch. 2.

12. Ibid., ch. 7 and Appendix I.

13. There are some exceptions, however. See Jorge Katz, "Cambio Tecnológico en la Industria Metalmecánica Latinoamericana," in Banco Interamericano de Desarrollo, *Industrialización y Desarrollo en América Latina* (Washington, D.C.: 1983), pp. 317–345.

14. Werner Baer, *The Brazilian Economy: Its Growth and Development*, 2d ed. (New York: Praeger, 1983) chap. 9; *La Empresa Pública en la Economía: La Experiencia Argentina* (Santiago: Naciones Unidas, Estudios e Informes de la CEPAL, 1983); Thomas J. Trebat, *Brazil's State-Owned Enterprises: A Case Study of the State as Entrepreneur* (New York: Cambridge University Press, 1983). p. 15.

15. Baer, *Brazilian Economy*, pp. 223–231.

16. Ibid.

17. Rhys Jenkins, *Transnational Corporations and Industrial Transformation in Latin America* (New York: St. Martin's Press, 1984), p. 115.

18. But these percentages rose substantially by the mid-1980s.

19. Jenkins, *Transnational Corporations*, pp. 117–118; see also *Political Industrial e Exportação De Manufacturados do Brasil* (Rio de Janeiro: Fundção Getulio Vargas/Banco Mundial, 1983), pp. 68–75.

20. *Desempenho Do Comercio Exterior Brasileiro* (Rio de Janeiro: FUNCEX, 1983), p. 134.

21. Jenkins, *Transnational Corporations,* p. 120.

22. United Nations, *Transnational Corporation in World Development, 1978;* Peter Evans, *Dependent Development: The Alliance of Multinational, State, and Local Capital in Brazil* (Princeton, N.J.: Princeton University Press, 1979); Richard S. Newfarmer and Willard F. Mueller, *Multinational Corporations in Brazil and Mexico*, Report to the Subcommittee on Multinational Corporations of the Committee on Foreign Relations, United States Senate (Washington, D.C.: U.S. Government Printing Office, 1975); Joseph LaPalombara and Stephen Blank, *Multinational Corporations and Developing Countries* (New York: The Conference Board, 1979); Raymond Vernon, *Storm Over Multinationals* (Cambridge, Mass.: Harvard University Press, 1977).

23. UNCTAD, *Dominant Position of Market Power of Transnational Corporations: Use of Transfer Pricing Mechanism* (New York, 1978).

24. Robin Murray, editor, *Multinationals Beyond the Market: Intra-Firm Trade and the Control of Transfer Pricing* (New York: John Wiley & Sons, 1981), p. 8. Jenkins, *Transnational Corporations;* p. 124, points to the rise of the import content of manufactured products as a result of an increased export orientation of Latin American industries, which can once again increase the opportunity for transfer price manipulations.

25. Arthur W. Lake, "Technology Creation and Technology Transfer by Multi-

national Firms," in *The Economic Effects of Multinational Corporations*, Research in International Business and Finance Series, vol. 1, ed. Robert G. Hawkins (Greenwich, Connecticut: JAI Press Inc., 1979), pp. 147–149; Richard S. Newfarmer, "Multinationals and Marketplace Magic in the 1980s" in *The Multinational Corporation in the 1980s*, ed. Charles P. Kindleberger and David B. Audretsch (Cambridge, Mass.: MIT Press, 1983), pp. 178–179.

26. Daniel Chudnovsky, "Pricing of Intra-Firm Technological Transactions," in Murray, *Multinationals Beyond the Market*, pp. 121–122. On page 124 Chudnovsky also makes some useful observations. He finds that "royalties are stated as cost items in balance sheets, and therefore the amount of taxable profits may be reduced. As they are usually stated as percentages of sales, they can also be transferred even in cases in which the subsidiary in question declares losses" and multinationals' "preference for intra-firm technological transactions can also be explained by some additional factors. One obvious but usually forgotten fact is that royalties are estimated on all sales, and run forever. This is seldom the case in inter-firm transactions. Secondly, it is harder to change inter-firm royalty rates than intra-firm ones. Thirdly, there is the possibility of capitalizing technology, i.e., the inclusion of patents, trademarks, know-how, or other intangible assets as part of the foreign firm's equity".

27. Ibid., p. 125. See also Lake, "Technology Creation," p. 151, and Newfarmer, "Multinationals and Marketplace," p. 178–179.

28. Evans, *Dependent Development*, pp. 121–143.

29. Jenkins, *Transnational Corporations*, p. 32.

30. Ibid., p. 38.

31. Newfarmer, "Multinationals and Marketplace," p. 168.

32. Ibid., p. 173.

33. For a number of case studies, see Paul E. Sigmund, *Multinationals in Latin America: The Politics of Nationalization* (Madison, Wisc.: University of Wisconsin Press, 1980).

34. Villela and Baer, *Osetor Privado Nacional*, ch. 3.

35. Peter Evans and Gary Gereffi, "Foreign Investment and Dependent Development: Comparing Brazil and Mexico," in Hewlett and Weinert's *Brazil and Mexico*, p. 126.

36. Sergio Bitar, "Corporaciones Transnacionales y las Nuevas Relaciones de América Latina con Estados Unidos," in *Economía de América Latina*, Instituto de Estudios Económicos de América Latina (1 Semestre de 1984): p. 106; Newfarmer, "Multinationals and Marketplace," pp. 182–184.

37. Bitar, "Corporaciones Transnacionales," pp. 110–111; Evans and Gereffi, "Foreign Investment and Dependent Development," p. 147; Newfarmer, "Multinationals and Marketplace," pp. 186–187.

Response: Panel*

Throughout the seminars, the discussion continually turned to the role of multinationals in Third World development and to how that role is shaped by host governments. This section draws on panel comments from multinational executives, Anthony G. de la Reza, John T. Ryan, III, and George Suter; a Mexican lawyer, Raymundo E. Enríquez; and a member of the United Nations Economic Commission for Latin America, Joseph Ramos. The range of views expressed reflects the wide diversity of participants in the seminar.

---

*Raymundo E. Enríquez is a lawyer in Mexico City. He has served as an associate with the international law firm of Baker and McKinsey, and as an assistant to the presidents of the Mexican Confederation of Industries and the American Chamber of Commerce in Mexico.

Joseph Ramos is a senior economist and assistant director to the Economic Development Division at the United Nations Economic Commission for Latin America, and a professor of economics at the University of Chile. He serves as a United Nations policy analyst and advisor in Latin America on issues dealing with employment, price stabilization, income distribution, and development.

Anthony G. de la Reza is president of Texaco Panama Inc. and chairman of the board of Refineria Panama S.A. He is also the senior executive for the group of Texaco companies operating in Panama and continues to serve as vice president of Texaco Caribbean Inc. with responsibilities for Texaco's interest in Costa Rica.

John T. Ryan, III, is the executive vice president of Mine Safety Appliance Company. He was previously the vice president for international operations with executive responsibility for South America, Asia, the Middle East, and export sales from the United States. Mr. Ryan is a member of the Advisory Council for the College of Business Administration at the University of Notre Dame.

George Suter is vice president–administration, Europe, Africa, and Middle East of Pfizer International Inc. He has resided and worked abroad for multinational firms in Thailand, Singapore, Malaysia, and Pakistan throughout most of his professional career, and was president of the American Chamber of Commerce of the Philippines on three separate, non-consecutive occasions.

59

THE IMPACT OF MULTINATIONAL CORPORATIONS

A number of panelists shared different perceptions of multinational contributions to Third World countries. Many of them were directed toward the Baer paper.

The balance of payments impact and transfer prices were major concerns. George Suter noted:

Comments as to the balance of payments drain in developing countries must be taken in the context of the contribution made to domestic economies by multinational corporations. Salaries and taxes, for example, are rechanneled into the economy; while they do not appear in the balance of payments, they make an important contribution to the gross national product.

Joseph Ramos stressed the future need for foreign exchange.

There is no question but that the critical bottleneck for now and the next ten years for most less-developed countries is going to be that of foreign exchange. Multinationals can be important not so much in their transfer of technology, their management techniques, or their bringing in new capital, but in that they have special access to world markets.

The marketing access of multinationals is their unique contribution for today's less-developed country. Here they will be helping solve the foreign exchange constraint, which is *the* critical bottleneck for growth and for employment today. If the multinationals can shift their less-developed country investment to exports, and if they can transfer important parts of their currently inward oriented less-developed country production to exports, they will be serving their best interest and those of the less-developed countries themselves.

Tony de la Reza sees profit remittances as under the control of Third World governments.

The major point of contention with resource companies is surely that of profit remittance. We have heard claims during these meetings that the majority of multinationals have as their primary objective the repatriation of large amounts of profit through schemes involving the pricing of intercompany transfers or payments for technology. These are all issues that have been subject to considerable speculation and misconceptions.

The fact, however, remains that, while some multinationals in the past may have utilized these schemes to remit foreign exchange or increase offshore business profits, most multinationals operating in Latin America are reputable and serious firms which have always operated completely within the laws of the countries. In my experience, host countries legislate fair rules and closely monitor profit or divided remittances.

Relative to transfer prices, George Suter stated:

Based on my experience, most governmental officials in the Third World understand the theories behind transfer pricing and know that value is received for the outflow of foreign exchange. In our experience, for example, we have shown that our transfer prices are consistent around the world and have documented the costs included in these prices. Today, it is really not a major issue in our operations.

The lack of research and development activities in the Third World continues to be a controversial issue between multinationals and host governments. George Suter commented:

Werner Baer is correct in his statement that the analysts in the quality control laboratories that he has observed in Latin America are not doing basic research. This is generally the case. In the pharmaceutical industry, for example, basic research is only successful if it is concentrated at a very few locations. A multinational must bring all of the scientists together so that they can interact twelve hours a day. It is impossible to have someone in Sao Paulo interacting with someone in Groton, Connecticut interacting with one in Sandwich, England. Therefore, at Pfizer, we have concentrated our basic research in two locations—Groton and Sandwich, although we do undertake some research in Japan. It would simply be nonproductive to attempt to diversify this work.

George Suter also responded to the charge that multinationals distort consumption patterns.

Distortion of consumption patterns is a fact of life in the United States as well as in the Third World. I just spent my first Christmas in the United States after an absence of twenty-five years. Frankly, I was appalled at the rampant consumerism here. Still, if this is what the citizens want, this is what they are receiving.

In the Third World, the distortion of consumption patterns cannot be attributed solely to the activities of the multinational corporations. This is a problem of the whole private sector. The majority of nondurable consumer products are manufactured by domestic corporations while multinationals are more involved in the essential goods or extractive industries. Thus, domestic firms probably bear a larger share of the responsibility than do multinationals. Thus, it is overstating the point to attribute distortion of consumption patterns to multinationals.

REGULATION OF MULTINATIONAL PRESENCE

In contrast to the discussion of the impact of multinationals in Third World development, the right and responsibility of host governments to regulate that influence was uniformly agreed upon. The efficiency with which this regulation is carried out, however, was the subject of some disagreement. George Suter noted:

Multinational corporations are invited to participate in economic development. None of us would go where we are not wanted. Governments issue invitations in the form of incentive programs to attract foreign direct investment, and to participate in the development of their economies. Multinationals enter under the rules of the host government, not their own. A multinational is a guest in the country and must represent the traditions, the culture, and the policies of the state. To do otherwise would violate the sovereignty of the country.

Joseph Ramos expressed his view as: "Of course multinationals are regulated." He presented four reasons why these firms tend to be so heavily regulated in the Third World, with specific reference to Latin America.

It is important to note that the pluses and the minuses of multinational corporations hold true for developed countries as well as for less-developed countries. Why, then, is it that Latin American less-developed countries look upon multinationals with so much suspicion and ambivalence, and why, therefore, tend to regulate them so much? Extensive regulation is inevitable in the less-developed countries for the following reasons: (1) Multinationals, obviously, are private firms, and capitalism is not such a good word in many parts of the world, including Latin America; (2) Multinationals are simply large, they stand out; (3) Multinationals tend to be capital intensive; (4) Multinationals are different, especially in less-developed countries.

It is important, especially for North Americans, to understand that the capitalist experience in Latin America is a poor and sad one. Capitalism was a success story, or is a success story, in Europe and in the United States. By and large, it has been a failure in Latin America. Keep in mind that this continent was colonized well before the United States, that it has a similar resource base, and while it is better off than Africa, its level of development is well below the poorest Western European countries — Greece and Portugal. It would be quite different if we were talking about the United States, where about 80 percent of the population is basically well-off and 20 percent is poor. In Latin America, the percentages are more likely reversed. Certainly no more than 20 percent have achieved United States–European living standards; whereas at least 50 percent by most standards are poor or very poor. The system strikes the eye as not having been a success. This unsatisfactory capitalistic experience colors the attitude of Latin Americans.

It is an unfortunate situation for multinationals. They are stuck with the bad reputation that capitalism acquired in its former four-hundred years before the multinationals arrived on the scene. Whatever the reason for the failures (a lack of entrepreneurial spirit, the bureaucratic centralizing and aristocratic ethos of Philip II's Spain, or the skewed concentration of wealth from the very beginning — like the plantation economy in the United States South rather than the West's family-farm economy), the market and the capitalist system failed to provide economic growth in Latin America, not to mention its further failure to provide a democratic system. These failures have led to increasing intervention and regulation of the economy. Multinationals are thus controlled and regulated because they are part of the capitalist system. Indeed they are the epitome of capitalism; they are its success story and therefore, as many Latins see it, something to be feared. Although this is not necessarily a correct reading of history, it is a common point of view in Latin America.

From this viewpoint, Latin America's unsatisfactory experience with capitalism has given rise to a "zero-sum" view of reality; that is, that if someone wins, it is because someone loses. For example, how many times has one heard the misleading simplification, "Multinationals take out more than they bring in." In reality, the issue is not whether a firm takes out more than it brings in. The issue is whether the firm creates more wealth than it brings in. If it brings in 100 and takes out 150 (which implies it has made a profit), but creates 300, that means it left 150 behind. So the zero-sum view of reality misfocuses the issues, thinking that if someone wins, someone else necessarily loses. This view is an unfortunate by-product of the region's historically slow growth.

Second, multinationals are regulated because they tend to be capital intensive. In all countries there is a tendency to regulate capital intensive enterprises. Multinationals are capital intensive in a region already scarce in capital because of its underdevelopment and, where moreover, that scarce capital is concentrated. Hence, the share of income that goes to labor is extraordinarily low. It is not just that the "pie" is small, but labor's share in that small pie is also small. Something on the order of 50 percent of the gross national product in the region goes to labor. In the United States, it is something on the order of 75 percent. Consequently, there is a tendency to regulate multinationals, not simply because they are multinationals, but because they are capital intensive.

Third, multinationals are large, and they are especially large in relation to less-developed countries. Obviously, bribes and corruption exhibit how size can be used in socially unproductive ways. Less obvious is what Baer called the first phase of capitalism—nineteenth-century natural resource and infrastructure investment. Infrastructure investments, such as railroads, electrical companies, or phone companies are normally natural monopolies. Natural monopolies need to be regulated one way or the other. It is not surprising, therefore, to find multinationals in those industries to be either nationalized or heavily regulated. The history of how some of these natural resource rights were bought is often sadly corrupt, but aside from the justice of the initial agreements, one has to keep in mind that natural resource investments in small countries, for example, Chilean copper and Venezuelan petroleum, have very important macroeconomic effects. From the host government side, it is impossible to ignore, for example, the effect of a devaluation on the copper sector. Inversely, the behavior of the copper firm and the behavior of the petroleum company have large microeconomic effects. This, consequently, leads to pressure to regulate or to nationalize.

The final reason that multinational corporations are heavily regulated is that they are different. They maximize globally rather than nationally. There is an inevitable conflict between multinationals and governments. One (the multinational) is maximizing *its* global profits; the other (the government) wants to maximize nationally. For example, if the Panama Canal Company were to have maximized profits, it would have charged much higher transit charges, which would have maximized benefits for Panama because it was its natural monopoly but at the expense of consumers. In fact, it maximized social benefits for consumers since it was basically run as a consumer cooperative of the United States and other world shippers. The policy was: Make no profits; just cover costs.

The issue of the future is, thus, not fewer or more, regulations. Regulations are here to stay. The issue is to stabilize regulations and direct them to specific objectives.

Raymundo Enríquez stressed the importance of strong host government regulation:

Yesterday one of our colleagues stated a phrase that struck me. He said that no developing country can afford not to have multinational corporations. That statement is correct. I would like to add a second sentence, however: No developing country can afford to have unrestricted multinational corporations. Multinationals are welcome as long as they adjust their practices and contribute in the overall and general objectives of each country. It would be risky to leave the responsibility of corporate behavior in the hands and in the conscience of multinational corporate managers. The responsibility lies in the hands of the host country.

The legal structure of the country is very important. It is the mechanism through which the practices of multinational companies are adjusted to serve the general goals of each country. While it is true that the complexity of Latin American legal systems might create problems for foreign investors, we cannot extend beyond our national boundaries. The real problem is that sovereign governments have not been able to utilize the international legal tools or international organizations adequately. Over the past years, all of the developing countries have fought on the various forums such as the United Nations for a code of multinational conduct. While a code would simplify the rules under which the foreign investors operate in our countries, unfortunately, the *developed* countries do not have the political will to commit to a code.

Third World governments must thus continue to rely on bilateral agreements. The history of these agreements indicates that they are designed and aimed to protect the investors, not the host country. What is missing is any real commitment for the United States to promote investment in the other countries. Moreover, we should note that most of these agreements were signed or executed when the bargaining power of the developing countries was very weak.

The main goal of government regulation is to teach multinationals to live like brothers with national investors. The legal structure must be aimed to accept the foreign investment as a means to complement national producers, not to let them be overwhelmed by massive size and power. Foreign firms can bring a great deal to a country and have much to teach national investors. This is welcome.

On the part of host governments, the regulations and legal systems have to ensure that national industries are protected and must be very selective in the objectives of this regulation. Alternatively, once the government accepts a foreign investment, they must promote it, foster it, and provide conditions under which it can grow. I do not accept the thesis evident in many countries that are presently trying to put a ban on foreign investment with bureaucratic barriers and red tape that limits their growth. Foreign investment is a two-way street. Once the investors accept the conditions imposed by the government, the government must accept that investment and promote it.

Tony de la Reza believes that multinationals are regulated effectively but that the global drive for efficiency will bring these firms into greater conflict with host governments.

From the perspective of the multinational energy business, mainly petroleum, most of our activities are highly regulated in virtually all developing countries. Those multinationals that do not comply with local laws can be challenged by the various governments. And, most of these countries have sophisticated means of legislating controls.

The relationship between host countries and multinationals, however, has undergone a revolutionary change since 1973. The shifting of oil prices and the recession of 1982 have forced multinationals to be lean and productive. In my opinion, the strains between host countries and multinationals will be even more evident in the future.

If multinationals are to stay in business in developing countries, they will need to emphasize low-cost operations. These firms must be efficient, lean, flexible, and highly productive if they are to maintain adequate returns on investment. This pressure will mean resistance to governmentally mandated salary increases, resistance to governmental pressure for increases in employment, and pressure to undertake the heavy cost in Third World countries of reduction in the work force. Multinationals have identified themselves with the developing nations for the last fifty to seventy years. They will continue to do so as long as they fill a need in these countries. If not, the system will ultimately reject these firms and ownership will transfer to local business or government. One dimension that must change is the paternalistic attitude multinationals exhibited in the past. With the new pressures for efficiency, the multinationals will be unable to bear the cost of paternalism. With the need for joint business-government efforts toward efficiency, multinationals will need to be more and more alert to the decision power of host governments.

John Ryan shared an example of how regulation can cause problems:

The reserved market philosophy for electronics in Brazil is a case of difficult host government–multinational corporate interaction. The reservation by a group called Secretariat Especial de Informatica (SEI) started out in terms of restricting microcomputers to protect a local producer with powerful supporters, but then developed for some time into restrictions that in some unpredictable ways affect the whole electronic industry. They control microprocessors and software besides minicomputers and threaten to impinge on "anything with a chip." Only recently given legislative approval, this is a group set up with the not very well defined power to decide which market should be reserved for Brazilian producers and which firms can compete.

Computers are not a natural resource industry where it can be argued that the natural resources belong to the country. Instead this is know-how that usually moves freely internationally. With SEI, there is a total emphasis on *nominal* ownership, and, in the view of many observers, SEI allows this factor to overwhelm consideration of the overall benefits, costs, and effects provided by alternative producers for Brazilian manufacturers and consumers. Downplayed is the alternative that competition would allow the customer to decide who is better (as well as creating the potential for abuses by "front men").

SEI could have accepted multinational companies either alone or in joint ventures. These multinationals would have brought the latest technology to Brazil, would have kept updating it in the future, and would have made or purchased most of the value added in Brazil. As an example, IBM's record of investing and developing in each country with substantial employment effects speaks well. IBM would have entered an export agreement as it later did in Mexico and assured that their prices would be fairly in line with the world market.

Most of the companies that were initially set up in the microcomputer business had no experience in computers. With little initial know-how, they purchased technology from overseas that many say was outdated. These companies have imported many more components than would have been the case with a multinational firm with superior computer know-how and a Brazilian manufacturing base. The former companies began in the assembly and charged high prices with uncertain quality and negligible exports. Given the short product life cycle in this industry and the extremely fast pace of technology, they may have to continue to buy technology from overseas. There may be continuing dependence on foreign manufacturers who will trade not-quite-up-to-date know-how for guaranteed sales to the associated company. The whole thing has the potential for ending up in a very nice, cozy oligopoly with a less-than-optimal level of technological development compared to alternatives, continued indirect dependence, and high profits for a favored few.

This group in the government has great and poorly defined powers with enormous economic consequences but little apparent real basis for making the decision as to who should be given the reserved market and who should not. Affected in this process is the Brazilian computer user, either industrial or consumer. Since many industrial and consumer products also use microprocessors as key components, those affected go well beyond the traditional computer markets. In the long term, Brazilian producers may be hampered in their efforts to export many valuable products by high-cost, unadvanced components.

I see the problem here as an overemphasis on *nominal* ownership as the be-all and the end-all of the decision, while a very low value was placed on consumer preference and the benefits of advanced technology, greater local manufacture, and export competitiveness for the economy in general.

PART III

The Cultural Interactive Context

When individuals come together, they each react out of their own set of values, attitudes, social and institutional structures — that set of variables we would identify as "culture." When the parties and the institutions they represent are steeped in different cultures, the interaction is strongly influenced by those often subliminal cultural variables. We found this to be the case in both our Mexican and Korean field research.[1]

In view of the many dimensions of what we call "culture," we must be selective in our coverage. The field experience clarified our choices. We found that religious traditions were a major influence on both the local corporate environment as well as on the interactions of individuals representing the corporations, and the host governments. A second observation was that legal traditions and structures were important components of the decision environment. The three narrowing cuts at the vast cultural context were as follows.

Asian and Latin Religious Traditions. The most pervasive influence of a people's culture is their religious heritage. Paralleling our field research, we considered the Confucian tradition of Asia against the Catholic tradition of Latin America.

The ancient Confucian tradition is still clearly in evidence in China, Japan, Korea, Taiwan, Vietnam, Hong Kong, and Singapore. It is a key component of all personal interactions, particularly when it involves the interface between those steeped in Confucian culture and those from the West. This is true even though the Confucian tradition has not been an important component of institutionalized religion in these countries for centuries.

Three observers comment on the Confucian tradition. David Steinberg presents a nuanced view of Confucianism in the fabric of

Asian societies with a focus on Korea, analyzing the factors that affect institutional and personal relationships. Against this background, Peter Moody discusses modernization especially as observed in China. Yusaku Furuhashi comments on how Confucianism may have influenced the economic-business contours of contemporary Japan.

In contrast to the influence of the ancient Confucian tradition in what are essentially still ancient societies, Catholicism in Latin America is an institutionalized religion in post-colonial societies. The Latin American Catholic Church provides an institutional affiliation with which members may find support and critics a solid target. Also, the Catholic Church, as an institution, has a definable doctrine that is changing at what appears to some as a rapid rate.

The social teaching of the Catholic Church, as it is evolving in Latin America today, and the implications for multinational corporations are reviewed by Archbishop Marcos McGrath, C.S.C., and Fernando Bastos de Avila, S.J.

Comments by Ernest Bartell, C.S.C., and Alexander Wilde conclude the presentation of religious traditions. They address the similarities and differences between the Confucian and Latin American Catholic traditions.

Latin American and North American Legal Traditions. The second cultural element faced by multinational managers is the different legal traditions and structures across the world.[2] The major distinction encountered in Latin America and Asia is between the common law tradition that the United States shares with other early members of the English empire and the Roman law basis of much of Europe and the Third World.

The focus of our inquiry was thus the Roman law tradition compared to the common law. Keith Rosenn traces the Latin American legal structure from its Roman and Iberian roots, analyzing how it fundamentally differs from the common law of the United States and the implications for the multinational firms. Two participants then comment, Trai Le from a United States, French, and Vietnamese view and Ricardo Arias from a United States' and Latin American legal background.

Bribery. In any close interaction and collaboration one participant can unduly influence the other. When the participants come from different religious and legal traditions, when the stakes are as high as they are with multinationals and host governments, and when we are suggesting a close collaboration, it is necessary to consider collaborations for other, more personal, ends. The issue of bribery has both religious and legal connotations. The notion has a long history in the Judeo-Christian tradition and, after centuries of little change in the common law tradition, the incidents of prosecution on charges of bribery in the United States over the past quarter-century have increased dramatically.

Moreover, with the passage of the Foreign Corrupt Practices Act, the U. S. position on bribery as it has evolved to the present time in this country has been set as the standard for U. S. multinationals and thus for other countries that are in different stages of their legal, and religious, notions of bribery. John Noonan outlines how the notion of bribery has changed over the centuries.

Throughout Part 3, the religious and legal cultures of Asia, Latin America, and the United States are interwoven. Together they set the context within which the interaction between United States multinationals and host governments in Korea and Mexico are examined.

NOTES

1. The importance of the cultural dimension did not come as a surprise. It had been a central dimension in our earlier study of a large multinational plantation in the Southern Philippines, see "The Dolefil Operation in the Philippine Islands," Yusaku Furuhashi, Don McNeill, C.S.C., and John P. Thorp in volume 1. Also see *Guanchias Limitada* by Carolyn McCommon, Norlin G. Rueschhoff, Lee A. Tavis, and Jean Wilkowski, A.I.D. Evaluation Special Study #22, U. S. Agency for International Development, March 1985.

2. Most notable in Korea was the lack of legal considerations as a significant component of the decision environment. Steinberg presents this as a factor of Confucian societies. The role of formal law in these societies is suggested by the low number of practicing lawyers compared to the U.S., as noted in the Korean study.

The Confucian Backdrop: Setting the Stage for Economic Development

*DAVID I. STEINBERG**

The purpose of this paper is to assess the influence of Confucianism on development and how the role of Western multinational corporations is defined in these societies. Neither of these relationships is analytically precise. Each must be viewed against the rich Confucian history and how it has been variously interpreted at different times in diverse cultures. Against this background, the factors of Confucian societies that affect development and multinationals will be analyzed. We must first, however, redress two deleterious imbalances in our thinking.

Asianists, a term better left undefined but one that conveys the flavor, if not the precision, of my background, tend to think in an intra-Asian context or at best in terms of what may be a spurious Asian-Western dichotomy on those few occasions when indeed we think in comparative terms. The discussion here plans to break that mold and deal both intellectually and pragmatically with more germane cross-cultural comparisons. It should, if we fulfill our obligations, tell us a great deal about the cultures we compare, the economic development process, and the nature of multinational organizations as well.

*David I. Steinberg is president of the Mansfield Center for Pacific Affairs where he assumes direction of the center's development and initiation of the full spectrum of the center's programs. He was a member of the Senior Foreign Service of the Agency for International Development, Department of State, and previously with The Asia Foundation. He has worked on economic, political, and development issues in Asia for over three decades.

As one steeped in public policy issues, our discussion may also help defuse a major, inchoate, but nevertheless real misconception prevalent in government and donor agencies, both bilateral and multilateral, that is, that there are universalistic answers to development issues. By contrasting the cultural context of both Mexico and Korea in the multinational context, we recognize the individuality of these societies, and by implication the generic issue, and thus the need for all organizations and analyses to also take this into account.

THE SETTING

Although our focus is on the multinational enterprise, the intellectual foundation transcends the corporate world, and indeed classical economics. That basis must be sought not only in the nature of and return on investments, but also in social, political, security, religious, and moral factors that impinge on and speed or impede economic growth. Without understanding the nature of the economic processes internal to these nations and how they perform in that societal context, and thus how local businesses and externally oriented organizations—such as multinationals—operate, the concepts of entrepreneurship, managerial styles, worker relations, to such pedestrian but essential elements as the granting of import and export licenses, and a myriad of other factors, will continue to remain a mystery. We should not forget that in this context it is not Asia that is inscrutable, it is our lack of understanding that makes it seem so.

The critical nature of the cultural context in which economics operates is evident. A Burman Buddhist with a little extra money to invest would either build a pagoda or go into the smuggling trade, but would not engage in any economically productive venture. In the former case, he would get a long-term return on his investment by building up karmic capital; in the latter, a short-term fiscal gain. Both are sound given the Burmese economic, social, and political environment, one that shapes interests and rewards, social esteem and values, as well as the gross national product.[1]

Let us also not ignore here the general issue of the peripatetic nature of capital. The Japanese multinational investments in the U.S. are but one example. Korean multinationals exist; four of the five leading companies from the LDCs on the Fortune 500 list are Korean *chaebol* (*zaibatsu* or conglomerates). As Japanese labor-intensive industry migrated to Korea following normalization of relations between the two countries in 1965, so now Korean capital is invested in Bangladesh spinning mills, and Singapore funds find their way to Sri Lanka. The multinational is increasingly an Asian phenomenon as well.[2]

In either case, the peripatetic nature of capital, Western or Eastern, raises profound questions of morality, for which answers are difficult at best. They involve conceptually the often conflicting issues of world market competitiveness, corporate profit margins, and returns to workers. At a more practical level, the issues not only include who gets what and how much from international investment and the development process, but who pays and how much for how long, and, perhaps equally important, for what societal or national ends. Confucian cultures have treated these issues in different ways, only some of which we will be able to explore.

In considering the issue of both institutional and personal relationships of multinationals operating in the Confucian environment, three broad issues might help structure the discussion. These are: 1) the key elements in the economic development process; 2) the key elements of Confucianism; and 3) the key elements of multinational organizations.

Only the second can be covered here, but the critical elements of developmental success, so long debated and subject to so much controversy, will be alluded to in the case of the Korea connection. As the efficacy of developmental agencies are affected by their organizational structure and relationships between home and field offices, we may hypothesize that similar tensions exist in the multinational field. Thus, there may be conflict between central management or administrative practices and local (Confucian) concepts of organization and hierarchy.

CONFUCIANISM RECONSIDERED

As little as a generation ago, the prevailing academic and popular position, both in Asia and among Western scholars and observers, was that Confucianism was a deterrent to modernization and development. It was, the argument went, hierarchical and authoritarian, when what was needed was egalitarianism and democracy. It based its intellectual model on the family and was unabashedly paternalistic, when the

West was thinking in national or global terms and rights. It harkened back to a golden age after which everything decayed, instead of forward to a more glorious future. It deified ancestors, denigrated commerce and trade, castigated the military, and centralized power and government in the hands of an administrative elite, defined by an outmoded concept of bureaucratic virtue. It subjugated women and was conceptually parochial.

This view was in part an outgrowth of the failure in China in the nineteenth century to harmonize the *chung t'i-hsi yung* dichotomy ("Chinese values, Western utility," also known in Korea as *dong-do so-gi,* "Eastern substance, Western vessel" and in Japanese as *wa-kon yo-zai,* "Japanese spirit, Western technique") or retain the sinitic Confucian essence or principles while employing Western material and practical technology, especially for defense.[3] It was a far cry from the days of Voltaire, when Chinese civilization became a rage of European intellectuals.

Only twenty years later we have reversed our views, and this reversal is shared by Asian governments and intellectuals. Confucian accomplishments are extolled broadly, including in the American managerial community, so that a common joke is that the American businessman would prefer to be shot, rather than listen to another lecture on the virtues of Japanese management practices.

This intellectual reversal is belated recognition that changes of great importance have taken place: in worldwide terms, the most remarkable economic development has occurred in those societies strongly influenced by Confucianism. These include not only China, but Japan, Korea, Taiwan, Hong Kong, Singapore, Vietnam, the overseas Chinese communities of Southeast Asia, and the growing East Asian population of the United States. With the exception of Vietnam, economic growth rates in these areas and among those peoples have been remarkable in spite of, in many instances, a paucity of natural resources. It is no wonder that the "Gang of Four" among the newly industrializing countries are Korea, Taiwan, Hong Kong, and Singapore. The hold of the overseas Chinese communities on the economies of Malaysia, Thailand, and Indonesia attest to their powerful influence. The remarkable economic and scholastic achievements of Asian immigrants in the U.S. also demonstrates the efficacy of Confucian-oriented, or sino-centric cultures.[4]

East Asian governments have recognized in the modern period

the value of Confucianism in supporting their perceived interests. Although Confucianism's economic implications will be discussed below, at the political level they include the retention of the status quo and loyalty to the state. From the Meiji restoration, perhaps the most famous example, and the Imperial Rescript for Education of 1890 in Japan, to the present, governments have used the Confucian concept for their own interests. The Japanese fostered and subsidized Confucianism in their colonization of Korea.[5] During the Chiang Kai-shek government in China, the New Life Movement was Confucian in overtones, as is education in Taiwan today. Through the *Saemaul* (New Village or New Community) Movement in Korea, as well as throughout the educational system and in goverment administration, Park Chung Hee fostered Confucian values, including filial piety and loyalty to the ruler. Confucian rites are officially sponsored by the government. Confucianism has recently and officially been introduced into the school curriculum of Singapore. We now give serious thought to the economic challenges of the "Post-Confucian" societies,[6] which may be more present and continuing and less "post" than previously thought.

Why have our attitudes changed toward the value of Confucianism? There is no question that the level of our analysis with regard to all aspects of East Asia has improved. We have progressed beyond the textual criticism school of Asian scholarship to delve into how concepts and institutions relate to societal and institutional change. Nevertheless, inferring causal relationships in nonlaboratory societal settings is often a tenuous exercise of dubious validity. We must be careful of succumbing to the dangers of developmental fadism, an insidious disease of reoccurring virulence, which skews thinking toward the fashionable. There is no question that East Asian successes have made Confucianism in vogue.

As we in the operational world of grant-giving institutions have denied the importance of cultural specificity, the admission of which would complicate the lives of bureaucracies by intellectually mandating the need for specific (as opposed to generalized) policies, administration, and personnel systems, so too we have searched for models of industrialization and development. For the former, we turn to Japan, and the latter is important for it enables us to prove our own efficacy and that of our institutions or governments, let alone our aid program. Korea is the primary example of such a model, especially in the United

States since our responsibilities and interests in Korea were so profound for many, varied reasons.

There are diverse explanations of Korean growth, and they range along the complete ideological spectrum, from revolutionary red to imperial purple, from class exploitation to autocratic rule, from the efficiency of the aid program to the observation that growth spurted after foreign aid diminished, from the agoraphobic relative efficiency of the public sector to the agoraphilic wonders of private enterprise. Some of these factors have been applied more broadly to the whole range of sino-centric societies. Especially prevalent are views concerning authoritarian governments and the role of the private sector.

The question might first be asked, however, whether the focus on Confucianism, while obviously germane, is the most appropriate construct for analysis. Some would maintain that there are broader societal issues into which Confucianism fits differently and with varying degrees of efficacy in each society. The patrimonial analysis is one such approach.[7] Some scholars argue that Confucianism has created the basis for effective modern state institutions,[8] while others would argue that this has not been the case for development, although it has fostered modernization.[9]

CONFUCIANISM DIVERSIFIED

Confucianism is not a monolithic ideological construct either viewed over time or by location. It has been modified historically in China by its bureaucratization, accretion of new ideas in response to changing needs, and through its dynamic relationship with Buddhism. In Japan, Korea, and Vietnam it has been indigenized and adapted to suit societal requirements that were quite different from its Chinese base. It has affected each people differently, in part the result of a variety of factors ranging from child-rearing patterns through familial socialization to concepts of national politics, and of course has in turn influenced those concepts as well. Although there are obviously shared core values in Confucian states, we must constantly recognize the importance of this cultural diversity. As we would view as absurd the notion that Christianity, or even any particular branch of that faith, remained untouched by local factors, and that it is everywhere constant, so we should treat the Confucian persuasion with the same degree of analysis.

Confucianism has been melded with traditional social structures that have profoundly affected its operations. The feudal society of Japan, in which primogeniture was the primary inheritance pattern, was quite distinct from the social organization of power and the inheritance of land in China, which in turn was different from that in Korea. As one author commented:

> Korean Confucianism was never a pale imitation of the Chinese Confucian social order; rather one should say that Confucian general principles were modified by prevailing Korean beliefs and practices.[10]

How deeply Confucianism penetrated to the lowest stratum of the society, when, and how evenly it may have spread geographically are all questions of some dispute, but there is no issue with the critical importance of the Confucian persuasion conceptually, at the acme of government, and among the upper classes and literati.

THE CONFUCIAN CONTINUUM

Although Confucianism changed historically and was variously interpreted at different times in diverse cultures, and thus might be analyzed by country or period, a thematic approach to describing issues in Confucian thought might be more helpful in conceptualizing its role in general, and in Korea in particular.

We are not engaged in some sort of exercise in Western-Confucian Manichean dualism, with dichotomies clear and distinct. We are attempting instead to examine a series of subtle differences along a set of idealized continua, tendencies rather than absolutes, gradations rather than precipices. There will be those who argue that some of these factors as evidenced in these societies are not Confucian in origin or indeed in primary emphasis, but rather have their genesis in other forces, such as the feudal society of Japan or the patrimonial one of Korea.[11] Some may be prevalent in other non-Western societies that are not Confucian in origin; others may predate Confucian influence and find beginnings in early shamanistic cultures. These analytical complications are welcome, however, for they indicate that our understanding is still in its formative period, and offer hope for future dialogue. These factors, whatever their origins, have their illustrations in both the classical and contemporary periods and affect both institutional and personal relationships.

The continua we shall sketch are those related to hierarchy and egalitarianism, power, centralization and pluralism, collectivity and individuality, and orthodoxy and heterogeneity.

Hierarchy and Egalitarianism

Hierarchy ideally is integral to the Confucian tradition to a degree and with a pervasiveness considered noteworthy in the West. The ruler is to treat his subject as a father his children. His role and rule are unquestioned. The wife is to be subordinate to her husband, the younger brother to the elder brother: there are no equals. Age is equated with superiority, and age and higher authority are evidence of greater moral virtue, the greatest of such virtue residing in the ruler.

Hierarchy creates strong elements of dependency that flow from the morally superior. In turn, these superior-inferior relationships determine who has power, the government having a formal monopoly on it legitimately. Those in power act according to established norms and become examples of conduct for others, thus influencing the latter's behavior, for good or evil.[12]

In the view of some scholars, in this superior-dependent relationship Korea exemplifies a patrimonial social and political order and results in a prebendial distribution of resources, but the same was not true in Japan with its feudal background.[13]

The pre-Confucian Korean social order was in fact more hierarchical than the Confucianism that was introduced. Early Korean states were organized along rigid class differentiations based on a "bone rank" system that eventually evolved into the *yangban* (gentry, both civilian and military) system. The *yangban* originally claimed status on the basis of aristocratic standing and lineage, but after the introduction of Confucianism, a "thin overlay of scholarship" was added to their legitimation.[14]

China maintained, by honoring in the breach, what we might call the "Abraham Lincoln scholarship myth" — that even the poorest person could theoretically pass the imperial examinations and thereby secure social and economic rewards on merit in the bureaucracy. Korea, when it introduced the Chinese examination system, modified it so that only the *yangban* were eligible to sit for the rigorous tests. The result was a self-perpetuating, but expanding, upper class that protected itself by limiting access to the lucrative perquisities of office and weeding out the *yangban* through vigorous and continuing factional strife.

Although the *yangban* system was formally eliminated, this has not prevented social ranking based on previous familial standing from remaining a significant force in the society. Depending on one's vantage point, Korean hierarchical structures have changed rapidly and pervasively, and essentially have been destroyed, especially by the Korean War and the military and economic changes since that time. One could argue equally cogently that the Korean class structure has remained remarkably intact. During the Japanese colonial period, many of the *yangban* were coopted into lower level functionaries, which enabled them to retain relative status under the Japanese overlords. Upper class status continuity has been maintained through judicious investments in modern education for their children (the equivalent of passing the imperial examinations is a U.S. doctorate) and in urban real estate. The past generation has, however, witnessed increased and highly significant mobility, first through the military channel since the coup of 1961, and more recently through business enterprise. Increasing social mobility, in which there was a great interest and for which there was great demand traditionally,[15] should not detract from the concept that hierarchy is still a critical force in the Korean context.

The sense of hierarchy is reflected in the Korean language itself, which like Japanese is pervaded by a complex system of honorifics that explicitly designate the relative status of each person referred to or involved in the conversation and the use of which is essential to any dialogue. The Chinese language uses many less such forms.

The equating of morality with political and social leadership has profound implications for all aspects of public and private life. It becomes evident that in Korea the concept of a "loyal opposition" is almost a contradiction in terms, no matter what the disiderata of internationally recognized legislatures and parliamentary unions may prescribe, and how many elections may be held. Elections in Korea may be ritualistic political legitimization, perhaps more for international respectability than for internal power changes, although recent elections have demonstrated that this view is not shared by a large segment of the population. It may be highly significant that no government (except during the U.S. military occupation of Japan) in any of the sino-centric societies has ever been ousted through an elective political process.

There is little wonder that under Korean law personal criticism
of the head of state in any form is illegal, although the issue of whether
Confucianism mandated such a concept or simply reinforced autocratic
tendencies in the government remains moot. So too a committee, commission, or other body containing heterogeneous levels of power (or
age) will rarely be able to result in spontaneous and equitable expression of divergent views; the younger will defer to the older, the
bureaucratically junior to those more senior.

Power: Infinite and Finite

Laswell has defined power as "participation in the making of
significant decisions,"[16] but the adequacy of this approach as a universal
definition has been seriously questioned. Others have argued that power
in the Asian context is more likely to involve the absence of or eleva-
tion above decision making, which can be left to subordinates. It may
be equally germane, however, to consider power in terms of its
magnitude. In a seminal article written on Indonesia,[17] but one with
broad implications, the concept was expressed that in Javanese society
power was considered finite, while in the West it was generally considered infinite. Thus, in the modern West it is possible bureaucratically
to accrue more power by sharing or delegating it, and because it is
infinitely replaceable, it is less personalized.

In many societies, if power is considered finite, then sharing that
power or delegating it (in the state or in the family) becomes difficult.
To acquire more power is to diminish someone else's stock; to delegate
it is to lose it. In a sense, this concept is quite similar to that of the
limited good in village economies or the zero sum game.

The implications for institutional and personal relationships of
this inchoate concept are profound. It could account for the tendency
toward centralized administration, the bureaucratic rigidity that is
characteristic of many governments, and the lack of interest in delegating authority on a personal level.

Whatever its origins, Confucianism reinforced it, but added to
it a moral imperative. The ruler who has such power must exercise it
in a moral manner, as a father would do toward his children. Social
responsibility was a cardinal, theoretical element of the Confucian
system of governance. Paternalism in organizations, rather than being considered pejorative and denigrated as in the contemporary West,

has been and continues to be an essential element in organizational relations. Indeed, if it is absent in Korea, the leadership is not considered quite human.

Centralization and Pluralism

The tendency to keep control of the process of government has its counterpoint in efforts to prevent alternative centers of power or authority from developing. Thus the concept, central to the American system, of a series of checks and balances between branches of government, between federal and local authorities, or institutionally in organizations from business to universities and non-profit organizations, is a traditional conceptual anathema.

Government views such autonomy as inherently destabilizing, diminishing its power, and in fact subverting the moral order, of which it alone is the guardian. Autonomous power is not always viewed as a threat, but certainly with suspicion, and through a complex, changing system of incentives and punishments, Korean officialdom has been able to maintain its power base. Park Chung Hee, following the coup of 1961, engaged in a sweeping, successful effort to centralize governmental (and many private) institutions.[18] He also eliminated elected local government in Korea, while Syngman Rhee before him had also attempted to manipulate and control it through rigged elections. The virtual, absolute control of private institutional credit by government and the profound and consistent government intervention into the private economic sector, from setting export targets and limiting or expanding competition in certain industries to intervening at all levels in the rural sector, are examples of a pervasive network that is in conformity with, if only partly caused by, the Confucian backdrop. The Korean actions can be attributed to military administrative "tidiness" (which may have played an important role), but the concept of a "Korea, Inc." and a "Japan, Inc."[19] indicate a strong historical basis for such public-private collaboration. This can, in a real Confucian sense, be productive for the society as a whole, but it also eliminates the pluralism so central to the American system.

Within this context, it might be useful to redefine our understanding of Confucianism as it applies to the private sector. If we think of private enterprise solely in terms of merchants and traders operating for their own private gain, the Confucian ideology offers little theoretical promise for development. If, however, trade, commerce, and production are considered as enhancing the status and moral legitimacy of the ruler, then fostering (but controlling) their development becomes a matter of appropriate national concern and Confucian statecraft. Thus political legitimacy pursued through economic channels is as much an integral part of the Confucian tradition as is policy formation.

Collectivity and Individuality

The relative strength of clan and family in each of the Confucian societies varies, but it is apparent that in all of them they are of far more important magnitude than in most Western societies and are more highly organized than in many traditional cultures. In Korea, perhaps, the family was most important, because Korean society lacked the Japanese system of setting up new family hierarchies.

The strong emphasis in Confucianism on the family as the intellectual and ideological analogy and the institution of primary loyalty has reinforced an earlier Korean emphasis on the clan and family. With few intermediate institutions between the state and the family, the family reinforced the function of protecting the individual family member, especially through the patriarchal line. The preeminence of the family, of course, also retarded the development of other institutional loyalties.

The result, reinforced by the generational role of Confucianism as a form of ancestor worship, has been the submerging of individual identity within the familial context, given special urgency by and the need to make offerings on behalf of one's ancestors. This collectivity is a pervasive phenomenon, and is illustrated by the continuous use of the Korean "we" when the American would normally use "I". What personal tensions this might create for Koreans caught in the process of change through foreign education or contacts is still conjectural.

Ironically, the submerging of the Korean individuality within the broader familial context has produced neither uniformity among Koreans nor a lack of personal incentive. In fact, an analysis of the Korean educational system,[20] which is still highly Confucian, hierarchical, group oriented, and traditional, has shown that even this system, seemingly archaic given contemporary needs, has produced Korean children with a highly developed sense of personal efficacy, initiative, drive, and entrepreneurial spirit. Some would attribute this risk-taking ability and interest to child-rearing practices that are somewhat different in Korea than those in Japan and China.[21] Whatever the causes, and however inconsistent individuality and collectivity seem to be, the system has produced both a personal and institutional dynamism which is the envy of many other developing societies.

The reverence for education as a factor of growth and development in Confucian-oriented societies is a trait now more widely recognized in the West. There are certainly few cultures in which the admiration for and role of the educated has been more extolled. The literati ideal, transformed into modern terms, has led to intensive, overwhelming familial pressures for individual student performance with overall remarkably effective results. Individual accomplishments, however spectacular, become an integral part of collective, familial status and pride, and a form of social security.

Collectivity exists at the national as well as at the family level. Constantly buffeted by superior foreign military pressures and various, pervasive foreign influences, (including that of Confucianism itself), Korea as a small nation has only survived because of a collective, cultural concept. In spite of the attempted cultural genocide during the later period of Japanese rule, Korea as a unique cultural unit has continued, and indeed been strengthened.

Orthodoxy and Heterogeneity

Equating morality with power has produced strong tendencies toward orthodoxy of a rigid variety. In China this was mitigated by vast distances, resulting in a degree of geographical obscurity which allowed non-Confucian intellectual movements, such as both Buddhism and Taoism. In Korea, however, orthodoxy was more pronounced. It was reinforced by geographic, social, and political factors. Korea is a relatively small nation in area, and thus strong separatist tendencies have not been apparent since the seventh century. The division of Korea into north and south today is regarded on both sides of the armistice line as a foreign-imposed aberration. Korea, in addition, is the only culturally, linguistically, and ethnically homongeneous nation in Asia. It has no significant minority groups. Buddhism as an intellectual (and economic) force was downgraded following the establishment of the Yi Dynasty in 1392 and the promulgation of Confucianism as the only court-sanctioned ideology. Korea, perhaps to gain favorable recognition of China, engaged in what was called *sadaechui*, or toadyism (serving the greater power—a term opponents of the present Korean regime sometimes use in describing Korean government attitudes toward the United States) and became more orthodox than its mentor.

The orthodoxy of the Korean court, together with strong centralist tendencies, produced a rigidity that exacerbated factionalism and forced intellectual endeavor into prescribed and accepted areas. Even officials in disgrace and exiled to the remote provincial areas played by the intellectual rules of the game when they wrote poetry.

The vitality of Yi Dynasty Korea in the arts was almost in inverse ratio to the artist's social distance from the court. Pottery, certain types of painting, village masked dance satirizing the society, and the *pansori* musical tradition belonged to those removed from court strictures.

The concept of a "virtuocracy" in which rulers were by definition more morally proper than the rest of society of course reinforced the intensity of orthodoxy. If one did not conform to the intellectual system, one had to leave it, in exile during the imperial period or in confrontation with established authority during the various republics. In this latter period, the mixture of traditional authoritarian attitudes with new participatory concepts created additional tensions, as the two intellectual systems were fundamentally in conflict, and remain so today. In some sense the task of the Korean government has been to fuse the aura of participation and the trappings of political representation with the Confucian concept of the authority of the ruler and the state.

This political tightrope, which is constantly subject to slippage, is in contrast with the lack of ideological rigidity in the sphere of economics. Korean economic planning is noted for its pragmatic approach to development issues, never allowing ideology to stand in the way of achieving economic goals. So Korea has a very large public sector, a vital private sector but with government planning and regulation of the economy, and a record of changing economic policies when the government feels that its interests are at stake. The explanation may lie in the role of economic development as a means to political legitimacy, and that economic growth is a facet illuminating the moral supremacy of the ruler, and by extension his regime. It is apparent, however, that this pragmatism is evident in the economic policies of other Confucian states, and even in the People's Republic of China, where it was belatedly introduced, it may eventually be considered more in the mainstream than the extreme socialist forms introduced since 1950.

Law and Morality

The "Rule of Law," the phrase so highly regarded in the United States, and equality before the law are two concepts that are antithetical to the Confucian system. Although it is true that China early developed a legalist school of thought, the central tradition in both Korea and China was that if the state's or the families' moral house was in order, then law would not be necessary. If law was required, it indicated that either the leader was deficient or the breaker of the law was morally depraved; thus law became punishment.[22] It is probably true that analyses of Confucian law have stressed too heavily the scriptural injunctions that morality should replace law, for later developments in China and Korea regarded law as important in the art of government.

The concept that law was a means either for a neutral confrontation between disputants, or between the individual and the state, was not developed. One could argue that the essential ingredient of the Western legal tradition is confrontation, while in many other societies along a mythical confrontation/non-confrontation continuum, non-confrontation is more the pattern. In some societies, the introduction of Western legal systems and courts has resulted in the use of such systems to reinforce traditional dispute settlement.[23]

The residual Confucian attitudes toward law result in the well-documented phenomenon in all Confucian societies of a paucity of lawyers (compared to the United States) and their relatively low status among professional groups.

Laws too are often facades that provide images divorced from the reality of decision making or power. Equality before the law is not widely practiced, and yet ironically law is used in the various constitutions to circumvent fundamental rights, which are articulated but often "subject to law." Law, rather than a refuge, is an overt reflection of the moral superiority of the regime and those who hold power.

The need for exports and imports has in part shifted concepts of contractual law, so that the Confucian tradition of gentlemen making binding agreements based on their word and the dire social consequences of breaking it has given way to internationalization of some of Korean business dealings. Yet there remain grey areas where Confucian attitudes may prevail, and law will give way to tradition.

The role of the Western multinational in Korean economic development has been economically marginal. Foreign investment from all sources is small in comparison with the size of the Korean economy. More important to Korea than the funds expended within the country or the numbers of people employed are perhaps several other factors that make the role of the multinational critical.

The multinational brings into Korea technology, technology that is imperative for Korea to internalize if it is to continue the economic growth on which the political legitimacy of the regimes since the Third Republic are based. Korea has largely been dependent on foreign firms, mostly trading organizations, for "product technology," the standards that foster international sales. It has great capacity for "process technology," the development of systems to produce more efficiently the products it plans to sell abroad.

Multinational investment in Korea is also a form of security insurance for Korea, for it is tangible evidence of the intent of the United States and the international community to come to the defense of Korea, should that become necessary. Such investment also demonstrates to the populace that the regime in power is accepted in international economic circles, and it enhances the legitimacy of the government.

None of these needs are inappropriate, nor are they unusual in many societies. In the Korean Confucian context, they fulfill certain requirements that in the shorter term may result in strengthening the modern adaptation of the Confucian system to developmental ends. Over a longer period, however, there is likely to be further erosion of Confucian political beliefs, their melding with international patterns, and the evolution, as in Japan, of an economic, social, and political system that will reflect certain basic attributes of the Confucian tradition as it evolved in Korea together with adaptation of international codes of operation of government and business. The Korean people have illustrated a remarkable capacity for inventiveness and entrepreneurship. Those traits will likely endure.

The strong circumstantial evidence is that the Confucian tradition, however it was adapted to and welded onto pre- or non-Confucian cultural elements, has played an important role in economic development and on the development of industrial and trade relationships in these societies. Exactly how this worked or why, is perhaps less clear, but its influence on the system of governance, on the bureaucracy, and on personal and institutional relationships is likely to continue.

Notes

1. This does not denigrate the importance of religious building to economic development. Writing on Buddhism in Burma in the 11 − 13th centuries, Aung-Thwin noted; "The more one devoted to the religion − the bigger the temple built, the larger the land and labor endowments are made − the more legitimate the king and the state became. The scale increased as others in the society followed the royal example. Initially then, there was a direct (and circular) relationship between spending and religion, increased agricultural production, proportional demographic expansion, and state development." Michael Aung-Thwin, *Pagan. The Origins of Modern Burma* (Honolulu: University of Hawaii Press, 1985), p. 27.

2. See, for example, Krishna Kumar and Kee Young Kim, "The Korean Manufacturing Multinationals," *Journal of International Business Studies*, Spring/Summer 1984, pp. 45-61.

3. See Byong-ik Koh, "Confucianism in Asia's Modern Transformation." Wilson Center Colloquium Paper, January 16, 1985.

4. This is not to argue that Confucian thought is the sole factor in such success. The roles of the Indian chettyar subcaste in Burma and Indians in East Africa, as well as the Lebanese in West Africa, attest to the operation of other elements.

5. Norman Jacobs, *The Korean Road to Modernization and Development* (Urbana, Ill.: University of Illinois Press, 1985), p. 242.

6. Roderick MacFarquhar, "The Post-Confucian Challenge," *Economist*, October 7, 1980.

7. Jacobs, *The Korean Road*, p. 242.

8. Lucian W. Pye, *Asian Power and Politics. The Cultural Dimensions of Authority* (Cambridge, Mass.: Harvard University Press, 1985).

9. Jacobs, *The Korean Road*, p. 242.

10. Ibid., p. 228.

11. Ibid.

12. Pye, *Asian Power and Politics*, p. 86.

13. See Jacobs, *The Korean Road*. His volume is devoted to this theme. He regards Korea as a patrimonial society, but Japan as a feudal and post-feudal one.

14. Pye, *Asian Power and Politics*, p. 83.

15. For a discussion of this issue, see Gregory Henderson, *Korea, Politics of the Vortex* (Cambridge, Mass.: Harvard University Press, 1968).

16. Quoted in Pye, *Asian Power and Politics*, p. 21.

17. Benedict R. O'G. Anderson, "The Idea of Power in Javanese Society," in *Culture and Politics in Indonesia*, ed. Claire Holt (Ithaca, N.Y.: Cornell University Press, 1972).

18. For example, see David I. Steinberg, *Foreign Aid and the Development of the Republic of Korea: The Effectiveness of Concessional Assistance*, Agency for International Development, Evaluation Special Study 42, December 1985.

19. Edward S. Mason, et al., *The Economic and Social Modernization of the Republic of Korea* (Cambridge, Mass.: Harvard University Press, 1980).

20. Noel F. McGinn, et al., *Education and Development in Korea* (Cambridge, Mass.: Harvard University Press, 1980). On the individual and the collective, see "I" and "We" in O-Young Lee, *In This Earth and In That Wind: This is Korea*, trans. David I. Steinberg (Seoul: Hollym Publisher for the Royal Asiatic Society, Korea Branch, 1967, 1983).

21. Pye, *Asian Power and Politics*.

22. For studies of law related to Korea, see *Traditional Korean Legal Attitudes*, Institute of East Asian Studies, University of California, Berkeley, Center for Korean Studies. Research Monograph 2, 1980, and David I. Steinberg, "Law, Development, and Korean Society," *Journal of Comparative Administration*, August 1971.

23. For an example from Thailand, see David Engel, *Law and Justice in a Thai Provincial Court*, Association for Asian Studies Monograph, vol. 34 (Tucson, Ariz.: University of Arizona Press, 1978).

Response: Peter R. Moody, Jr.*

Basically, Confucianism is a very broad, very long-lived tradition. If we are to understand it in current society, we have to understand it as it functions rather than as an abstract set of principles. In this sense, it becomes fair to ask whether a Confucian society today is really Confucian, in the same sense that it is fair to ask whether Christian societies have ever really been Christian. There is more in all these societies, and when any particular result is viewed, it is difficult to know whether it is a product of Confucianism or of something else.

We can talk about the West in terms of Christendom. The term "Christendom" never really implied that everything going on within that region had to do with Christianity. It was a way of identifying a relatively distinct culture on the world stage. In the same way, I think we can talk about Confucian and post-Confucian society as a distinct cultural form.

As Steinberg brings out, in Vietnam, in Korea, in Japan, Confucianism was imported and imposed over an older folk society, although it has been very well absorbed into those societies. In China, where Confucianism originated, it has never been the single tradition; there have been competing traditions. And again, when a set of people will say of a certain thing, "Well, it is our Confucian tradition," it is difficult to know if they know what they are talking about. Is it really Confucianism? How do we know? How do they know?

Alternatively, in looking at the societies that call themselves Confucian, we do in fact begin to see similarities. In the process of modernization, all have done well in terms of income growth and equity growth. That seems to be a rather distinctive characteristic of all of

*Peter R. Moody, Jr., is a professor of government and international studies at the University of Notre Dame. An authority on the relationship between traditional patterns of thought and culture in East Asia and contemporary Asian politics, he is the author of four books on China.

91

these societies, socialist and nonsocialist, with the nonsocialist states having more spectacular success in recent years.

One reason is that these states have been forced by world circumstances to engage in the world economy and perhaps the Confucian tradition has somehow helped them. In each case, however, it has been done reluctantly, it has been done with very bad grace, it has been done with a lot of grumbling, it has been done with a sense that they have sold their souls in order to achieve this spectacular growth.

In China a few years ago, there was a major campaign organized around the issue of spiritual pollution. One thing it apparently addressed was the bad influence of Western ideas which accompanied Western investment. There have been similar concerns in all of these societies, whether Communist or not, that somehow modernization was destroying a lot of good old customs and attitudes.

Steinberg points to the tendency in the olden days to see a contradiction between Confucian society and the demands of modernization. Even though it has passed out of fashion among Western analysts, who now believe that Confucianism really fits in with the demands of modernization, that contradiction is still perceived in East Asia. In most East Asian societies, perhaps even including Japan, there is a tendency, at least among intellectuals, to see the contradiction between what they consider to be the traditional practices and the demands of modernization. At the same time, there is a tendency to see anything that they believe to be blocking a better life for them as a residue of tradition. A Chinese, for example, whether inside or outside the Communist Party, tends to identify as obstacles to growth, factors that most of us would consider standard Marxist-Leninist practices. But, they see them as part of their feudal heritage.

A case can be made that the traditional Confucian state structure has been relatively hostile to modernization. The Chinese obviously have shown a great ability to adapt to the modern world. The greatest ability in adaptation has been among the overseas Chinese and the smaller Chinese communities, areas not under the central control of the Chinese state.

In the West, liberalism and industrialism developed together. In Confucian society they did not, and Confucian societies did not industrialize spontaneously. With liberalism in the West came not only individualism and political liberty, but also a growing abstraction of human relationships, people losing touch with each other except in the usual terms of conducting business. Confucianism, on the other hand, is built upon human relationships, which are never abstract. Parents and children, for example, are engaged in concrete, specific relationships. The importance of personal relationships pervades the society. This personalism also interrelates with the weakness of law in these societies.

It may be that modernization is no longer necessarily liberal. As a hypothesis, there may be a correspondence or affinity between what is sometimes called post-industrial society and the modern version of Confucian society. This combination might have a superiority over the West in that there is the post-industrial pattern without the abstraction, without the depersonalization that accompanies Western society. This means that rapid post-modern growth and change take place in a situation where there is still relatively well-developed, well-articulated, sound, personal relationships, both in families and in organizations.

Moreover, we must note that, while these post-Confucian societies are able to adapt to the post-liberal, post-industrial, post-modern world and achieve success in economic growth, every one of them has grave and chronic problems of political legitimacy.

An important aspect of Confucianism is that it is a very moralistic tradition. All political and economic behavior is judged in terms of morality. This can be high-minded, but it also can mean simply that the rulers would prefer that status come from education and bureaucratic position rather than from making money. This moralism, while serving a social function, also means that economic activity is not always judged in terms of efficacy. If that were the case, if government were judged solely in terms of efficacy or efficiency, the state would begin to lose legitimacy. In other words, it would be seen as the selling out of what had been the moral way.

Response: Yusaku Furuhashi*

At the conclusion of the realistic assessment of Confucianism in East Asian countries, Steinberg states:

> The strong circumstantial evidence is that Confucian tradition . . . has played an important role in economic development and on the development of industrial and trade relationships in these societies. Exactly how this worked or why, is perhaps less clear, but its influence on the system of governance, on the bureaucracy, and on personal and institutional relationships is likely to continue.

The following comment tries to speculate briefly on "how" Confucianism may have influenced principal aspects of the economic-business contours of contemporary Japan as an example. Thus, the comment that follows is more an extension of Steinberg's paper than a comment on specific aspects of his paper.

CONFUCIANISM AND SINITIC CULTURES

Confucianism is a nice summary way of describing Sinitic cultures and societies, but representing manifold interconnections of East Asian societies by this one dimension alone may be misleading. What then are the common features of the East Asian peoples and societies? Someone has perceptively described them as chopsticks, Chinese ideographs, and abacus. And a contemporary pundit has cryptically portrayed the two most common features of the fast-growing East Asian societies as chopsticks and baseball.

A list of salient characteristics common to these societies most likely includes the following four: First, East Asian peoples share gen-

---

*Yusaku Furuhashi is the Ray W. and Kenneth G. Herrick Professor of International Business and dean of the College of Business Administration at the University of Notre Dame. He serves as a consultant for both American and Japanese business firms.

erally common physical features and thus all look alike. Second, these peoples use Chinese ideographs as a common storehouse of ideas and written symbols. Although not a means of perfect communication, they make mutual communication and learning much easier. Third, they use chopsticks and eat rice as the mainstay in their diet. Wetfield rice farming in densely populated areas as the common, central agricultural endeavor may have facilitated the adoption of many features of the Chinese culture, family and lineage organization as well as political and economic organizations, in these societies. Last, they all share the similar religious and ethical heritage derived from the amalgamation of Buddhism, Confucianism, and Taoism. "Confucianism" seems to have been used as a handy way to describe many of these characteristics common to East Asian societies.

GENERAL ROLE OF RELIGION IN JAPANESE ECONOMY AND BUSINESS

While religion plays only a peripheral position in Japanese personal life, it can play a crucial role in the economic or business life of a society. Karl Marx contended that ideology and ethics were no more than the reflection of underlying material conditions, in particular the economic conditions. Max Weber, in his *Protestant Ethic and the Spirit of Capitalism*, made the case for the existence of quite the reverse situation. In reality, political and economic choices may depend on the dominant ideology and ethics; conversely, these may be influenced, modified, and even destroyed by shifting political and economic conditions as well.

The influence of religion on economic and business development thus can be negative, neutral, and/or positive. Further, the relative strengths of these influences differ among different societies and undergo changes in a given society.

Religion had a *negative* influence in the economic life of feudal Japan in the sense that the private accumulation of wealth and pursuit of profit was viewed with considerable distrust, and merchants were given the lowest social status. While these negative influences have subsided to a large extent, they continue to play an important role in contemporary Japan, providing restraints on the *excesses* in economic and business activities such as selfish profit-seeking and excessively competitive behavior of both individuals and firms.

Religion also has had a *positive* influence on the economic and business aspects of Japanese society. For example, during the eighteenth century, Japanese Buddhists and neo-Confucianists such as Seisan Suzuki and Baigan Ishida advanced some creative reformist ideas to bring the work ethics in line with their ideologies. They asserted that money-making and saving activities aimed at accumulating capital to be invested for public purposes were by no means base. Rather, through honesty, frugality, busy work, and honest profit-making, an individual can attain spiritual enlightenment, harmony with nature, and service to the society. Thus, work came to be seen as not purely an economic act but a spiritual and moral experience as well. The business and work ethics of Seisan and Baigan became the ethics of Japanese business and eventually offered a rationale for the *samurai* to become business-men themselves in the early modern Japan.[1]

Eiichi Shibusawa, a giant figure in both government and business in the Meiji Japan, was a Confucian who refined the business and work ethics of Seisan and Baigan and applied them to the world of developing modern Japanese business and industry. He felt that business needed the Confucian ideal of strong mutual relationships and service to keep it from degenerating into selfish profit-making. To him learning was as much a part of business as sound morality, and productivity was a way of practicing virtue. Such work ethics and ideologies as Shibusawa's continue to exert a strong influence on contemporary Japanese economy, business, and society.[2]

Religion in Japan has come to have a decreasing influence on peoples' lives as the trend toward secularization, which began in the seventeenth century, continues to accelerate. Religion thus has come to occupy a peripheral position in peoples' lives, resulting in a general emphasis on "now" and the experiences of life in this world rather than in the "hereafter." Thus, religious ideologies have become increasingly *neutral* toward economic changes in the sense that religion does not constitute a barrier for political and/or economic changes.

PRINCIPAL ASPECTS OF JAPANESE CONFUCIANISM

Confucianism, in the Japanese context, is a philosophy rather than a formal religion. In the irreligious, contemporary Japanese society, "Confucianism probably has more influence on them than any of the traditional religions or philosophies."[3] Even then, contemporary Japanese are obviously not Confucianists in the sense of the pre-Meiji period, but they are still permeated with Confucianism. Such Confucian ethical values as belief in the moral basis of government, emphasis on interpersonal relations and loyalties, and faith in education and hard work still lurk beneath the consciousness of the Japanese. No contemporary Japanese considers himself a Confucianist, but in a sense almost all native-born Japanese are.

Japanese Confucianism was primarily concerned with three-dimensional, mutual relationships: vertical order, horizontal web, and continuity. The vertical order is concerned with a sense of hierarchical order in the society in which primacy of public over private is clearly defined, and each individual is assigned a relative position with respect to another on the basis of seniority and/or the degree of importance toward the "public." The horizontal web is concerned with a sense of the complementarity of relations. The emphasis here is on interchangeability and cooperation among complementary elements. Here the major identification is with one's role in the organization, and decision making is based on principles of solidarity rather than majority. Continuity refers to a unity of nation, village, and family through a common flow of blood from the ancestors to the present.

In this framework, each individual's rights and duties result not so much from principles of an individual's conscience as from the external formalistic demands to which each must submit. Thus, primacy of human harmony and of living up to the expected role is recognized. Further, one's role connotes the public, not the private, aspect of oneself.

EFFECTS OF CONFUCIANISM IN JAPANESE SOCIETY

The effects of these characteristics on the Japanese people have been the creation of an educated people with the enhanced sense of commitment, organizational identity, and loyalty to various institutions. The other side of the Confucian influence has been the failure to evolve a liberal, progressive, and self-asserting mentality on the one hand, and the Japanese tendency to be anti-individualistic, conservative, and paternalistic on the other.

The effects on the macropolitical-economic system have been the emergence of state capitalism guided and driven by a national bureaucracy. In line with the Confucian political thought of government by men of education and superior ethical wisdom, elite national bureaucrats are respected and accorded the most important position in the society, amassing power, authority, and prestige. They are strictly and competitively selected. They are believed not only to be intelligent, competent, dedicated, and cohesive, but to have the strong sense of group mission needed to concentrate on what is good for the nation as a whole. Thus, the strategic directions for the national economy given by the ministerial bureaucrats have the general support and trust of the population. The result is the Japanese brand of guided capitalism in which the national government bureaucracy provides central strategic *developmental* (vs. regulatory) directions and the action framework, and implementations are carried out largely in the hands of local governmental and business organizations. In this Japanese brand of capitalism, *symbiotic* (vs. adversarial) relationships between government and business have been recognized and accepted on both sides.

The general pattern of industrial organizations may be seen as reflecting the Confucian philosophy. Within an industry, companies are classified and ranked according to their sizes and ages. Thus, it is generally assumed that the bigger (and older) a company, the better its quality and the higher its prestige in the society of industries and the society in general, thus resulting in concentration of power and wealth in large business firms. Further, business firms both large and small are organized into webs of horizontal business groupings such as the prewar *zaibatsu* or postwar *keiretsu* and vertical groupings such as subsidiaries, affiliated companies, and subcontract manufacturing networks.

Confucianism's influence may be discernible in a wide range of management practices including organizational structure, decision-making processes, and employment practices. Given the strong emphasis placed on solidarity, group consciousness, and loyalty to their own kind as the key building blocks in the society, individuals are ideally at one with their group. In other words, human value based on familistic values form the core value of Japanese organizations, including the business corporations themselves and their managerial practices. The latter include, among others, employee recruitment, so-called permanent or life-time employment, seniority-based pay, enterprise union, and consensus decision making as well as the corporate family structure.

Business corporations often are affiliated with industrial group-ings on the one hand and a vertical network of closely knit groupings such as manufacturing subcontracting networks on the other—usually on a long-term personal basis. The Japanese company itself is perceived as not merely a functional organization or amalgamation of pieces of property of its shareholders, nor as the merging of talents and func-tions of interchangeable, technically qualified people. Rather, it transcends the ideas and objectives of a mere economic organization; it is a community, an organization in which the people factor is critical. Stated differently, if we view a firm as a set of people and simultane-ously a set of roles to be performed by this set of people, each of the two sets is organized to form a complex whole in an organization. In the Japanese system, the human or people system dominates the role system, in which a set of people is formed which then explores what it can and should do. This may be contrasted to the individualistic Western system where role system dominates human system, in which acceptance of a role by an individual is made via a formal contract.

The Japanese have transplanted to the modern corporation many social values and habits of the *ie*, or households of the rice-farming village, such as dedication to group goals, the task-sharing, and the sense of mutual obligation. This pattern is manifest in the way business offices are organized: few private offices, mostly open-space offices where desks are arranged in such a way as to facilitate communication and interpersonal interactions as well as constant, intimate evaluation of subordinates by superiors. In fact, the typical layout of Japanese offices looks like a giant organization chart. The office layout sym-bolizes the deeper attitudes toward these relationships.

These attitudes toward relationships and pervasive values are clearly seen also in human resource management practices. While ac-tual practice may deviate considerably, idealized Japanese human resource management practices typically involve periodic induction (once a year) of new graduates (of both high school and/or college) via elaborate selection and formalistic induction rituals, periodic rota-tion of jobs, slow but periodic promotion and increase in compensa-tion (up to certain levels) based on the *nenko* seniority system, life-time employment (typically until the set retirement age of fifty-five, now moving toward sixty), and enterprise unionism. Enterprise or com-pany unionism refers to an approach in developing a community of faith in the firm's survival based on "one company, one union in a sort of union shop." In other words, the Japanese version of communism in the corporate community envisions and tries to pursue the ideals of (1) linking the interests and fortune of employees with those of the company as a whole, and (2) paying each according to his needs and expecting from each work efforts according to his ability. Such ideals, while not fully realizable, can be pursued only in the context of long-term dedication to group goals, task sharing, and a sense of mutual obligation on the one hand, and the employee's internalization of the values, roles, functions, and systems of his firm on the other.

The "*ringi*" system is much discussed as a salient feature of decision making in Japanese organizations. It refers to a process of obtaining approval on a proposed matter through vertical, and sometimes horizontal, circulation of documents to the concerned members in the organization in order to build a consensus around major decisions. It may be time-consuming and politically delicate, but it is appropriate for the Japanese organization based on and protected by a seniority system. In the Japanese business organization, which is viewed primarily as a social entity rather than overwhelmingly an economic entity, decision making is not merely a matter of transforming information, it is a political activity. Long-term stability within the tightly knit group requires constant effort, long discussions, concern for minority views, and explicit compensation for disappointments and other contributions to group solidarity. But the payoff is expected in results, the ultimate reward for good teamwork. Thus, if management is to be measured not only by the time needed for making decisions but also by the time needed for implementing the decisions made, this system is efficient as well as effective.

One of the major challenges for survival, vitality, and growth of these organizations is the issue of how to introduce the competition and social mobility so vital for change and progress into the system effectively while maintaining the Japanese primacy of human harmony and of living up to the expected role of individuals. This is accomplished by basing the entry into the group on individual ability and the principle of survival of the fittest — primarily through a series of competitive examinations. Once the individual enters the group, the group takes over under the principle of human harmony. The competitive struggle continues, however, between groups, making use of the tremendous force of solidarity and role expectation.

CONCLUSION

It is safe to state that Confucianism is too narrow a concept to be truly meaningful when applied to analyze and discuss the syncretic Japanese situation, although it may be a handy way to describe the complex religious and ideological phenomena commonly found in the East Asian societies. The discussion here is not intended to evaluate the comparative merit of these with those of the United States or more generally the West. Where some comparisons are made, they are intended only to show the differences. Unquestionably, there are some fundamentally different values and ideologies as well as cultural and social institutions embodying such differences. But at the same time, there exists a wide range of similarities in these cultures and societies. Because of the orientation of this discussion, these have not been explored.

An increasingly strong interest has been shown in recent years in the East Asian economies and business performance. It is possible that Confucian values and ideologies as well as cultural and social institutions found in the contemporary Asian societies may be better suited to (1) the pursuit of rapid growth in an economy, and (2) efficient and effective operations of highly interdependent complex business and industrial systems. Designating the economic systems of Japan and the Four Little Dragons of East Asia as "East Asian Capitalism," Peter L. Berger states that:

> certain components of Western bourgeois culture — notable activism, rational innovativeness, and self-discipline — are necessary for successful capitalist development. Specific elements of East Asian civilization, be it in the "great traditions" or in folk culture, have fastened these values and have consequently given the societies of the region a comparative advantage in the modernization process.[4]

Before an attempt is made to compare the merits of these different systems, one must come to a good understanding and appreciation of the differences and similarities that exist among these systems. Moreover, having a good understanding of Confucianism and its apparent manifestations in economic and business systems in the East Asian societies does not necessarily provide sufficient explanation for the rapid growth of their economies and the high performance of their businesses. For that we must seek additional causes and explanations as well.

NOTES

1. Based on Shichihei Yamamoto, *Nihon Shihonshugi no Seishin (The Spirit of Japanese Capitalism)* (in Japanese) (Tokyo: Kobunsha, 1979), pp. 113–168.

2. Based on Johannes Hirscheimer, S.V.D., and Tsunehiko Yui, *The Development of Japanese Business 1600–1980* (London: George Allen & Unwin, 1981), pp. 101–132 *passim*.

3. Edwin O. Reischauer, *The Japanese* (Cambridge, Mass.: Harvard University Press, 1977), p. 214.

4. Peter L. Berger, *The Capitalist Revolution* (New York: Basic Books, Inc., 1986), p. 166.

Multinationals and Catholic Social Teaching in Latin America

THE MOST REVEREND MARCOS G. McGRATH, C.S.C.,

AND REVEREND FERNANDO BASTOS DE AVILA, S.J.*

It was after the Second World War that the Holy Father, Pope Pius XII, began to call the attention of Catholics in Western Europe and North America to the situation of the Church in Latin America, where, already at that time, about 40 percent of the Catholics in the world lived. By the end of this century, perhaps closer to 50 percent of the world's Roman Catholics will live in Latin America. This is an astounding figure. All the more so when we consider that Latin America is the only area of the so-called Third World which is predominantly Christian, and in this case, Christian Catholic. Given this large and growing Catholic population, Catholic social teaching will surely be a critical factor in shaping the role of the private sector and of the direct investment climate in Latin America. If Catholic social doctrine is to impact the development of Latin America in general and multinational investment in particular, it is important to first investigate the nature and history of the region and the doctrines this scenario involves.

---

*The Most Reverend Marcos McGrath, C.S.C., the Archbishop of Panama, has served as a member of Vatican Council II and on the steering committees of the Second and Third General Conferences of Latin America Bishops. He was also the dean of the theology faculty at the Catholic University of Chile. The Archbishop is on the Board of Trustees at the University of Notre Dame.

Fernando Bastos de Avila, S.J., is a professor of social ethics on the graduate faculty of theology at the Catholic University in Rio de Janeiro. He is co-author of *Christian Faith and Social Commitment* published by the Latin American Episcopal Council (CELAM).

MULTINATIONALS AND THE THIRD WORLD

The Third World Condition

What characterizes the Third World is its underdevelopment. Whether measured by quantitative economic criteria such as income per capita, gross national product, savings, or investments or by social criteria in terms of literacy or infant mortality this underdeveloped condition is clearly visible. The question is whether Third World areas are moving toward some further goal, some breakthrough, some new form of organization of society; or whether the state of the developing countries is a global pattern which will continue. Does the world economic structure *necessitate* underdevelopment in some areas in order for other countries to be developed?

The distinction between the developing and developed countries is not the same as the distinction between the rich and the poor countries. There is the breakthrough of some Third World countries, particularly the oil nations, into wealth without thereby becoming developed. Nor is it wise to suppose, as some have done in the past, that development must or will take the same shape everywhere — and that, therefore, the so-called developing nations are simply "behind" and the whole job is to help them catch up to the northern models.

In the pattern of development, the Western world has been established as a metropolis, a center of development. On the periphery are the developing nations, held in a state of dependence. This dependence can easily present an opportunity for the exploitation of the Third World by the First World.

This exploitation need not be interpreted as some kind of diabolic conspiracy of evil minds to subject the peoples of the Third World to nondevelopment, poverty, and oppression. It can simply be viewed as a mechanistic pattern of Western development which has been operating in the last two centuries.

Involvement of Multinationals in Third World Development

The Third World has tried to break this pattern by diversifying its imports and exports: importing capital as well as consumer goods and exporting finished products produced from such imported capital.

Developing countries have also set up protective barriers to enhance their internal industry and agriculture, too often provoking retaliation.

The principle characteristics of multinationals are that they are enterprises which have the capacity to administer factors of production and resources wherever found within or beyond national frontiers. They are enterprises which can also take their product—output, goods, and services—into or out of any country. Secondary characteristics of multinationals are their great economic and financial potential, their capacity for administration, their use and development of advanced technology, and marketing power.

Multinationals are not necessarily bound by national obligations or mentalities. With their pragmatic approach, they have been able to leap over protective barriers and install themselves in developing nations. They have established their own industries and their own commerce within the Third World economies. In this process, multinationals have helped the Third World produce manufactured products and diversify imports and exports. In large measure it is the multinationals which have brought about the industrial growth of Latin America. In a certain sense, multinationals de-nationalize capitalism. However, it is also true that the bases of the major multinationals are in the First World. There they receive the larger profits and control advanced technology.

The multinational presence in the Third World has both positive and negative aspects. Their investments in Third World countries have created jobs, paid salaries, and trained human resources. They have increased the value of natural resources for which there was no indigenous technology. The traditional price-setting pattern which has been one of the major complaints of the developing nations—prices set in the North, both for exports and for our imports—has been somewhat broken by the operation of multinationals. This is particularly true for petroleum prices but has occurred in other areas as well. The multinationals have brought new technological and organizational procedures, while competition between multinationals has given the countries of the Third World a certain liberty of option between the various firms seeking a place in their markets.[1]

Foremost among the negative aspects of multinational involvement in the Third World is the fact that multinationals tend to transfer industries rather than technology. For example, Brazil does not have technology in the automobile manufacturing but manufactures a lot of automobiles. In other words, the whole factory has been brought in but not the infrastructure by which the imported technology may be duly assimilated. This infrastructure is composed of trained human resources, the universities, and the public and private enterprises that promote scientific and technological research.

Multinationals can prove to be a drain on Third World reserves, absorbing local credit and competing with national enterprises. Undesirable ecological consequences may well follow the installation of industries banned in the First World due to attendant environmental hazards. Further, while competition among multinationals does allow Third World countries to choose among corporations, such decisions are not necessarily made wisely. Some multinationals have proved themselves expert in exploiting the weakness of Third World bureaucracies—particularly those of authoritarian regimes—by tendering unwritten advantages such as bribery and by associating themselves with the local oligarchy.

In the effort to evaluate multinationals operating in the Third World in general, or Latin America in particular, one must consider whether or not these corporations have helped increase the growing gap between the rich and the poor nations, and between the rich and the poor in the poorer nations. It is this increasing gap that leads to the accusation prevalent throughout much of Latin America, and so often expressed by religious leaders, that multinationals operate as part of an international system which exploits the dependence of the poor for the benefit of the rich, both within each country and on the international level.

A Lack of Judicial and Ethical Guidelines

In an effort to enhance the positive impacts and mitigate the negative, two voids must be faced—the ethical and the judicial vacuums. Multinationals, like all enterprises, do not function primarily from an ethical point of view, but rather on the level of *praxis*. The determining factor in their conduct is efficacy for profit. However, when operating in a nation, even a large enterprise must submit to certain ethical patterns. It has duties toward fiscal authorities, suppliers, competitors, consumers, the labor force, and the general public. Each of the units or branches of a multinational submits to those ethical patterns imposed by the nation in which it is located. Yet, even while complying with these norms, a multinational may perform on the international level without any ethical consideration at all. The ethical demands on this level are not the sum of the individual ethical performances followed at the national level. Rather, a multinational, by its own transnational nature, has a global ethical responsibility, even though there is no such thing as an ethical code for fulfilling these demands.

Multinationals similarly evade judicial regulation. While national enterprises perform according to duties and rights contained in national laws (e.g. the anti-trust law in the United States), once they become multinationals they do not operate within a nation. Their nation is the world. There is no such thing as an international juridical order capable of establishing rights and duties for them.

At the national level an enterprise may file for composition of creditors or file for bankruptcy. These are situations ruled by laws. At the international level firms do not file for bankruptcy, but call a moratorium without any kind of regulation. Again at the national level loans are regulated, a transgression of which constitutes a crime of usury or speculation. At the international level, interest rates freely fluctuate without any input by the debtor nations. In Brazil, for example, a one percent increase in the London Interbank Offered Rate (the accepted measure of global short-term interest rates) would increase the external debt by $500 million. The international legal order lacks the institutions to regulate these situations. Disputes are resolved through bargaining and compromise where the power of the strongest prevails.

CATHOLIC SOCIAL DOCTRINES

If the juridical void remains as a challenge to international law, the ethical void is a challenge to the social doctrine of the Church. It is time to review the history of this doctrine, its sources, its development, and its evolving engagement with the multinational situation, particularly in Latin America.

The Sources of Social Doctrine

The fundamental source of Christian social teaching is obviously divine revelation as contained in the Bible and in Apostolic Tradition.[2]

In this view all human destiny springs from the notions of God and creation and of our common vocation to really be children of God, interrelated to all peoples in a more than creative sense, in participation with divine nature. Each person is called to be co-creator of the world and its development. As imitators of God and lords of the world, all are called to imitate His love and its qualities of justice, pardon, and mercy. This involves the fullest development of each human being. There is no utopia on earth. Only imperfect kingdoms are being developed here, but they are the stuff of which the Kingdom will be made.

The reality of sin is very much a part of social thinking. Sin is in the world. Original sin is the sin in each person which darkens the horizon, the heart, and the mind. It constantly creeps into individual actions and social relationships. Sin projects itself not only as personal sin, but also as social sin where its effect is injustice. Sin creates structures of injustice and violence. If the structures are simply eliminated, yet nothing attacks the roots of those structures, little is accomplished. Other forms of oppression or injustice will simply spring from those same or other similar roots.

The desires of humanity will never be fully realized individually or collectively in this world. Therefore, any goal, definition, or pattern of society which presents itself as *the* full answer to the desires of humanity cannot be accepted. Everything that is accomplished is a preparation for the world to come. This does not detract from the internal significance of the present task but, rather, gives it a larger significance. There is a tendency to view this projection toward a life to come as converting religion into an opium of the people, a distraction from the secular task of building a more just world. This tendency is not a biblical vision. It is an accretion of some forms of expression of Christianity which distract people from their secular task. The whole thrust of the Church today is that through the secular task the Kingdom of God is attained, beginning on this earth and reaching perfection only at the end of time, when it is consummated by the action of God Himself in Christ.

Every major modern document on Church social teaching, going back to the very first, *Rerum Novarum* (the 1891 encyclical of Pope Leo XIII, "On the Social Question"), begins by justifying the Church's concern for social issues. The Vatican Council is no exception. It states the modern crisis of values dramatically:

Never has the human race enjoyed such an abundance of wealth, resources, and economic power. Yet a huge proportion of the world's citizens is still tormented by hunger and poverty while countless numbers suffer from total illiteracy. Never before today has man been so keenly aware of freedom. Yet, at the same time, new forms of social and psychological slavery make their appearance. Although the world of today has a very vivid sense of its unity and of how one man depends on another in needful solidarity, it is most grievously torn into opposing camps by conflicting forces. For political, social, economic, racial, and ideological disputes still continue bitterly and with them the peril of a war which would reduce everything to ashes. True, there is a growing exchange of ideas but the very words by which key concepts are expressed take on quite different meanings in diverse ideological systems. Finally, man painstakingly searches for a better world without working with equal zeal for the betterment of his own spirit.[3]

This presentation in the pastoral constitution of "The Church in the World Today" introduces a call to illustrate the problems of today in light of the Gospel and to do so with a real understanding of the problems seen *in themselves.* There is a need to experientially bring the Gospel to bear upon real life situations: by *observing* these first in depth, then *judging* them morally in the light of the Gospel, then *acting* in accord. This Pastoral Constitution is an urgent call to incorporate our religious beliefs into professional and social living, to bridge that gap between faith and life which the same Council document calls the heresy of our time.[4]

By the same token, the Council calls for a closer look at all the temporal and social problems and values in their own context. This means quite clearly that along with its call to integrate religious, professional, and secular lives, the Council insisted upon the autonomy of the secular order. It stated that the Church as *church*, through its official representatives, should not pretend to present any specific economic nor political model for society. Christians should try to develop these models and try to do so in the light of their Christian inspiration, but with the freedom to differ in the applications of the models. No Christian should pretend that any one person or group exhausts in any way the possibilities of Christian reflection on the different economic, social, and political models of society. At the same time, the document strongly rejects the kind of secularism that would attempt an absolute exclusion of religious values from temporal concerns — this would be the converse of the integration of the Gospel into our personal and social lives.

While, in effect, the Council was placing heavy stress upon effective and realistic moral thinking in the social areas, quite paradoxically there were strong criticisms, even during the Council sessions (1962 to 1965), about how this was being done in the manuals or handbooks of "Catholic Social Doctrine," which had been developed especially in the two or three preceding decades. The criticisms were several: 1) The manuals, and to some extent the Social Encyclicals, took their principles too directly from *Natural Law*. The "return to the sources" stressed by the Council called rather for principles reflecting directly the biblical vision of God, man, and society. 2) The manuals were becoming too pat, too static, too dogmatic — as reflected in the very name, "Catholic Social *Doctrine*." The critics preferred to speak of "Catholic Social *Teaching*" and stress the need for a more supple approach: applying principles of revelation and faith to the new and evolving world situations.

As a result of these criticisms, Catholic social teaching waned for a decade following Vatican II in Latin America as well as on other continents. Those who were fighting to have a Christian presence in labor unions, in organizations of entrepreneurs, or in professional organizations found themselves bereft of guidance. They were given the Bible and told, "Go ahead." There was no coordinated thinking, no development of patterns of action that would correspond to a Christian inspiration in Christian social teaching. In the last several years, under the guidance of John Paul II and, in Latin America, under the impetus of the last General Conference of Latin American Bishops in Puebla at the beginning of 1979, more of a balance is becoming evident.

What is to be said of the criticism of the previous social teaching of the Church? Like many criticisms, it possesses a great amount of truth, but was often overdone in its consequences. Earlier doctrine did tend to give formulas or recipes for social problems, based on natural law. As a result of the Council, the presentation of social teaching, just as of Christian living, has become much more rooted in the Scriptures, where it should be. The sound effort of the Second Vatican Council was to return to the sources of Christian living, particularly in the Word of God and the early example of the Church, and then to take this out to the world as something which sprung from the sources of

Christianity rather than from the philosophical manuals upon which we had come to rely.

There was also a certain lack of adaptability, a lack of growth in social teaching. Implicit in this is the charge that a historical perspective was missing — that Catholics lacked historical categories for the illustration and the dynamics of their thinking. In Latin America, this criticism has led some to adopt Hegelian patterns of conflict within society or to embrace a more explicit Marxist critique.[5] The return to the biblical vision is, at the same time, a return to a historical dynamic and to the perspective of the growth of the Kingdom of God in many different patterns, tending toward the final revelation of Christ. This vision has injected a dynamic into Catholic social teaching which, before the Council, was lacking.

In the years following the Council, several key documents expressed and guided this pursuit of a more adequate expression of what Catholic Social Teaching (or Doctrine) is, and how it is developed. Perhaps the best formulation yet is the one given us by the Third General Conference of Latin American Bishops in Puebla, 1979:

> Attentive to the signs of the time, which are interpreted in the light of the Gospel and the Church's magisterium, the whole Christian community is called upon to assume responsibility for concrete options and their effective implementation in order to respond to the summons presented by changing circumstances. Thus these social teachings possess a dynamic character. In their elaboration and application lay people are not to be passive executors but rather active collaborators with their pastors, contributing their experience as Christians, and their professional, scientific competence (GS:42).[6]

The Evolution of Latin American Social Doctrine

There is a great difference between the churches North and South. The Catholic Church in the Northern Hemisphere has been much affected in certain directions by the Protestant Reformation, more than the Church in the South, and has taken on many Northern European and North American cultural, ethical, and social patterns. Consideration of the social doctrine of the Church as it has evolved in Latin America must be set against the cultural-religious background of the Church and the people of Latin America. This teaching has been formed in an environment chafing against the traditions and culture of the

United States. It has developed uniquely in this century, with a pace accelerating since the Second Vatican Council. A synopsis of this history is thus a necessary background for the discussion of present teaching.[7]

The Latin American Church's social teaching of the present day can be traced to a period of renaissance of the Church, beginning in 1899 when Pope Leo XIII convoked all the bishops of Latin America to the Vatican for a special Synod. One can trace a progressively energetic renewal of the Church in Latin America from that date onward—in Scripture, in liturgy, in social action, in lay participation, in ecumenism—all very much under the impulse and guidance of the Holy See.

Thus, when bishops from Latin America went to Rome for the Second Vatican Council in 1962, they took with them the efforts of several generations of Catholics at a renaissance in the very direction embraced by the Council. The Latin bishops were very present at the Council. Of the 2,800 bishops there, some 750 were from Latin America. While they raised a lot of questions and influenced many of the documents, the most important impact of the Council was that they took to heart its call for renewal.

The Church of Latin America sensed its unity in Rome, at the Council, as its bishops joined together constantly to discuss the major issues at stake. They began to form a more united Latin American point of view due to their close proximity while in Rome, much more than when they were dispersed over the entire continent. Following the Council, the Council of Latin American Bishops (CELAM, created in 1955, at the First General Conference of Latin American Bishops) convened meetings across the continent on a range of subjects: catechetics, universities, social action, and many other topics.

These meetings led to the Second General Conference of the Latin American Bishops, which took place in Medellin in 1968.[8] Its grand purpose is summed up in the overall title placed upon the sixteen brief documents which it approved: "The Church in the Present Day Transformation of Latin America, in the Light of the Council."

The Medellin meeting was revolutionary in a real sense of the term. It brought together for the first time a large representation of bishops from all of Latin America who spoke clearly in the line of the Council on their vision of the Church in Latin America in the religious sphere, in the sphere of faith and church organization, and in the sphere of justice and peace on the continent. This had never happened in such a way before. Medellin was truly the beginning of a new history of the Church in Latin America.

The individual bishops and episcopal conferences took the Medellin documents[9] home. They became the subject of reflection and application on the part of priests, religious, and lay people throughout Latin America. A decade later, in 1979, the bishops joined in their Third General Conference in Puebla.[10] The Puebla discussion, based on fourteen years of experience after Vatican II, was a more reflective, more mature approach to the same subjects. The signposts which had been raised at Medellin in 1968 had now been converted into well-trodden roads during the ten years of experience in each of these areas, particularly in the lay participation in the Church. The Church was going out from itself, not remaining within the temple or within the parish house, and not content to say that in Latin America all are Catholics. Instead, the Church went out to the people in an effort at evangelization and social awareness with large participation of the laity. There has been a revolution of participation in the Church in Latin America occurring throughout the structure but particularly at the grass roots and among the poor.

The Latin American Church insists very much upon the question of the poor. This is, of course, profoundly biblical and evangelical. But the emphasis in Latin America today is particularly acute for a genuine historical reason: There are so many poor. And this in a continent that calls itself Christian, but where much of the poverty is obviously due to injustice resulting from the obvious lack of Christianity in the people, in the continent, in the nations and governments, indeed, in all those who are responsible for the making of a better society.

The Latin American Church documents—both continental, like Puebla, and those of local Catholic churches—speak a great deal about "evangelizing the poor" as a mission priority given to the Church by Our Lord.[11] They also take up the exhortation of Puebla to evangelize the whole of society *from* and *through* the poor ("a partir de los pobres" is the common expression). This is, in fact, occurring. The Church in Latin America, as a structure, is much less linked to the centers of political and economic power and prestige than in the past. In the 1920s and thereafter, most countries sundered the colonial and early republican union of Church and State. In recent years, especially since the Council, the local churches in Latin America have been working religiously and socially more and more with the poor, and drawing more of their leaders, including priests and bishops, from among the poor—including the "Indian" and "Afro-American" groups, which were so generally marginal or passive in the past.

The Church continues to be a strong and vocal opponent in Latin America to the Marxist promotion of class warfare, and the violence this invokes; but at the same time it recognizes the sharp and often tragic class distinctions which condition and prolong the poverty of so many millions in the continent, and calls for those personal and structural changes which are so essential for justice and for peace among our peoples and on the international level.

Thus the well-known "preferential option for the poor," so characteristic of the Church in Latin America, and so highly recommended by Pope John Paul II as well, is more and more *effective* in many areas, while at the same time it is not *classist* nor exclusive and seeks social reconciliation rather than social conflict.

The evangelizing of the middle and the upper classes, particularly in terms of Christian social awareness, was more effective in the 1940s and 1950s than since the Council. This is partly due to the decline and confusion surrounding Catholic social teaching after the Council. However, there are hopeful signs of new efforts and better hopes in this regard in recent years.

CATHOLIC SOCIAL DOCTRINE AND MULTINATIONAL CORPORATIONS

The multinationals have come upon the scene of late, and the Church's reaction even later. This delay is normal, since as the phenomena appear, reflection begins and reaction follows. While we cannot expect the institutional Church to provide a full-blown code of conduct for multinationals, Catholic social teaching has begun to address their presence.

The first Church text to mention multinationals was in 1971 when the Church began to react to their reality. It is in a document of Pope Paul VI to Cardinal Roy, who was at that time the head of the Papal Commission on Justice and Peace.[12] The Pope was very critical, pointing out the danger of the multinationals as instruments of exploitation of the Third World nations. It questions, it does not affirm. After that, there began a series of other statements in Papal documents and from the Latin American bishops, particularly the Puebla and Medellin

statements. The Puebla document is specially attentive to multinationals, declaring that they are at the root of the situation in the Third
World.

> There is the fact of economic, technological, political, and cultural
> dependence: the presence of multinational conglomerates that often
> look after only their own interests at the expense of the welfare of the
> country that welcomes them in; and the drop of our raw materials as
> compared with the price of the finished goods we buy.[13]

In a direct reference to the multinationals, the document regrets that

> unfortunately, in many instances this reaches the point where the
> political and economic authorities of our nations are themselves made
> subject to even more powerful centers that are operative on an interna-
> tional scale. And the situation is further aggravated by the fact that
> these centers of power are ubiquitous, covertly organized, and easily
> capable of evading the controls of governments and even international
> organisms.[14]

> Latin Americans see a society growing more and more unbalanced in-
> sofar as shared life is concerned. There are mechanisms that are im-
> bued with materialism rather than authentic humanism, and that there-
> fore lead on the international level to the ever increasing wealth of the
> rich at the expense of the ever increasing poverty of the poor.[15]

> These mechanisms manifest themselves in a society that is often pro-
> gramed in terms of egotism, in manipulations of public opinion; in
> invisible expropriations; and in new forms of supranational domina-
> tion, since the gap between the rich nations and the poor nations grow
> greater. And we must add that in many cases the power of multina-
> tional business overrides the exercise of sovereignty by nationals and
> their complete control over their natural resources.[16]

Regarding the organization of international society, the document
affirms:

> It is the right of each nation to defend and promote its own interest
> vis-à-vis multinational enterprises. On the international level there is
> now a need for a set of statutes that will regulate the activities of such
> enterprises.[17]

The positive aspect of the social teaching of the Church on the
multinationals is the development of the social teaching of John Paul
II. Before John Paul II, the social teaching of the Church, in large

measure, centered upon private property, and the just participation and distribution of property on a national level. The ideas of property and its use were clearly stated by Pope John XXIII in *Pacem in Terris*[18] and *Mater et Magistra*[19] in which social doctrine of the Church widens its vision of the social question. It is no longer centered around the dispute between capital and labor for the ownership of the means of production, but rather it becomes a dispute between developed and underdeveloped nations for the valuation of the resources available on earth. The social question acquires a planetary dimension although remaining tied to the issue of ownership.

Pope Paul VI's *Populorum Progressio*[20] extended these ideas to a world level. These encyclicals espoused the vision of a global society in which there would be serious efforts to achieve social justice.

Pope John Paul II, building upon the previous vision of the social dimensions of productive property, places a new emphasis on work as the source of property value. Human work — human endeavor — is the center of his social thinking, because this is the person and the product of the person's endeavor. His encyclical *Laborem Exercens*[21] extends from "things" back to humanity as the center of all social concern.

> Work is a good thing for man — a good thing for his humanity — because through work man not only transforms nature, adapting it to his own needs, but he also achieves fulfillment as a human being and indeed in a sense becomes "more a human being."[22]

In the same encyclical the Pope calls attention to the great paradox of the modern world.

> While conspicuous natural resources remain unused there are huge numbers of people who are unemployed or underemployed and countless multitudes of people suffering from hunger. This is a fact that without any doubt demonstrates that both within the individual political communities and in their relationships on the continental and world levels there is something wrong with the organization of work and employment, precisely at the most critical and socially most important points.[23]

Pope John Paul II presents a much broader historical perspective and a new kind of dynamic vision in which each individual is co-creating with God. All, from the artisan to the senior executive of the largest multinational corporation, are developing a world in a co-creative process in which all can participate and look for the basic values that will help each to be more human and all to participate in the benefits of the society. This means, therefore, that there is greater emphasis on being than having. There is not merely a quantitative question of producing, but the issue of what is being produced. Who is being served? What are the goals? What are the cultural values involved? *Laborem Exercens* poses a new dimension, opening new kinds of consideration for Christians as persons dedicated to human and social development for the multinationals.

CONCLUSION: MULTINATIONALS AND CATHOLIC SOCIAL DOCTRINE IN THE POST-INDUSTRIAL ERA

Society is at the end of the first development experience, the industrial era, and the beginning of a new experience, the post-industrial era, also called by some "the technocratic era." Multinational corporations are in a unique and powerful position within the private sector of the economy to help make the transition from the first development experience to the second one in a way that would minimize if not correct the negative results of the first era, while at the same time increasing the potential for positive results in the second one. The question now is whether in the new post-industrial era, the multinational corporations will be capable of fostering a sensitivity toward the basic needs of the poor in the Third World and, in answer to these, promote new developmental schemes; or will those corporations prefer to stimulate an artificial demand for sophisticated goods and services that ultimately favor the Third World oligarchies — demands that in the short run might prove more profitable but that will maintain the area in its present underdeveloped reality. Multinational corporations during the new post-industrial development experience have the enormous potential for initiating corrective measures that could erase the negative end-results of the industrial era, but they also and equally have the same potential for amplifying and augmenting these negative effects to a point of no return, promoting an ever-increasing gap between the First and the Third Worlds. The price and consequences of this gap are the contrasting realities of affluence in the First World and of poverty in the Third World that is shaping a kind of universal apartheid.

In Latin America, that portion of the Third World which is preponderantly Catholic, the institutional Church, and multinational corporations are challenged to pool their understanding and resources, ensuring that this new era does indeed see a narrowing of the developmental gap between the First and Third Worlds. This is the ethical challenge confronting both the Catholic Church and multinational corporations in Latin America today which Catholic social doctrine is evolving to meet.

Pastors and bishops have a particular role as the authentic interpreters of the tradition, the revelation, and the teaching of the Church. Alone they cannot work this into a social teaching of the Church; social teaching must come from a confrontation with the problems. It is the interpretation of the problems, in the light of divine revelation, which is social teaching of the Church. The liberation thinking in Latin America on the whole is positive. It is the sign of a Church that is very much alive.

As doctrine evolves, it will take on different tendencies, interpretations, and applications. If there are some branches of this expression which the Holy See and bishops have rightly criticized, the concern lies with the ideological deviations that can take place in liberation thinking, not with liberation thinking itself.

One of the important issues in the area of social teaching is that social teaching in the Church is not merely doctrine; it is doctrine and life. In an exaggerated, characterized sense of the word, ecclesiastics generally have the doctrine, and those working in the business community have the life. We must put them together. It is out of that combination that social teaching evolves. It is not a question of dictates coming out of the Vatican or any other moral center. All peoples must integrate and be faithful to the principles, values, and Christian vision, but they must be developed in practical terms. All must continue to work together.

NOTES

1. For a more complete review of the multinational contribution to development, see Werner Baer, "Industrial Structure of Latin America and Multinationals," this volume.

2. For an extended dimension of this point, see the El Valle document, *Hacia*

Una Economía Más Humana: Reflexiones Cristianas Para El Desarrollo de Panamá con Prioridad en los más Pobres (Panama: Editorial Litografica, S.A., 1985), ch. 6.

3. *Gaudium et Spes* "Pastoral Constitution on the Church in the Modern World," *The Documents of Vatican II*, (December 7, 1965) New York: American Press, 1966 no. 4.

4. *Ibid.*, no. 43.

5. For a thorough criticism of Marxist elements of liberation theology, see Joseph Ramos, "Reflections on Gustavo Gutierrez's 'Theology of Liberation' " in Michael Novak, ed., *Liberation South, Liberation North* (New York: American Enterprise Institute, 1981). Cf. the two recent statements on this matter issued by the Vatican Congregation for the Doctrine of Faith: *Instruction on Freedom and Liberation* (Aug. 6, 1984) and *Freedom and Christian Liberation* (March 22, 1986).

6. *The Puebla Document* (Maryknoll, N.Y.: Orbis Books, 1979), no. 473.

7. For a more complete, synoptic approach to Latin America and to the Church in Latin America, see "The Church in Latin America" by Archbishop Marcos McGrath in *Latin America, Dependency or Interdependency?* ed. Michael Novak (New York: American Enterprise Institute, 1985).

8. Medellin Documents "Justice, Peace, Family, and Demography Poverty of the Church" (September 6, 1968) in *The Church in the Present-Day Transformation of Latin America in the Light of the Council*, vol. 2, *Conclusions*, Latin American Bureau of the United States Catholic Conference and the General Secretariat of the Latin American Episcopal Council (CELAM), 1970.

9. Ibid.

10. *Puebla*, no. 473.

11. Cf. Isaiah 61:1; Luke 4:18.

12. *Octogesima Adveniens*, "The Eightieth Anniversary of *Rerum Novarum*" (May 14, 1971) apostolic letter of Pope Paul VI to Cardinal Maurice Roy, president of the Council of the Laity and of the Pontifical Commission Justice and Peace (Vatican Polyglot Press, 1971).

13. *Puebla*, no. 66.

14. Ibid., no. 501.

15. Ibid., Pope John Paul II Opening Address: III, 4.

16. Ibid., no. 1264.

17. Ibid., no. 1277.

18. *Pacem in Terris* "Peace on Earth" (April 11, 1963), encyclical letter of Pope John XXIII (New York: America Press, 1963).

19. *Mater et Magistra* "Christianity and Social Progress" (May 15, 1961), encyclical letter of Pope John XXIII (Glen Rock, N.J.: Paulist Press, 1961).

20. *Populorum Progressio* "On the Development of Peoples" (March 26, 1967), encyclical letter of Pope Paul VI (Vatican Polygot Press, 1967).

21. *Laborem Exercens* "On Human Work" (September 1981), encyclical letter of Pope John Paul II, United States Catholic Conference: publication no. 825 (Washington, D. C.: Office of Publishing Services, 1981).

22. Ibid., no. 9.

23. Ibid., no. 18.

Comparative Religious Traditions

ERNEST J. BARTELL, C.S.C. *

As a priest I am concerned about the influence of religion and the philosophic groundings of religious beliefs on economic growth and social reality. As an economist, I continue to be intrigued by the experience of rapid development in the group of four newly industrializing Asian countries and their neighbors as opposed to the variable experiences within Latin America. So, I listened to the Steinberg and McGrath — de Avila papers with those two perspectives in mind. I appreciated hearing the disavowal of any ability to identify in a clear-cut fashion what exactly Confucianism contributes to a development model. Certainly I have never been able to specify what Christianity, either the Catholic or Protestant version, has contributed to economic development in the West. My kindred spirit on that point enables me to continue.

CULTURAL SIMILARITY

There is an awareness within Latin America of the geographic diversity of the countries and of cultural diversity between the indigenous peoples and the people of Spanish and European origin — a whole range of cultural differences. It is interesting that in a country like Chile, despite its distance from the U.S., one perhaps finds a more pronounced cultural influence of the U.S. in popular culture, such as popular music, than one does next door in Mexico where there has been more emphasis on development of indigenous popular culture.

*Ernest J. Bartell, C.S.C., is a professor of economics and the executive director of the Helen Kellogg Institute for International Studies at the University of Notre Dame. He also serves as overseas mission coordinator for the Congregation of the Holy Cross, Indiana Province (C.S.C.) with missionaries in South America, East Africa, and South Asia.

In spite of cultural diversity, there are common patterns that can be observed. Indeed, at core, I see similarities in the development-related aspects of Latin American and Confucian cultures. Steinberg stressed paternalism, hierarchial authority, centralization, and the family as the social unit. All of these have played a big part in the traditional understanding of the famous trilogy of Latin America—the church, the military, and the landed aristocracy. In all of these, there was centralization, there was hierarchial authority, and certainly a good bit of paternalism.

The family continues to be a strong social unit. While Cuba has retained very few overt expressions of its Catholic traditions and culture, many traditional social values continue to perdure, and family ones seem exceptionally strong. It is impressive to discover parents selling their own valuable apartment, because of the housing crunch there, common to so many socialist countries, just to help a newly married son get housing for his own family. In this case, they don't actually sell, but rather barter the apartment to get two smaller ones. They move into the smaller one and give the other to the son in a display of strong traditional family ties.

Steinberg spoke of the finite sense of power in Confucian countries. This same perception of power as finite can be observed in the social struggles of Latin America.

There is also a strong sense of class distinction across Latin America. This antedated the Marxist rhetoric of more recent years. Twenty years ago, when working with Notre Dame students in a rural, low-income area of central Mexico, we were all amazed to find that the children of the moderately prosperous families who were our hosts had never walked the few blocks to the orphanage for the poor where we were working. Elitism is also entrenched in the educational system. Thus, at these levels of abstraction, I see as much similarity between the Confucian and Catholic-influenced cultures as I do among the various Latin American countries themselves.

Different Economic Results

The economic results arising from the development of these Asian and Latin countries, however, are vastly different. At this point, the paradox remains unanswered.

One source may be in the child-rearing practices stressed by Steinberg. This may be the source of individual initiative and drive, entrepreneurial spirit, and efficiency. Perhaps there is something different between Asian and Latin American family structures. Even though family is important in both places, there may be a significant difference in the way in which family members relate to one another.

A second possible cause of such diverse economic results could be in a sense of intellectual orthodoxy versus intellectual dissonance. Steinberg stressed the intellectual orthodoxy of Confucian cultures as evidenced by authoritarian regimes surrounding themselves with a thick and heavy cloak of moral justification and moral legitimacy. This is certainly observable in Latin America from Chile on one end of the political spectrum to Nicaragua on the other. Still, I would argue that, in spite of the fact that we do find morality and authority linked in Latin America, there is a lack of intellectual orthodoxy. Dissent is everywhere. In some areas such as the universities, there is often serious conflict. In a number of Latin American countries, the universities are being subjected to heavy controls. There is a growing conflict between the moral claims of authoritarian superstructures and the desire for intellectual autonomy. Today much of the creative intellectual activity in countries as politically diverse as Chile and Cuba is taking place outside the established national institutions of learning.

Why do we observe this intellectual dissonance in Latin America as opposed to the orthodoxy of Asia? Perhaps it is a result of the Western, secular, liberal, intellectual revolution that came to Latin America in the nineteenth century but not to the Confucian countries. Throughout Latin America we are left with conflicting patterns of traditional, cohesive institutions set against the intellectual currents of liberal individualism.

RAMPANT PRAGMATISM

The Steinberg paper clearly stresses pragmatism as a factor in Confucian societies. Apparently, in spite of ideological superstructures, when the chips are down, good old-fashioned economic pragmatism takes over.

Economic pragmatism is certainly present in Latin America as well. The Latin Americans have inherited an abstract sense of intellectualizing and reasoning. In a typical Latin American economic conference, the first day and a half is spent discussing the nature of man, society, and the universe. But, under pressure, the Latin Americans can behave very pragmatically on their own account, and in the name of larger values they will wheel and deal just like anyone else.

It concerns me as an economist, as much as a priest, that there exists a pervasive pragmatic rationality that creeps into so many cultures worldwide. We may try to attribute it to the local inherited religious or philosophic traditions. However, in our own social sciences, we see the theories of rational choice applied to everything from how to run world governments to deciding how many children to have. The discussion is cloaked in jargon and special vocabulary but the methodology is built upon maximization of self interest in one way or another. So, self-interested pragmatism seems able to transcend cultural diversity.

THE CHURCH

As for the Latin American Catholic Church itself today, it is worth noting that the traditional notion of the church as one of the forces of hierarchial authority and centralized power conflicts with recent history in Latin America. The contemporary Latin American church has become, in so many places, the outsider rather than the insider. Rather than the protector of the status quo, of the established system, it has become an agent of change. There is concern from the hierarchial heights right down to the basic Christian communities about the creeping secularism of modern society and its impact on people. There is a religious concern at various levels of society for the kinds of values that are being transmitted with economic growth. Michael Novak likes to say that the Latin Americans are so concerned with distributional questions and social justice that they forget that there has got to be economic growth as well. I don't know that Latin Americans forget the need for growth, but what they are sometimes saying is that there are moral priorities and trade-offs. Therefore, they are not willing to buy growth at any social cost, but are concerned about larger issues of justice. Thus the distributional questions do rise in priority, and that does suggest a perduring moralism as noted by Moody, but a moralism that within the Catholic tradition now takes a critical stance toward society. If contemporary Confucianism tends rather to reinforce and support dominant social institutions, there may be a significant difference in social outlook between Confucianism and Latin American Catholicism that has escaped our attention here and deserves further investigation.

Comparative Religious Traditions

ALEXANDER W. WILDE*

In comparing development in Latin America and Asia, there are interesting parallels between the alleged impact of Catholicism and Confucianism, as Father Bartell has pointed out. They are very different religious traditions, however, and operate in societies shaped quite differently by history. I would like to highlight just a few of those differences in order to illustrate a contrast which seems to me very deep.

LATIN AMERICA: SOCIETIES OF THE NEW WORLD

The most obvious difference between the societies of the two regions is that Latin America is part of the New World, and historical experience is that of the Americas, not of Asia. Latin American societies originated in relatively recent (by Asian standards) imperial ventures, while those of Asia are ancient. In Latin America, the native peoples were consistently defeated and their societies were in effect replaced by new ones with a mixture of European, Indian, and African elements. At the time of Independence, what might have been "wars of national liberation" of the native peoples were suppressed, most clearly in Mexico. The result has been a far more fragmented, individualistic culture in Latin America than in Asia.

---

*Alexander W. Wilde is a senior fellow and associate academic director of the Helen Kellogg Institute for International Studies at the University of Notre Dame. He holds degrees from Lawrence University, Oxford University, and Columbia University.

LIBERALISM AND ITS SUCCESSORS AS SECULAR ALTERNATIVES TO CATHOLICISM

A second difference resides in the historical alternative posed by liberalism and other organized forms of secularism to the institutional influence and cultural hegemony of Catholicism. In the newly independent countries of Latin America in the nineteenth century, the Catholic Church was frontally challenged from the left not only by secular values but also by secular movements and secular institutions. In many cases, the secularizing process was ultimately successful. Many corporate entities in society — the Church and Indian communities among them — were in effect disenfranchised in the name of an individualist ethic of economic liberalism.

The Church lost most of her economic wealth, and was removed from her predominant position in education in most countries. At the same time Latin Americans attempted to create liberal, proto-democratic political systems. While today some sneer at "Latin American democracy" as a contradiction in terms, they miss the fact that in Latin America the ideas and institutions of democracy were installed only a century ago and, despite the lack of achievement, embody a continuing aspiration. Thus, liberalism and its successors in the twentieth century — anarchism, Marxism, socialism, and other modern forms of secularism — have offered alternatives to Catholicism in terms of institutions as well as of values as part of Latin American society and culture. For a good deal of history, the Church has reacted defensively, attempting to resist modernity rather than adapt to it.

THE CHANGING RELATIONSHIP OF THE CATHOLIC CHURCH TO SOCIETY

In the highly institutionalized character of Catholicism, in contrast to Confucianism, is inherent a third important difference: its capacity to change its ideas and action in a conscious, directed, relatively rapid way. While obvious, this is a central point when we are comparing it to the much more diffuse processes of change in Asian religions. McGrath and de Avila outline the changes in Catholic social doctrine beginning even before the Second Vatican Council. The ferment is observable in many places in the Catholic world since that time, but surely in no place has it been stronger or more intense than in Latin America.

The Church has reinterpreted its social magisterium in a basic way. It has taken a newly critical stance toward its societies, while at the same time assuming a greater responsibility for their development. The Vatican Council and its interpretations in Latin America — notably at Medellín in 1968 and Puebla in 1979 — have legitimated the cries for fundamental social change. The continuing debate about liberation theology should not obscure the broad area of consensus within the Latin American Church around social ideas quite different from those of the Confucian tradition. Orthodox, free-market economics, for example, is strongly condemned in the Puebla documents, an attitude found even among conservative Latin American bishops.

Another clear contrast with the Confucian support for authority and order can be seen in the Latin American Church's courageous opposition in many places to authoritarian rule. It has taken this position both out of its commitment to humane values in society and, in my view, in order to retain its own autonomy as an institution. It has seen the seeds of totalitarianism in the National Security Doctrine invoked by many military regimes. Against a historical tradition going back to the French Revolution, the Church has in the last twenty years become a champion of pluralism and political democracy. Again, these are positions held even by many conservatives within the Latin American Church. Support of democracy is now a point of unity, allowing the Church to distance itself from partisan involvements and dangers of internal division.

There has been reaction in recent years, in the Vatican and in Latin America itself, against what some have seen as excesses of social activism among some Catholics. However, this does not signify a return to anything like the Church's traditional alliances and the status quo ante. With the new basic Christian communities, the Church has changed not just its social ideas but its institutional linkages with society. The extraordinary vitality at these lower levels is a new reality and ensures continuing change. They have given the Church a new basis of authority in Latin America's fragmented, rapidly changing societies and are a foundation for its future.

A Comparison of Latin American and North American Legal Traditions

KEITH S. ROSENN*

The U.S. businessman's first contact with Latin American law is likely to be a bewildering one. Not only are there inevitable difficulties resulting from language, distance, and varying business practices, but the legal rules, procedures, and institutions are quite different. Even securing adequate translations of the relevant laws and regulations can be difficult, in large part because equivalent concepts often do not exist.[1] More importantly, the legal culture — the generalized set of lay and professional values and attitudes toward law and the role of legal process in society[2] — is strikingly different in Latin America. This essay will compare the realities of contemporary legal practice in terms of the differing historical, social, and cultural factors that have shaped Latin American and U.S. law, and suggest some of the more important implications of these differences for multinationals operating in Latin America.

Latin America traditionally comprises twenty countries that differ substantially,[3] and the expression Latin American law is likely to convey a uniformity that simply does not exist. Nevertheless, just as it makes sense to talk about U.S. law despite significant differences among the laws of the fifty states and the federal government, it makes sense to talk about Latin American law, particularly for certain analytic

*Keith S. Rosenn is a professor of law and director of the Foreign Graduate Law Program of the University of Miami Law School. He has extensive legal experience in Latin America and the United States, and is also director of the Brazilian-American Chamber of Commerce, a member of the American Law Institute, and a director of the American Society for the Comparative Study of Law.

127

purposes. As a region, Latin America shares a common Roman law heritage, a common Iberian colonial past, and present-day patterns of social organization. The region's nations also share a considerable number of basic codes. More importantly, they share a common set of attitudes about law, legal institutions, the legal profession, and methods of legal education.

Latin America and the United States are heirs to two different legal traditions. Latin America inherited the tradition of the civil law, while the United States inherited the tradition of the common law. The civil law tradition is much older, more widely distributed, and more influential than the common law tradition. The civil law tradition goes all the way back to 450 B.C., when the Twelve Tables, the first Roman law code, appeared. The common law tradition, on the other hand, did not begin until more than fifteen centuries later. The customary starting point for the common law tradition is the Norman Conquest in 1066 A.D. Not only Latin America, but most of Western Europe and many parts of Asia and Africa adhere to the civil law tradition. Until recently, the civil law was also the dominant legal tradition in the Soviet Union and most of Eastern Europe. A much smaller part of the world—consisting of Great Britian, Ireland, the United States, Canada, Australia, New Zealand, and some of the nations of Africa and Asia—adheres to the common law tradition.[4]

The distinguishing features of the civil and common law traditions are complex; here only some of the highlights will be covered. One of the most important differences is the role of court decisions. In the civil law tradition, a basic dogma is that the legislative will is supreme, and that the legislature has a monopoly on the business of lawmaking. Legislative power can be delegated to the executive, and regulations or decrees promulgated by the executive may therefore have the force of law. Lawmaking cannot, however, be performed by the judiciary because in this area the civil law operates with a stricter concept of the separation of powers. Therefore, judicial decisions are not regarded as a source of law, and the familiar common law doctrine of *stare decisis*—that the courts must decide similar cases in the same fashion—is rejected, at least in theory. In practice, civil law courts tend to follow prior decisions even if they are not obliged to do so.

A second important difference is the civil law notion that legislation is to be comprehensive, providing solutions for the entire array of problems likely to arise. Both common law and civil law countries have codes, but civil law codes are much more systematic and comprehensive than common law codes. A common law lawyer is likely to look first to cases and then to statutes to solve a given problem, while a civil law lawyer is likely to look first to a code or statute, then to scholarly commentary on that legislation, and finally, if at all, to cases.

A third important difference is the relatively reduced role and power of the civilian judge. The Roman law judge (*iudex*) was originally a lay person, appointed as a special master to resolve a particular dispute. The Romans developed a tradition in which judges relied heavily on legal scholars, called jurisconsults, for advice in deciding cases. That tradition has continued to this day. The opinions of scholars are given much greater weight by civil law judges than by common law judges. It is not uncommon for lawyers involved in important litigation in civil law countries to pay substantial sums to distinguished jurists for their written opinions advising the court how to resolve the particular dispute. In the civil law tradition, the legal scholar generally has more prestige than the judge. The judge is regarded as a glorified technician, whose job consists of essentially applying the law to the facts of a particular case.[5] The scholar is regarded as the creative thinker, and the task of drafting important legislation is usually entrusted to legal scholars. In many civil law countries, one becomes a judge by taking competitive examinations immediately after completing law school. The best and brightest of the young lawyers are usually not attracted to the judiciary. Very few civil law judges have significant practice experience, and even fewer have any independent political base or broad political experience.

In no civil law country does the judge have the power, prestige, and deference enjoyed by the U.S. judge, particularly at the federal level. Unlike his common law counterpart, a civil law judge does not have the power to punish disregard of his orders by jailing the recalcitrant party for contempt of court. Although a number of civil law countries have imported the institution of judicial review from the United States, many restrict the power to declare statutes unconstitutional to the Supreme Court or a Constitutional Court.[6] This is in large part because of more rigid adherence to separation of powers theory, lack of *stare decisis*, and a serious concern that civil law judges lack the experience and training necessary to perform adequately the value-oriented quasi-political functions involved in judicial review.[7]

A fourth basic difference is the nature of the litigation process. Generally speaking, civil law courts do not hold trials in the common law sense of focusing the production of evidence and witnesses into a single concentrated hearing. Common law procedure is, to a large extent, shaped by the widespread use of the jury, an institution seldom used in civil law countries. In civil law courts, evidence comes in piecemeal, starting with documents attached to the complaint and the answer. A series of mini-hearings before the judge and his clerk account for the rest. Perhaps because surprise is not a serious concern, civil law countries have nothing like the broad discovery (depositions, interrogatories, requests for production of documents) that exists in the U.S. Unlike common law countries, where complex rules of evidence have been developed to prevent juries from being misled, civil law countries have few rules of evidence; virtually anything the judge deems relevant is admissible. On the other hand, many civil law countries still have detailed rules of legal proof that tell the judge what weight to attach to evidence, while common law countries give judges and juries virtually unfettered discretion to evaluate the evidence. In contradistinction to the common law world, most civil law countries will not permit parties and their close friends or relatives to testify under oath, and their testimony is regarded with suspicion. Civil law courts have a decided tendency to believe written documents and to disbelieve oral testimony.

The great weight given to documentary evidence is in part a function of the very different roles of the notary in civil and common law systems. In the common law world, the notary public's principal function is the minor clerical task of authenticating signatures on certain types of documents. In the civil law world, the notary is a lawyer who occupies a very important office. In addition to preparing wills, deeds, and contracts, the civil law notary authenticates documents. An authenticated document, which the civilians call a public act, is conclusively regarded both as genuine and as reciting accurately what was said and done before the notary. In ordinary judicial proceedings, a litigant cannot attack the authenticity of a public act.[8] The lesser weight accorded to oral testimony in the civil law countries is in part due to the lack of cross examination and an emphasis upon the written record, an emphasis that makes demeanor of the witness irrelevant.

Another distinguishing feature of civil law litigation is abundance of opportunity to appeal. Most civil law countries operate with the principle of the dual instance. The case is initially heard by a single judge, called the court of the first instance. Not only his final decisions, but many of his interlocutory orders are appealable to the court of second instance, usually a three to five judge tribunal. Because all evidence is reduced to writing, frequently by the clerk rather than the judge, civilians refer to the "documentary curtain" that separates the court from the witnesses.[9] The court of second instance, therefore, regards itself as equally competent to review the evidence and in effect accords a trial *de novo*. In some cases, new evidence will be admitted by the appellate court. Review of decisions of the courts of second instance by the supreme court or court of cassation is usually possible, but that review is usually limited to questions of law and not of fact. Often even decisions by the highest court are not final, and further litigation in lower courts or before another part of the highest court will be necessary.[10]

Because of the less focused nature of the trial, procedural systems that grant more power to the parties than to the judge, and the plethora of appeals and collateral attacks permitted, litigation often seems interminable in civil law countries. Litigation can also drag on for years in common law countries, but it is not as common. Long delays are exceedingly common in Latin American capitals, where huge increases in population have greatly overburdened the court system. In some Latin American countries, galloping inflation has combined with the lengthy delays of the court system to produce veritable denials of justice.[11]

On the other hand, civil law countries have summary proceedings, which have no analogue in the common law system. In contradistinction to the lengthy ordinary proceedings, summary proceedings provide a rapid means of disposing of claims supported by highly probative evidence, such as negotiable instruments, notarial documents, or official obligations like tax assessments. Plaintiffs in summary proceedings are placed in the same position as litigants who are suing to enforce a judgment, and the range of defenses is quite limited.

Finally, civil law lawyers tend to be astonished by the size of damages awarded by courts and juries in common law countries, while common law lawyers tend to be surprised by the size of court costs in civil law countries. Damage awards tend to be much more modest in civil law countries. Generally, one can recover only compensatory damages in civil law countries, and not the punitive, exemplary, or treble damages sometimes awarded in common law countries. In civil law countries, costs are generally fixed as a percentage of the amount in controversy and can easily amount to sizeable sums. In addition, civil law courts tend to rely heavily on court-appointed experts, whose fees are added to costs. Unlike the United States, where each party generally pays his own attorney's fee, the rule in civil law countries is that the loser pays the winner's attorney's fee as well as the court costs. Contingent fees are not used in civil law countries, and courts generally fix attorneys' fees as a percentage of the verdict or in accordance with a statutory fee schedule for the type of service rendered. This does not mean, however, that you will owe your attorney nothing if you prevail, for in many civil law countries good lawyers often insist upon fee agreements allowing them to charge fees higher than those set by the courts.

These distinguishing features of the civil law tradition require some qualification for Latin America. Latin American countries are in certain respects hybrids because of the influence of the law of the United States, particularly in the area of public law. The U.S. Constitution has served as a model for Latin American constitutions, and virtually all Latin American countries have adopted some form of the U.S. institution of judicial review. Four Latin American countries follow the U.S. model of entrusting the power to declare laws and decrees unconstitutional to the entire judiciary, while eight countries restrict the power of judicial review to the supreme court. Mexico is unique in conferring the power of judicial review on the entire federal judiciary but denying it to the state judiciary.[12] Chile, Guatemala, Ecuador, and Peru are also unique in having special constitutional tribunals.[13]

A form of *stare decisis* exists in Argentina, Brazil, and Mexico. The constitutional decisions of the Argentine Supreme Court and the *en banc* decisions of appellate courts are regarded as binding on the lower courts.[14] Since 1964, Brazil has instituted a system of precedent known as the *Súmula*, consisting of a collection of case law rules enunciated by the appellate courts that are, as a practical matter, binding on the lower courts.[15] Five consecutive *amparo* decisions by the Mexican Supreme Court or Collegiate Circuit Tribunals constitute *juris-*

prudencia, a case law rule binding upon the courts.[16] Declarations of unconstitutionality are binding *erga omnes* in Costa Rica, Guatemala, Chile, and Panama,[17] and may have an *erga omnes* effect in Brazil, Colombia, El Salvador, Peru, and Venezuela,[18] depending upon the type of procedure utilized. In some of the Latin American countries, namely Argentina and Brazil, the highest courts have displayed considerable independence by declaring important legislation unconstitutional. They have, however, paid a significant price for assertion of their independence. Since 1945, the Argentine Supreme Court has been impeached *en masse* once, summarily dismissed *en masse* twice, and has resigned *en masse* three times. The Brazilian Supreme Federal Tribunal has been treated like a suitcase by the military governments, who summarily packed it in 1965 and unpacked it in 1968.

THE LARGE GAP BETWEEN THE LAW ON THE BOOKS AND THE OPERATIONAL CODE[19]

The foregoing comparison of basic differences between the civil and common law traditions glosses over one of the most striking features of Latin American legal institutions. While there is some gap between the law on the books and the law in practice in all countries,[20] that gap is notoriously large in Latin America. Despite great concern for the appearance of legality, an impressive number of legal rules are honored only in the breach. One of the leading commentators on Latin American law, Phanor Eder, long ago pointed out the paradox.

> How can we reconcile and understand the curious combination of an outward respect for legal formalities and rituals, evidencing a real reverence for law, and a complete disregard of the substance and essence of parts of the written law?[21]

Much of the explanation for this wide disparity between the law on the books and the operational code lies in a complex of historical and cultural factors that have conditioned Latin American attitudes toward law and the role of legal process.

The roots of the Latin American legal culture run deep into the Iberian past. During the critical formative era, Iberian attitudes toward law were fundamentally influenced by Roman law, theories of natural justice, Catholicism, and legal pluralism. Because of Spanish and Portuguese colonization, these same influences shaped Latin American attitudes toward law. Latin American attitudes toward law were also shaped by the Catholic Church and the peculiar character of Iberian colonial rule, as well as three cultural characteristics bequeathed by the Iberians: high tolerance for corruption, lack of civic responsibility, and profound socio-economic inequality.

The Dual Roman Law Heritage

Iberian legal culture has been heavily influenced by Roman law. Roman law was originally steeped in custom and experience; consequently, it displayed remarkable adaptability and practicality. It was a vital legal order that developed as Rome developed into the center of a vast empire. During the Classical Period (27 B.C. to 235 A.D.), solutions to legal problems were worked out on a case-by-case basis in the opinions of practicing jurists. By the time of the late Empire, however, Roman law had begun to diverge from socio-economic reality and to take on an imposed and rigid character. With the development of an absolute monarchy, republican forms of judicial administration were replaced by imperial courts. During the post-Classical Period, the source of legal growth shifted away from the opinions of practicing jurists to imperial legislation. The three hundred years preceding Justinian's reign has been labeled "the bureaucratic period" because the lawgivers became the faceless officials and jurists who drafted statutes for the imperial chancellery.[22]

Justinian was a reactionary who regarded the Roman law of his time as decadent and technically inferior to the Roman law of the Classical Period. He set out to reform it by codifying the best legal scholarship of the Classical Period and imposing it as the living law of the Roman Empire. Much that Justinian preserved in the *Corpus Juris* never had any practical application in his own time because the doctrines and concepts were grounded in a much different age. With the overthrow of the Roman Empire, Roman law was lost to the West until the eleventh century. When it was rediscovered, the Glossators and Commentators, the medieval scholars who sparked the revival of the study of Roman law in the West during the eleventh through thirteenth centuries, were oblivious to the gap between the *Corpus Juris* and the Roman socio-economic reality of Justinian's time, a gap even more striking for their own times. They regarded the *Corpus Juris* as living law and slavishly attempted to decipher the true meaning of its text and to arrange its principles into systematic form. Both the Glossators and the Commentators focused on the abstract, formal rules themselves rather than the socio-economic context for which they were formulated.

Spain and Portugal were two of the countries most profoundly influenced by the scholasticism of the Glossators and the Commentators. The Roman law scholarship of the Glossators and the Commentators was primarily concerned with constructing a harmonious and universal system of ethical guides of conduct. This was largely accomplished by reasoning deductively from abstract moral postulates found in the *Corpus Juris*. The end product was displacement of local and customary rules of law by unrealistic ethical standards of conduct that reflected goals to be attained.

Iberia has a dual Roman Law heritage. It inherited the living Roman Law from the six centuries of Roman occupation, in time modified by custom and Gothic superimpositions. It also inherited an idealized Roman Law, culled by academicians from the texts of Justinian's *Corpus Juris*. This pattern of dualism — law as an ideal versus law as a practical system for ordering affairs — persists in Latin America today.[23]

The Primacy of Natural Justice

The idealism and unreality of Iberian law were accentuated by Spanish and Portuguese political theory. The Iberian monarchs were beneficiaries of the "divine right of kings" theory of sovereignty, which had developed during the Middle Ages. In the Peninsula, as in the rest of Europe, the theory operated to strengthen royal power. Since the king was God's representative on earth, disobedience to royal command became sinful as well as unlawful. Obedience to the king as well as the church was a concept inculcated by a loyal clergy. Iberian colonial rule, therefore, was the product of an absolute monarchy, with "the King as its head, chief, father, representative of God on earth, supreme dispenser of all favors, and rightful regulator of all activities, even to all the personal and individual expressions of his subjects and vassals."[24] ". . . [T]he Christian monarch claimed total control in the name of God and the pursuit of justice. In the performance of the royal *officium*, he relied upon Christian dogma and his sense of equity.

His duty was to promote the common good which, once translated into Christian terms, meant the salvation of the soul."[25]

Iberian political thought has long conceived of the primary purpose of government as the dispensation of justice on earth. That one owes allegiance to an abstract nation state is not an Iberian tradition. Traditionally, Iberians have viewed the state as "a federal unity of the diverse yet interconnected interests of men, directed and held together by the sovereign who was to be the arbiter to resolve their conflicts and the dispenser of justice which should define the order in which they were to function. . . ."[26] This theory of the state was transmitted intact to the colonies.

In a brilliant essay on Hispanic-American cultural history, Richard Morse has suggested that the postmedieval jurist who most clearly recapitulated Hispanic-Catholic legal and political thinking during the formative period of the New World colonies was Francisco Suarez (1548–1617), a Jesuit professor of theology at the University of Coimbra in Portugal.[27] The importance of Suarez's jurisprudential views lies primarily in their reflection of deep-seated attitudes toward law and assumptions about the relationship of man to the state which still pervade much of Latin American society. Suarez perceived of law as a moral system, grounded on eternal law. Eternal law is known to us through natural law, which in turn is known by the dictates of right reason. To be law, secular rules must accord with eternal truths. In other words, to be a law a rule must be moral and just. "Strictly and absolutely speaking, only that which is a right and virtuous rule, can be called law."[28] Suarez also theorized that the people do not delegate but alienate sovereignty to their prince. If, however, the prince acts tyrannically, the people have the right to rebel and seize control of the government.[29]

The implications of this view of law are continually reflected in Ibero-American experience. If every citizen is authorized to make an independent determination of the justice of any particular law, those entrusted with the task of administering the law feel few compunctions about amending legislation to conform with their own assessment of what is right or expedient. Indeed, the Crown not only expected colonial officials to disobey laws that they found to be unjust but also specifically enacted an administrative formula for their doing so. The Recompilation of the Laws of Spain expressly recognized the right of Spanish colonial viceroys and other officials to stay the execution of royal commands whenever the circumstances made implementation inopportune by invoking the curious formula: "I obey but do not execute."[30]

If the real source of law lies in "right reason," a natural law concept external to societal consensus, the notion that legislative enactments are to be obeyed because they represent the will of the majority must sled uphill. Important Latin American legislation has historically been drafted by distinguished jurists in an atmosphere far removed from the clamor of special interest groups. Draftsmen have typically consulted the various solutions to the problem that have been enacted in other countries (with little awareness of how these solutions operate in practice) and selected the solution that logically appeared best. Seldom has anyone conducted a fact-finding inquiry about the peculiarly local economic, social, political, or administrative problems involved, or made an attempt to crystallize local custom or practice. To be sure, disputes have been common among jurists and law professors about the particular rules that have been drafted, but generally these have been technical, doctrinal arguments. The end product of this process has been legislation of idealized standards of behavior, continuing a tradition that harks back to late Roman law.

If the legal culture emphasizes the right and duty of citizens to rebel against unjust governments, one can expect a high degree of political instability. While the tendency to overthrow governments by force rather than overhaul them by votes involves many factors, not the least among them is this natural law heritage.

The Intertwining of Law and Religion

Historically, law and religion have been blended in Iberia. Roman law and canon law were taught together at the universities, and the cross influences have been substantial. That there should be "a wall of separation" between church and state, an idea embodied in the First Amendment of the U.S. Constitution, is not part of the Iberian tradition. Law, religion, and the force of arms served as the bases for the Spanish and Portuguese conquests, and religiously inspired legislation has been a long-standing tradition. The Church, with its rigid dogmas, moral intolerance, and slowness to change, has often been responsible for the enactment and maintenance in secular law of ideal standards of behavior that many people, particularly in modern times, find impossible or distasteful to meet.

The Iberians have had a long tradition of paying only lipservice to religiously inspired legislation. Thus, the *Fuero Juzgo*, the Visigothic Code promulgated in final form in 694, contained a set of prescriptions prohibiting Jews from practicing their religion, but these were apparently honored only in the breach.[31] Similarly, the more humane, Church-inspired laws for the protection of the Indians in the New World were widely disregarded by colonists bent on enslaving the Indian population.[32]

Even today, a number of Latin American countries still do not permit absolute divorce out of deference to the Church. Citizens of these countries do, nevertheless, divorce and remarry. Legal separations are often in practice treated as if they were absolute divorces, and new marriages are contracted abroad or in foreign embassies. In Chile, where absolute divorce is still prohibited, the custom has developed of falsely stating one's residence on the marriage application to facilitate subsequent annulment if the marriage does not work. Since 1925, the Chilean Supreme Court has cooperated in this obvious charade by holding such marriages void for want of jurisdiction. Thousands of Chilean marriages, even those with children, are annulled each year for misstatement of residence.[33]

Legal Pluralism

The Romans also bequeathed Iberia a tradition of profound juridical inequality. Roman law recognized the principle of the personality of laws, which meant that the law applicable to a particular person depended upon the group to which he belonged rather than the territory in which he happened to live. Roman law was reserved for Roman citizens, while the Iberians were governed by their own customary law.[34] The Visigoths, who overran the Iberian Peninsula in the fifth century, also applied the principle of the personality of laws. For much of their reign, the Visigoths were governed by the Code of Euric, while the Hispano-Romans were governed by the Breviary of Alaric (a crude restatement of Roman Law), as modified by Celto-Iberian custom.[35] The Moors, who invaded the Peninsula early in the eighth century, followed the same principle, applying Islamic law to their own population and the Visigothic Code to the Roman-Gothic population.

The critical part of Latin American legal culture was formed during the Reconquest, a state of more or less permanent war that lasted nearly eight hundred years. Its termination in 1492, when the Moors were finally expelled from Spain, coincided with Columbus' departure for the New World. The tradition of legal pluralism continued during the Reconquest. Iberian kings customarily granted special legal privileges, embodied in municipal charters called *fueros* or *forais*, to cities and towns as they were freed from Moorish control. The *fueros*, which were contractual in nature, contained detailed rules and privileges for self-governance of the locale. In addition, Iberian kings granted special legal privileges to the multiplicity of corporate estates that made up medieval society. The nobility, military orders, clergy, university faculty and students, merchants, and various other guilds were generally exempted from the ordinary jurisdiction of the king's courts and governed by their own *fueros*, which created special laws and courts.[36]

Thus, long before Latin America was discovered, Spain and Portugal were characterized by profound juridical inequality. During the Reconquest and for many centuries thereafter, Spain and Portugal had the antithesis of a universalist legal system. The *de facto* legal pluralism so often found in Latin America is firmly rooted in the *de jure* legal pluralism of Iberia's past.

The Legacy of Patrimonialism

Portuguese and Spanish rule was essentially patrimonialist.[37] Administrators were tied to the king by bonds of personal loyalty and profit rather than official duty. All taxes, tributes, and monopoly profits were the personal income of the sovereign rather than the nation. Patrimonialism produced widespread corruption, an incredible penchant for bureaucratic red tape, and a highly unpredictable and personalistic legal system.

Corruption

Patrimonialist regimes generated relatively low expectations that government officials would act honestly and in the public interest, for the concepts of the public service and public office were alien to patrimonialism. An administrative position or office was regarded as a personal privilege granted or purchased from the king. Citizens could claim no rights in a patrimonial regime. Instead of public services, citizens sought favors from the government. These were dispensed on a personal basis, often in return for graft. Because patrimonialism encouraged colonial administrators to view their office as a franchise for private gain, Latin American history abounds with tales of official corruption and dishonesty. In addition, Spain and Portugal's strict mercantilist policies and heavy taxation gave the colonists strong economic incentives to avoid compliance. Tax evasion and smuggling became a way of life in Latin America.

Bureaucratic Red Tape

Patrimonialism also produced a superabundance of red tape, for the Spanish and Portuguese sovereigns delegated no real decision-making powers to their colonial administrators. Their function was simply to execute royal commands. Seemingly interminable delays and endless red tape were produced by the exaggerated centralization of bureaucratic power in Spain and Portugal. The paternalistic preoccupation of the Spanish Council of the Indies and the Portuguese Overseas Council in regulating virtually all aspects of colonial life, down to its pettiest details, and their seemingly interminable procrastination, resulted in voluminous correspondence and incredibly lengthy delays.[38]

The Ad Hoc Administration of Justice

Patrimonialism produced a judicial system in the Spanish and Portuguese colonies that was essentially inefficient and venal. Lack of justice was a constant complaint. Justice was regularly bartered like any other commodity, albeit delivered more slowly. Judicially collecting a debt was an extremely onerous, time-consuming, and expensive proposition, subject to many exceptions and much paperwork. The decisions of the magistrates were never really final, for everyone had the right to appeal any decision directly to the King, who dispensed justice as he or his top aides saw fit that day. Supervision over the notaries and judicial clerks was practically nil. Since these offices were frequently leased or subleased, often for more than the position's salary, the investment in the office was commonly recouped through acceptance of bribes. That most colonists preferred the justice of their own (or hired) hands, family, or friends to that of the King's magistrates was hardly surprising.

Much of the law that governed colonial Latin America was personalized and ad hoc. Laws and decrees were often tailored for a particular individual or situation and had no more universal application. Scanning the confused and contradictory mass of statutes, letter laws, orders, opinions, regulations, decrees, edicts, and instructions through which the sovereign transmitted his will to the colonies, one is amazed that the administrative machinery functioned at all.

Underlying this special legislation was the legislation of Spain and Portugal. In neither country was the basic legislation really codified. The New Recompilation of the Laws of Spain (*Nueva Recopilación de las Leyes de España*), published in 1567, was the usual starting place for one seeking an answer to Spanish law. The New Recompilation was badly organized and gathered together only the most important laws. Earlier compilations were left in force. To determine the applicable law, a lawyer had to sift through the unindexed royal letters and ordinances, the Laws of Toro (83 laws promulgated in 1505), the *Ordenamiento de Alcalá*, the municipal *fueros*, the *Fuero Real* (to the extent one could prove it still in use), the Visigothic Code, and the *Siete Partidas*. Not until 1680 did a compilation of legislation for the Spanish colonies appear. Known as the *Recopilación de Leyes de los Reynos de Indias*, this monumental work distilled some 400,000 royal *cédulas* (regulations issued by the Spanish government to the colonial viceroys, etc.) into 6,400 items. This alleviated the legislative confusion for a while, but it was soon rendered obsolete by the steady stream of new legislation. In 1805, another effort at compiling the jumble of Spanish legislation appeared. Known as the Newest Recompilation (*Novísima Recopilación de las Leyes de España*), this effort was even more unsatisfactory than its predecessor.

At the heart of Portuguese legislation was the *Ordenações Filipinas*, which was promulgated in 1603. Although often referred to as the *Código Filipino*, the *Ordenações* was not really a code. Rather it was a compilation of prior compilations, which, in turn, had awkwardly amalagated Roman law, the *forais*, customary usage, the Visigothic Code, the *Siete Partidas*, canon law, and the general legislation of Portugal since 1211. Much of its draftsmanship was unclear to begin with, and it soon became such a hodgepodge of overlapping and inconsistent amendments that a divining rod seemed as sure a guide to legal research as any other method. Nevertheless, the *Ordenações* remained the bulwark of Brazil's civil law until 1917, almost a cen-

tury after independence and a full fifty years after Portugal had relegated the *Ordenações* to the statutory scrapheap.

Paternalism

The paternalism that stemmed from the Iberian monarchy, the
Catholic Church, and the extended patriarchal family still permeates
Latin American society. It is commonly expressed in the *patrón* complex. In return for fealty and service the *patrón*, a member of the local
elite, customarily looks after the interests of his employees, tenants,
and followers. The *patrón* plays the role of protector, interceding with
the authorities when any of his flock is in trouble. This aspect of the
patrón system serves to personalize and particularize legal relations for
the lower class. The ultimate patrón is the state, from which Latin
Americans seem to expect virtually everything.

Authority is tightly concentrated in Latin America and is delegated
most reluctantly. As with many developing countries, almost all decisions, even the most petty, must come from the top.

> The concentration of the power of decision at the highest levels was,
> and still is, the most serious ill of the country's administrative organism.
> The repugnancy for delegation has been responsible for the incredible
> delay in solving the most routine matters, for the interminable routing
> of processes for "higher consideration", and, in the final analysis, for
> the demoralization of those governing, who see themselves separating
> from the governed by a veritable bulwark of paper.[39]

Lack of Civic Responsibility and Personalism

The Spanish and Portuguese handed down to the colonists a weak
sense of loyalty and obligation toward the society in which they lived,
and a strong sense of loyalty and obligation toward family and friends.
In comparing the Portuguese character with the Spanish, Marcus Cheke
noted:

> . . . The trait that is common to both peoples is their lack of what may
> be termed "civic sense". Even more than the Spaniard, the Portuguese
> is kind and charitable to five categories of persons: to his family, to
> his friends, to the friends of his family, to the friends of his friends,
> and lastly, to the beggar in his path. But to other fellow citizens he
> acknowledges little obligation.[40]

The proposition that the law should be applied even-handedly and impersonally to all citizens conflicts with this Iberian heritage. The dominant attitude is reflected in the familiar Brazilian adage: "For friends, everything; for strangers, nothing; and for enemies, the law." Family and friendship ties very frequently impose on bureaucrats the duty to bend the law, for much of Latin America social organization is still based upon the extended family and personal relationships. Direct personal relations, based upon affection or family ties, are above the law.

Profound Socio-Economic Inequality

From its inception, Latin American society has been characterized by profound socio-economic inequality. The initial colonization scheme began the pattern by conveying enormous areas of land and effective sovereignty over these areas to a select group of royal favorites. The pattern was continued in the socio-economic system of the *latifundia*, large agrarian estates that still dominate much of the countryside. To this day income is highly concentrated in Latin America, with a huge gulf separating the small upper class and the burgeoning middle class from the great mass of the population.

This profound socio-economic inequality has been accompanied by *de facto* juridical inequality. Latin America has always had one law for its elite and a very different law for its masses. Despite the constitutional rhetoric of equality, in Latin America, as in much of the world, one's status and connections are critical variables governing actual application of the law. Particularly in dealings with the bureaucracy and the police, the rules applied to the upper and middle classes differ from those applied to the lower class.

Legalism and Formalism

Latin American legal culture is highly legalistic and formalistic; the society places great emphasis upon seeing that all social relations are regulated by comprehensive legislation. A feeling exists that new institutions or practices ought not be adopted without prior legal authorization. Latin Americans abhor a legal vacuum. The region has reams of laws and decrees regulating with great specificity seemingly every aspect of socio-economic life. It often appears that if something is not prohibited by law, it must be obligatory.

Another facet of this legalistic mentality is the tendency to regard as done that which is enacted into law. Latin America inherited from Spain and Portugal the naive faith that almost any social or economic ill can be cured by legal prescription. Latin America has continually repeated the pattern of Spanish and Portuguese colonial rule by enacting laws with little regard for the prospects of enforcement. Unenforceable laws have typically been remedied by new laws, most of them equally unenforceable. The persistence up to the present of the assumption that all problems can be solved on a legal level is remarkable. Whether the society is willing and able to shoulder the costs of enforcement is seldom a suitable topic for discussion.

Lawmakers are generally not content to set forth desired conduct in general terms. They seem driven to try to anticipate and regulate all possible future occurrences with detailed, comprehensive, and occasionally incomprehensible legislation. Situations that in common law countries would be left to judges or administrators to work out on a case-by-case basis under the rubric of "reasonableness" are preordained by statute. This legislative style reflects a deep-seated mistrust of those administering and interpreting the laws, as well as the entire legalistic and codifying tradition of the civil law, which exalts certainty as a supreme value.[41]

In much the same fashion as the conquistadors brought along notaries to certify the legality of the *requerimientos* read to the Indians,[42] present day Latin Americans display a prodigious concern with ascertaining the existence of formal legal authority for almost any act. Notaries do a land office business, and even their signatures may occasionally have been authenticated. Official forms typically come with half a dozen copies attached, all of which must be duly signed, authenticated, and stamped. Some of this is obviously bureaucratic featherbedding, but some of it is due to the old Iberian habit of requiring several persons to perform the same task, with each checking on the others.

Governmental action, even when plainly arbitrary or tyrannical, is likely to be spelled out in startling specificity in official gazettes. Latin American regimes frequently appear more concerned with ensuring the formal legality of their actions by putting them in black and white in an official gazette than concealing their arbitrariness. One explanation for exaggerated concern with legal formalities in modern Latin America has been offered by Professor Morse:

It is because the lawmaking and law-applying processes in Latin America do not in the last instance receive their sanction from popular referendum, from laws and constitutions, from the bureaucratic ideal of "service," from tyrannically exercised power, from custom, or from scientific or dialectical laws. As Gierke said of the Middle Ages: "Far rather every duty of obedience was conditioned by the rightfulness of command." That is, in a patrimonial state, to which command and decree are so fundamental, the legitimacy of the command is determined by the legitimacy of the authority which issues it. Hence the importance of sheer legalism in Latin-American administration as constant certification for the legitimacy, not of the act, but of him who executes it.[43]

Every nation has some formalistic behavior, but Latin American concern with authenticity and verification is both impressive and oppressive. One must produce a plethora of legal permissions and official documents even for simple transactions. Latin American legal systems display a decided tendency to honor form over substance. Elaborate simulations to bypass particular legal rules are fairly common.[44] The authorities frequently, although by no means always, display remarkable tolerance for such maneuvering.

Lack of Penetration

The formal legal systems of Latin American countries are modern, developed institutional structures. Disputes are resolved by a hierarchical arrangement of courts on the basis of the wording and legislative history of legal norms, scholarly doctrine, opinions of distinguished jurists, and prior court decisions. Official determinations of the rights and obligations are based upon the application of impersonal, universalistic principles by professionals trained in the system. This formal legal system has failed, however, to penetrate very far into most Latin American societies. With the exception of the elite and the still relatively small but burgeoning middle class, the great bulk of the population does not actively avail itself of the formal legal system. Their disputes have been resolved by the *patrón*, *paterfamilias*, or local leaders.

Even today penetration of the formal legal systems is quite limited. Some Latin Americans still live in remote and inaccessible areas, for all practical purposes outside the market economy. Much of the rural interior still is only nominally under the control of formal authorities; real power lies in the hands of local landholders. Typically, the latter have rendered justice to their friends and applied the law to their enemies.

Not only in rural regions has the penetration of formal legal systems been limited. Millions of urban Latin Americans dwell in the squatter settlements that ring all major cities. It is clear that one of the basic mechanisms for transference of land in many parts of Latin America is by invasion.[45] Penetration of the formal legal structure into these settlements is often incomplete, perhaps in large part because such a settlement itself is of doubtful formal legality.

Penetration of the formal system into even the modern, urban sectors is greatly hampered by difficulties in ascertaining its provisions. Discovering the governing law in Latin America today often seems as perplexing and difficult a task as it was in colonial times. One looks in vain for comprehensive digests, citators, a key-number system, or an index to legal periodicals. Official gazettes are typically unindexed and undigested. Whether one finds a particular law or decree frequently depends on luck and the caption's phraseology. Decisions of important tribunals, including many supreme court decisions, remain unpublished. It is common to find several decisions by the same court on different sides of an issue. Instead of repealing obsolete or inconsistent statutory provisions, Latin American practice is generally to adopt supplemental legislation, which, in turn, is amended and reamended. Frequently, one is forced to read a host of separate statutes and decrees regulating a given subject (and many others as well) and then undertake the jigsaw job of piecing together the provisions still in force to find the governing law. Even the authorities charged with administering a particular body of law are often unaware of significant changes in the statutory or case law. Inertia, ignorance, and inability to keep abreast of rapid-fire legislative change frequently combine to produce substantial differences between formal rules and the law actually being applied.

The Calculated Gap

It would be misleading to suggest that the gap between the law on the books and actual practice in Latin America is always unintentional. This gap is sometimes intentional. Formalism can be a useful strategy for averting social change, managing social conflict, or improving a government's bargaining position. In many countries, particularly those undergoing wrenching societal clashes, it is easier and less socially divisive to prevent or limit implementation of redistributive or regulatory legislation inimical to powerful interest groups than to prevent the enactment of such legislation. Proponents of such legislation are afforded a symbolic victory, but in practice little or nothing changes. A number of Latin American agrarian reform statutes have been of this "lyrical" variety.[46] Occasionally, some of these "dead letter" laws are resuscitated and utilized as means for effectuating significant socio-economic change when reformist groups succeed in capturing the executive but not the legislature.[47]

In other situations the calculated gap may serve as a strategy for promoting social change or improving the government's bargaining position. Obviously unenforceable provisions may be written into constitutions and laws in the hope that some day social, economic, or political conditions will evolve sufficiently to permit implementation. From time to time such essentially aspirational or hortatory provisions eventually bear fruit. Developing countries frequently attempt to regulate foreign investment by legislation that is so restrictive that if applied literally, little new foreign investment would be forthcoming. In practice, the restrictive rules are relaxed by *ad hoc* negotiations.[48]

A more sinister aspect to structuring a high degree of noncompliance into the legal system is the inhibition of the rule of law and the facilitation of authoritarianism. A system in which most economic actors must break or bend the law in order to do business dramatically increases the government's power to discourage legitimate opposition by merely threatening to investigate activities where violations are notorious. In a very real sense, widespread and notorious violations of certain kinds of laws creates a large group of hostages to threats of governmental retribution and may serve to dampen open opposition to governmental policies.

IMPLICATIONS FOR THE MULTINATIONALS

It is easy to draw inaccurate conclusions from the above description of Latin American legal culture. One conclusion that should not be drawn is the Latin American judiciary and legal profession are corrupt, incompetent, or poorly trained. As a rule, Latin American judges and lawyers are dedicated, scrupulous professionals. Indeed, many Latin

American jurists deservedly enjoy international repute for their scholarship and dedicated work on international legal projects.

On the other hand, one must recognize that Latin American courts do not have the power and prestige of U.S. courts. It is, therefore, unrealistic to expect Latin American courts to provide as effective protection against arbitrary governmental action as U.S. courts.

One should also be more reluctant to engage in litigation in Latin America as a means of protecting one's rights. Disputes in Latin America are more likely to be resolved through the mediation or influence of family, *patrón*, or friend. In urban areas, court congestion and poorly functioning procedural systems often make litigation drag on for decades. Court clerks are often poorly paid, and payments of speed money, delay money, and "make the file disappear" money are common. Tort recoveries tend to be low, and the amount of recovery is often not worth the hassle of litigating. On the other hand, from the standpoint of a company that is a potential defendent, the low damages, lack of discovery, and potential for delay make Latin American courts ideal forums for litigation. This is why it is so critical to structure commercial transactions, if possible, in a manner that guarantees one's legal rights with a document such as a negotiable instrument that will enable the holder to resort to summary proceedings.

Although the law on the books appears to be universalistic, in practice it is not. The tradition of one law for the elite and another for the masses is alive and well in most parts of Latin America. The foreign investor usually discovers fairly quickly that there is considerable play in the joints of the foreign investment statute and that disputes are likely to be resolved through *ad hoc* negotiations rather than through the formal legal system.

One must rely heavily upon local counsel in the Latin American country or countries in which one is operating. Not only do business people have pressing needs to be kept aware of rapid-fire legal change, but they need continual guidance in dealing with unfamiliar laws and ways of doing business. For example, if one cannot count on the court system to protect one's patent or copyright, a licensing transaction may have to be structured in a very different way.

One should also carefully explore possibilities for dispute resolution before U.S. courts or arbitration panels as an alternative to litigation in Latin American courts. But one also has to be careful to ensure that a Latin American court will recognize the judgment or award if one has to sue to enforce it in Latin America.

Long-term business planning in Latin America is extraordinarily difficult because of both the difficulty in knowing what the law is and the frequency with which it changes. Business decisions, therefore, should be made with a relatively short time frame. One also needs more elaborate contingency planning for changes in laws and regulations.

Finally, one has to learn to understand the underlying legal culture in Latin America and to distinguish between the myth system as expressed in the law on the books and the operational code. In some situations, doing business in association with a local partner may be a virtual necessity for dealing with the government. The local partner may possess a network of friends and local contacts that can be invaluable in avoiding or resolving disputes. On the other hand, a local partner's different cultural perceptions and different legal constraints can easily become new sources of disputes.

NOTES

1. A substantial number of Latin American juridical terms have no counterpart in English, just as a substantial number of English juridical terms have no counterpart in Spanish, Portuguese, or French. Common examples of terms that have no English counterpart are *mandado de segurança* (the Brazilian writ of security), *amparo* (a combined form of appeal, habeas corpus, injunction, and writ of prohibition that developed first in Mexico and has spread to other Latin American countries), and *cause* (the generalized motivation of the transaction in French contract law). Similarly, terms like "estoppel," an estate in real property, or "trust" (even though adopted in a few civil law jurisdictions, including Mexico and Panama) have no civil law counterparts. Habeas corpus, borrowed originally from Anglo-American law, has been stretched beyond recognition in some Latin American countries. Peru, for example, has allowed habeas corpus to be used to challenge the fairness of an agrarian reform expropriation. Adding to the confusion is that even when the equivalent concepts exist, one sometimes has to resort to Latin to translate accurately. For example, the Spanish *cosa juzgada* or Portuguese *coisa julgada* is best translated as *res judicata* in English. Even then, significant technical differences between the concept of *cosa juzgada* and *res judicata* exist. *See* R. CASAD, CIVIL JUDGMENT RECOGNITION 45–46 (1981).

2. *See* Friedman, *Legal Culture and Social Development*, 4. L. & SOC. REV. 29, 35 (1969).

3. Argentina, Bolivia, Brazil, Chile, Colombia, Costa Rica, Cuba, Dominican Republic, Ecuador, El Salvador, Guatemala, Haiti, Honduras, Mexico, Nicaragua, Panama, Paraguay, Peru, Uruguay, and Venezuela.

4. J. MERRYMAN, THE CIVIL LAW TRADITION 1–4 (2d ed. 1985). A few jurisdictions, such as Louisiana, Puerto Rico, Quebec, Scotland, and South Africa, share both traditions.

5. *Id.* at 36–37.

6. *See* M. CAPPELLETTI, JUDICIAL REVIEW IN THE CONTEMPORARY WORLD 46–66 (1971).

7. *Id.* at 54–63.

8. J. MERRYMAN, *supra* note 4, at 106.

9. *Id.* at 114.

10. *See generally*, Herzog & Karlen, *Attacks on Judicial Decisions*, in M. CAPPELLETTI (ed.), CIVIL PROCEDURE, 16 INT'L ENCY. COMP. L. 60–66 (1982).

11. J. LOPEZ–SANTA MARIA, LE DROIT DES OBLIGATIONS ET DES CONTRATS ET L'INFLATION MONETAIRE 111–27 (1980); K. ROSENN, LAW AND INFLATION 221–29 (1982); Rosenn, *Expropriation, Inflation, and Development*, 1972 WIS L. REV. 845, 860–62.

12. R. BAKER, JUDICIAL REVIEW IN MEXICO 198–207 (1971).

13. Rosenn, *Judicial Review in Latin America*, 35 OHIO ST. L. J. 785, 788 (1974); Carpizo and Fix-Zamudio, *La Necesidad y la Legitimidad de la Revisión Judicial en América Latina*, 52 BOL. MEX. DER. COMP. 31 (1985). Chile's 1980 Constitution permits judicial review to be exercised by both the Supreme Court and the Constitutional Tribunal. Ecuador's 1978 Constitution provides for a unique form of judicial review. The Supreme Court is granted the power to declare unconstitutional at any time, whether in conjunction with a case or *ex officio*, any law or decree and to suspend its operation. The Supreme Court also has the power to refuse to apply any law or decree to a concrete case on the ground of unconstitutionality. The Supreme Court's decision, however, is not final; it must be submitted to the National Chamber of Representatives, which has the final word.

14. 1 S. LINARES QUINTANA, DERECHO CONSTITUCIONAL E INSTITUCIONES POLÍTICAS 666–68 (1970); TORRES-LACROZE & MARTIN, MANUAL DE INTRODUCCIÓN AL DERECHO, 337 (4th ed. 1983).

15. As one Brazilian commentator explained, the *Súmula* is technically not legally binding, but it has created "a kind of *de facto stare decisis.*" Sampaio, *O Supremo Tribunal Federal e a Nova Fisionomia do Judiciário*, 273 REV. FOR. 29, 35 (1981). A rule of law is published in the *Súmula* only after a series of decisions on the point indicate that the court has definitively adopted a position.

16. Ley de Amparo, arts. 192–94 (as amended 1968).

17. Const. of 1980, art. 83 (Chile); const. of 1949, art. 10 (Costa Rica); const. of 1985, art. 268 (Guatemala); const. of 1983, art. 203 (Panama).

18. *See* Rosenn, *supra* note 13, at 790–91, 804, const. of 1980, art. 301 (Peru).

19. The analysis in this section draws heavily on K. KARST & K. ROSENN, LAW AND DEVELOPMENT IN LATIN AMERICA 15–69 (1975) and Rosenn, *Brazil's Legal Culture: The Jeito Revisited* 1 FLA. INT'L. L. J. 1 (1984).

20. W. M. REISMAN, FOLDED LIES: BRIBERY, CRUSADES, AND REFORMS 15–36 (1979). Reisman differentiates between countries' myth systems and operational codes.

For an intriguing application to Mexico, *see* Gordon, *Of Aspirations and Operations: The Governance of Multinational Enterprises by Third World Nations*, 16 INTER-AM.L.REV. 301, 325–352 (1984).

21. Eder, *Law in Latin America*, in 1 LAW: A CENTURY OF PROGRESS 39, 42–43 (N.Y.U. ed. 1937).

22. H. WOLFF, ROMAN LAW: AN HISTORICAL INTRODUCTION 127–30 (1951).

23. Moreno, *Justice and Law in Latin America: A Cuban Example*, 12 J. INTER-AM. STUD. & WORLD AFF. 367f, 374 (1970).

24. C. PRADO JUNIOR, FORMAÇÃO DO BRASIL CONTEMPORANEO 297 (1942).

25. F. MORENO, LEGITIMACY AND STABILITY IN LATIN AMERICA: A STUDY OF CHILEAN POLITICAL CULTURE 18–19 (1969).

26. M. MADDEN, POLITICAL THEORY AND LAW IN MEDIEVAL SPAIN 14 (1930).

27. *The Heritage of Latin America*, in L. HARTZ (ed.) THE FOUNDING OF NEW SOCIETIES 123, 153 (1964).

28. Cited in Scott, *Francisco Suarez: His Philosophy of Law and of Sanctions*, 22 GEO. L. J. 405, 414 (1934).

29. F. SUAREZ, TWO SELECTIONS FROM THREE WORKS 854–55 (J. Scott ed. 1944).

30. Law 24, Book II, title 1. Writing in 1616, the great Spanish jurist, Castillo de Bavadilla, explained the reasoning underlying this formula:

> By laws of these realms it is provided that the royal provisions and decrees which are issued contrary to justice and in prejudice of suitors are invalid and should be obeyed but not executed . . . and the reason for this is that such provisions and mandates are presumed to be foreign to the intention of the Prince, who as Justinian has said, cannot be believed to desire by word or decree to subject and destroy the law established and agreed to with great solicitude.

Quoted in C. HARING, THE SPANISH EMPIRE IN AMERICA 122–23 (Harbinger ed. 1963).

31. S. SCOTT, THE VISIGOTHIC CODE xiii (1910).

32. S. SCHWARTZ, SOVEREIGNTY AND SOCIETY IN COLONIAL BRAZIL 122–39 (1973). Resistance to Hapsburg Indian policy was so strong among Brazilian colonists that the Crown was eventually forced to repeal this legislation as unenforceable. *Id.* at 137.

33. *See* B. GESCHE MULLER, JURISPRUDENCIA DINAMICA 128 (1971).

34. K. RYAN, AN INTRODUCTION TO THE CIVIL LAW 6 (1962). In 212 A.D., an edict of Caracalla extended Roman citizenship, hitherto reserved for a privileged few, to all inhabitants of the Roman Empire. H. JOLOWICZ & B. NICHOLAS, HISTORICAL INTRODUCTION TO THE STUDY OF ROMAN LAW 345–47 (3d ed. 1972).

35. K. KARST & K. ROSENN, LAW AND DEVELOPMENT IN LATIN AMERICA 231 (1975). This dual legal system was eventually abrogated in the reign of Chindasvinth (641-652). *Id.*

36. M. CAETANO, HISTÓRIA DO DIREITO PORTUGUÊS 235–39 (1981); L. MCALLISTER, THE "FUERO MILITAR" IN NEW SPAIN 5 (1957).

37. R. FAORO, OS DONOS DO PODER: FORMAÇÃO DO PATRONATO POLÍTICO BRASILEIRO 15–22, 130–31 (3d ed. 1976); M. SARFATTI, SPANISH BUREAUCRATIC—PATRIMONIALISM IN AMERICA (1966); F. URICOECHEA, THE PATRIMONIAL FOUNDATIONS OF THE BRAZILIAN BUREAUCRATIC STATE (1980); E. WILLEMS, LATIN AMERICAN CULTURE: AN ANTHROPOLOGICAL SYNTHESIS 89–98 (1975). Patrimonialism is an archetypical form of

political system in which a traditional sovereign, such as a king, either personally or through his administrative staff, determines all political and administrative decisions. The sovereign, however, gives up some of this absolute power by ceding to certain officials or private individuals special rights or privileges, in exchange for goods or services, thereby creating estates. In this form of organization, the "legal order is rigorously formal but thoroughly concrete and in this sense irrational. Only an 'empirical' type of legal interpretation can develop. All 'administration' is negotiation, bargaining, and contracting about 'privileges', the content of which must then be fixed." M. WEBER, ON LAW IN ECONOMY AND SOCIETY 263 (M. Rheinstein ed. 1967). *See also* 3 M. WEBER, ECONOMY AND SOCIETY 1010–42 (G. Roth & C. Wittich eds. 1968).

    38. C. HARING, THE SPANISH EMPIRE IN AMERICA, 100 (Harbinger ed. 1963); C. PRADO JUNIOR, *supra* note 24, at 303.

    39. Statement of Hélio Beltrão, until recently Minister of Debureaucratization in Brazil, quoted in *O Globo*, Aug. 24, 1970, at p. 23.

    40. *The Portuguese Character*, in PORTUGAL AND BRAZIL 42, 45 (H. Livermore ed. 1953).

    41. J. MERRYMAN, *supra* note 4, at 50–51.

    42. *See* KARST & ROSENN, *supra* note 35, at 31–33. Another revealing example of the Conquistadors' exaggerated concern with formality is Pedrarias Davila's celebrated reenactment before notaries of Balboa's immersion in the Pacific so that the Spanish claim to possession of the new territory and sea would be entirely legal. E. CRUZ, DERECHO, DESARROLLO E INTEGRACION REGIONAL EN CENTRO AMERICA 13–14 (1967).

    43. *Supra* note 27, at 174.

    44. *See* Kozolchyk, *Law and the Credit Structure in Latin America*, 7 VA. J. INT'L L. 1, 10–13, 34–35 (1967).

    45. *See* Falcão, *Justiça Social e Justiça Legal: Conflitos de Propriedade no Recife*, in CONFLITO DE DIREITO DE PROPRIEDAD: INVASÕES URBANAS 79, 96 (J. Falcão ed. 1984); K. KARST et al., THE EVOLUTION OF LAW IN THE BARRIOS OF CARACAS (1973).

    46. A. HIRSCHMAN, JOURNEYS TOWARD PROGRESS 107–58 (1963).

    47. A particularly striking example was Allende's use of previously slumbering statutes to nationalize a substantial part of Chile's economy, despite a hostile legislature. *See* Petras, *Political and Social Change in Chile*, in LATIN AMERICA: FROM DEPENDENCE TO REVOLUTION 9, 24–25 (J. Petras ed. 1973).

    48. Gordon, *supra* note 20, at 325–40.

Response: Tang Thi Thanh Trai Le*

Dr. Rosenn presented a clear and precise overview of the salient features of the Latin American legal and administrative system. He has covered a complex comparison clearly and completely. Based on my experience in a civil law country, Vietnam, as well as with the common law tradition of the United States, I would underscore three conceptual differences between these two systems, and comment on the role of the lawyer in these systems.

The concept of property ownership is not the same in the common law tradition as in civil law. In the common law tradition, due to certain historical and sociological factors of past English history, property ownership was conceived as a bundle of rights. The tenure of the land is given but not the ownership of the land. With the tenure of the land are a number of rights over the land which are similar to those of an owner — the right to dispose of the land, the right to mortgage the land, the right to transfer the land. When those rights are taken away, however, one no longer "owns" the land. To the civil law lawyer, this interpretation does not make sense. Ownership is one thing, rights are another. An owner may give up all the owner's rights but still retain ownership.

We see the same distinction between rights and remedies. In the common law tradition, rights are equated with remedies. If one has no remedies, one has no rights. In the civil law tradition, however, rights still remain if there are no remedies.

Multinationals doing business in a foreign country usually operate through a subsidiary, i.e. a corporation incorporated under the laws of the host country. The term "corporation" in common law has a dif-

---

*Tang Thi Thanh Trai Le is a professor of law in the University of Notre Dame Law School with doctorates from the United States and France. She is the former dean of the Law School, University of Hue, Vietnam, and the founder and senior partner of a law firm specializing in corporate law and international business transactions in Saigon.

ferent meaning from the term "corporation" (the French term: *societe*) in the civil law tradition. In the common law tradition, a corporation is a creature of the sovereign. The corporation owes its existence to the sovereign's will which approves the corporation's charter through the process of incorporation. In civil law, on the other hand, a corporation is simply a contract between the parties. Article 1832 of the Napoleanic Code, which also influences Latin American law in this area, defines a corporation as: "A contract by which two or more persons agree to put something in common with the purpose of sharing the profit arising therefrom." Therefore, in civil law countries, the corporate entity is formed on the basis of personal and mutual trust.

While a country like the U.S. stresses the rule of law as a cornerstone of its legal and political system, many Third World countries emphasize trust and harmony. We see this difference in thinking reflected in many business practices. A U.S. business entity dealing with a foreign counterpart will feel secure only if it can surround itself with legal counsel and substantial legal protection. This attitude of the U.S. corporation is often not understood by the foreign counterpart. In Third World countries, and in many European countries, lawyers do not play the same role as in the U.S. A lawyer often means distrust and trouble. In such countries, one goes to a lawyer as a last resort in order in fight an opponent in litigation or to be represented in a criminal case. One does not normally use lawyers between business partners, who in that tradition are contracting parties, any more than a wife would use a lawyer to deal with her husband unless she means trouble. Of course, presently, U.S. business practices are widespread, and lawyers are accepted with less misgiving.

In light of these differences in the concept and practice of law in these two systems, some corporations insist upon going to U.S. forums when drafting a contract concerning the application of U.S. laws. Besides the fact that such an insistence may denote a lack of trust in the host country legal system, U.S. law may not always work to the advantage of the multinational. Such a stipulation may not be upheld in a foreign court if litigation takes place outside the U.S. The foreign court could dismiss the provision of applying considerations of public policy or danger to the public order. Third, insistence on U.S. courts, even if upheld, might be downright counterproductive. A corporation may find a favorable judgment in the U.S. court unrecognized or unenforceable abroad, and the foreign entity may have no assets in the U.S. against which the judgment might be executed.

Response: Ricardo A. Arias*

These comments represent, of course, my private perspective. I was trained in law in Puerto Rico, where they have a dual system of civil law and common law, and where both systems seem to prevail and work efficiently. In addition to studying both systems of law, I have practiced law in Panama and in the United States.

The Rosenn thesis is that U.S. businessmen are bewildered by Latin Amerian law. He proposes that one of the reasons for this bewilderment is what he called the distinguishing differences between the civil law and the common law, primarily in codification and the judicial system. However, Rosenn affirms, and I agree with him, that these distinguishing features of the civil law tradition require some qualification in Latin America; Latin American judiciaries are, in certain respects, hybrids, sharing some features from the common law and civil law courts. Further, and I believe that Rosenn will agree, basic legal concepts such as contracts, property law, banking systems, negotiable instruments, etc. are all very similar in Latin America and in the United States, and U.S. businessmen from multinational firms are comfortable with those concepts. While, in principle, I must give due respect to the distinguishing features outlined by Trai Le, in my opinion they are more theoretical than practical and are aspects that preoccupy lawyers more than businessmen.

A second reason for the bewilderment of U.S. businessmen suggested by Rosenn is what he calls the cultural heritage, or the Iberian legacy of Latin America. While Rosenn does not come out and explicitly say so, his position can be summarized as follows: This Latin American Iberian legacy has created a paternalistic, autocratic society where there is little respect for the rule of law and a great degree of

---

*Ricardo A. Arias is a partner in the Panamanian law firm of Galindo, Arias, and López. He is a graduate of Georgetown University School of Foreign Service, the University of Puerto Rico Law School, and the Yale University Law School.

155

corruption, a situation which can be confusing for the Anglo-American multinational manager. In my opinion, the existence of a paternalistic, autocratic society in Latin America can be traced to factors different from our cultural heritage.

At least two political factors have significantly contributed to this situation. One of them is the human aspect of Latin American colonization, which was quite different from the colonization of the United States. In the U.S. the colonizers were civilians, who arrived with their families in the new land, and consequently did not comingle with the Indian population. Regretfully, this led to the elimination of a great part of the Indian population of North America. The Latin American colonization process was undertaken by governmental employees or military men who came alone, not to stay but only to comply with a mandate from the government. It was natural for these military and government officials to impose an autocratic regime.

A second political factor contributing to a paternalistic, autocratic society appeared during the post-colonial period—the United States colonial imperialism. After the Latin American wars of independence, enlightened national leaders attempted to create democratic and liberal institutions. These efforts, difficult enough given the autocratic social structure prevalent at the time, were confronted with the expansion of United States capitalistic imperialism. The corporations which came to Latin America in those days had not only little or no concern for democracy in our countries, but actually preferred to deal with the autocratic regimes. These corporations found that the autocratic systems were more efficient, more stable, and most importantly, could be controlled. The U.S. businessmen were not bewildered by these autocratic regimes; on the contrary, the businessmen were an important factor in promoting their existence. Unfortunately, essentially the same situation endures today. While the colonialistic expansion is no longer in evidence, the rise of socialist countries in Latin America—like Cuba, Chile, and Nicaragua—has encouraged the United States government to be more willing to back military rather than democratic regimes.

While I accept that there are certain differences between the civil law and common law traditions, I do not believe they are so important as to bewilder the U.S. businessmen living in Latin America. Rather, I believe that the existence of autocratic regimes, at least in certain countries, is due in no minor way to the policy of the U.S. government and to the past behavior of U.S. businessmen.

Bribery in the Judeo-Christian Tradition and the Common Law*

*JOHN T. NOONAN, JR.***

My subject is the concept of the bribe. Its development will be set out both in moral and in legal terms, the two of them shading into one another.

THE MORAL DEVELOPMENT OF BRIBERY

To generalize about moral ideas and their development, the major origins in Western tradition have been divine instruction and divine example, earthly interests, and the elaboration of the basic insight. Elaboration goes in one direction by a kind of expansion — an expansion in the direction of "purity," that may or may not have a solid basis. In another direction expansion is provided by human experience. This direction always has a basis because experience furnishes it. In the following examples, you will see these elements at work.

At the beginning of the Western tradition one gets back to the Ancient Near East where our moral ideas originated. In the Ancient

---

*Copyright 1986 John T. Noonan, Jr. These remarks are drawn from his book, *Bribes*, McMillan Publishing Company, New York, 1984.

**John T. Noonan, Jr., is a judge of the U.S. Court of Appeals for the Ninth Circuit and the Robbins Professor Emeritus at the University of California, Berkeley. A recognized scholar in the areas of church history, canon law, and theological development, he has served as a consultant to the Papal Commission on the Family, the Presidential Commission on Population and the American Future, and the United States Catholic Conference. In 1984, Judge Noonan was awarded the Laetare Medal by the University of Notre Dame.

Near East the concept of the bribe does not exist. The bribe is not known. When people relate to each other outside of the family or the tribe, they relate to powerful strangers. If one wants to meet a powerful stranger without a hostile reaction, one must bring an offering. To go empty-handed to a powerful stranger is unthinkable. Peace requires a gift. The aim is reciprocity. One comes with something to give. One expects something in return. That is the way life is. Reciprocity is the rule. It is unnatural to depart from reciprocity.

To give an example of the ethic that prevails in that kind of civilization, consider a story from Mesopotamia about 1500 B.C., "The Poor Man of Nippur." The man's name is Gimil Ninurta. He wants to rise in the world. All he has is a goat. He takes the goat and visits the mayor of Nippur. The mayor at once asks, "What is your problem that you bring me an offering?" The mayor accepts the goat, but he is a poor reciprocator. He has a feast and he gives Gimil Ninurta only stale beer and a bone of the goat and has him thrown out. As the story continues, Gimil Ninurta through other means acquires a fortune. He comes back in disguise as a royal emissary and tricks the mayor and finally has the mayor beaten. The whole point of the story is that the mayor was a bad reciprocator and was justly rewarded for his bad reciprocation. The mayor did not know what he was supposed to do when he received an offering. There is no sense in this story that there is anything wrong in trying to influence the mayor with a present. The story hinges on the churlish behavior of the mayor in failing to reciprocate.

Glimmerings of an idea of something different are apparent at about the same time in Egypt. In Egypt, Books of the Dead were provided to royalty and nobles with illustrations to instruct them on their passage into the next world. One of the great illustrations in a Book of the Dead for an nobleman named Ani shows him going to the Judgment Hall. In the first scene Ani's hands are filled with gifts. Ani is at the entrance of the Judgment Hall. In the second scene Ani's soul is being weighed on scales. The gifts are over at one side. The gifts are not in the hands of the judging god, a subtle indication that the moment of judging is not the moment at which gifts are to be presented. In the third scene Ani's soul has been weighed and been found to balance with truth and so he has been admitted and received by Osiris. In this last scene he presents the gifts to Osiris. The scenario, one supposes, is based on the court etiquette of Egypt. Gifts are not presented to the judge at the instant of decision. But if the decision is favorable to the petitioner, the petitioner gives gifts to the judge. The beginning of a different approach from that prevalent in the past can be seen.

In definitive form, as far as our culture goes, the break in the pattern occurs in the Hebrew Bible. A very powerful force was necessary to break the ordinary relationship of reciprocity. That powerful force is the example of God. Most significantly, the image of God as example in relation to gifts is presented in Deuteronomy 10, where the people of Israel are told "The Lord your God is God of God and Lord of Lords; the great, mighty and terrible God, who does not lift up faces and who does not take *shohad*, but secures justice to widows and orphans." *Shohad* is an ambiguous Hebrew word, best translated as "offering." God, Deuteronomy tells the people of Israel, does not take offering. The context of the statement is provided by the accompanying declaration that God does not lift up faces. The expression means "reaching out one's hand to the face of another for whom one is going surety." God does not go surety for another in judgment, that is, God does not identify himself with a litigant and so he does not take offerings in judgment.

The image of God is used as an image for the judges of Israel. They are told to imitate God and in judgment not to lift up faces and not to take offering. This message is presented within the context of the religion of Israel, where in fact there is a great deal of gift-giving to God. The concept of God as the receiver of gifts coexists with the notion that God as judge does not take offering. The picture is mixed and complicated. The paradigm of a judge in taking offering is weakened by the total context. The message translates as a bending of the rule of reciprocity rather than a breaking of the rule. Only in the very specific context of judgment is the rule of reciprocity questioned or discarded.

Nothing in the Hebrew Bible condemns the gift-giver. In a number of texts the person who does give a gift to secure official influence is praised. Nowhere in the Hebrew Bible are there sanctions against giving or receiving offering except that a judge who receives an offering has a sanction of conscience—a sanction of great weight but different from any material sanction. Nowhere in the Hebrew Bible is there an example of anyone being caught, tried, and punished for taking bribes. Moreover, the material interests of anyone are not enlisted in the effort to prevent bribery. No class of persons has an interest in preventing bribery, detecting it, or even avoiding it. The idea of the bribe as bad is presented, God is given as an example, there is divine example and instruction, but the idea is at such a level of abstraction that one suspects that the anti-bribery rule could not have often been observed.

The next step in this formation of the concept of the bribe occurs in Roman civilization where Hebrew ideal is joined to Roman experience. The Romans had the same basic insight that the Hebrews had — that in giving judgment one was acting for God or the gods and that one's judgment should not be influenced by a bribe from the person seeking the judgment. What the Romans did which the Jews had not done was to enlist the professional interest of a class of orators whose business was to argue cases and whose profession would have been meaningless if the cases could have been decided by the highest bidder. Without the concept that bribes to judges were something to be avoided, the whole Roman system of law would have been a marketplace. For the first time, at least in Western tradition, a class was constituted which was professionally opposed to giving offerings to judges.

When the Christians appeared in the Roman Empire, they inherited the Hebrew idea and the Roman professional practice. They added to what they had received. First, they had the idea that the briber as well as the bribee is doing something wrong. This notion appears in the specific context of an attempt to purchase the Spirit. The story is told in Acts. Simon Magus wants to buy the Spirit from Simon Peter. Simon Peter repudiates the attempt with some of the harshest words in the New Testament: "You and your money go to hell!" It is a stunning repudiation of the person who wants to buy something that seems to be good and should be for sale. With this repudiation of the wrongful offeror goes a teaching that there are some things that cannot be purchased. In the view of the Christians the Spirit cannot be purchased. Market reciprocity is wrong in relation to the Spirit.

The teaching of the episode in Acts receives a general form in the saying of Jesus which establishes a new law of reciprocity. That saying in the Gospel of Luke is: "You have received freely. Give freely." The rule of reciprocity is raised to a higher level. The recipient of a free gift is told to give freely. The teaching relates to an even more fundamental theme in Christianity — the meaning of redemption. The Christian teaching on redemption, reciprocity, non-saleability, and the wrongfulness of offering to obtain what is not for sale — these additions fill out the concept of bribery derived from the Hebrew Bible and Roman legal practice.

Brought together by the Fathers of the Church, most notably Saint Augustine, these notions became the ideas of Roman Christian civilization. The ideas then encountered the new peoples who came into Europe, the barbarians — the Germanic, Celtic, and Hungarian peoples who entered Europe from the fifth century to the tenth century. The new peoples had never heard of such ideas. Their way of relating to powerful strangers was the old way — come with a gift, expect reciprocation, avoid war. Clashes occur between the Jewish, Roman, and Christian ideals and the ordinary practices of the new peoples. The barbarians are surprised. They cannot believe that this is the way things are done. In general it is not the way things are done among them. The Roman traditions are perpetuated by the monks and sometimes lived by saints. On the whole, the old-fashioned way of reciprocity prevails.

The next major moment in the evolution of the bribe occurs in the eleventh century when European civilization revives. The Christian ideals are now being systematically inculcated. A new Europe is being formed. Wave after wave of reform occurs. One of the great battle cries of the reformers focuses on the elimination of bribery, especially in the Church. For the first time a specific concept is formed of bribery within the Church. The word "simony" is coined, based on the story of Simon Magus. The practice of buying the Spirit is treated as a serious sin. Simony is stamped as heresy. The reformers pitch their hopes on the papacy as the institution that will eliminate it.

Simony is a subspecies of bribery. Some theological writers advance the proposition that justice itself is spiritual. If one attempts to purchase justice, one commits the sin of simony just as if one were attempting to buy the grace of ordination in the Church. The campaign against simony broadens into a general realization that it is a serious sin for Christians to sell or to buy justice.

The process of reform goes on for over five centuries. The waves of reform continue. The papacy, once the leader in stamping out corruption, becomes corrupt itself. The last wave — the Reformation — attacks simony in the Church and particularly in the papacy. By this time the ideal excluding reciprocity in certain transactions has been accepted everywhere. No one contests that non-reciprocation in certain contexts is right. Grace cannot be sold in the Church. Justice cannot be sold in the courts. The European mind is formed. A concept has been ingrained.

The greatest single embodiment of the tradition is formed by Dante in *The Divine Comedy*. In *The Divine Comedy* the sin to which the greatest attention is given — the sin which takes up three and one third of the thirty-three cantos of the Inferno — is the sin of bribery, both ecclesiastical and secular. Dante indeed puts the secular bribe-takers in a lower position in hell than the ecclesiastical bribe-takers. As Dante uses the physical sufferings of the sinners as signs of the real nature of their sins, the bribe-takers live in pouches. They are so busy that they are scarcely ever seen. At times their backs appear but not their faces. They are compared to frogs and otters. They live in a sticky, viscous pitch that covers them. The dirt covers them because they are bribe-takers. Describing the city of Lucca, Dante provides the single most succinct definition of a bribe: Lucca is "where No becomes Yes for money." The definition is comprehensive. An intense spiritual hatred of bribery animates Dante's depiction.

The anti-bribery tradition — the Christian tradition — gained the mind of Europe. In English probably its strongest embodiment can be found in Shakespeare. The anti-bribery tradition is an ironic undercurrent in *The Merchant of Venice*. It reaches full resonance in the play that turns on notions of bribery, *Measure for Measure*. Shakespeare does for English-speaking readers what Dante did for European literature in general.

The Legal Development of Bribery

To shift now from the moral development of the concept of bribery to its legal development, I have found no instance in English literature or English legal practice where a bribe-taking judge was actually tried, convicted, and punished prior to Francis Bacon in 1621. The ideal was there. Application of the actual sanction was certainly rare. Bacon's trial and conviction constituted a great turning point. One of the most literate and intelligent people in England, the Lord High Chancellor was convicted of taking bribes. He was brought down by his rival, Sir Edward Coke. Wits in England had been saying "This Bacon is too hot for this cook," but in the end, Coke got Bacon. He organized the prosecution, achieved Bacon's indictment by the House of Commons, and kept the pressure on until the House of Lords convicted him.

Bacon's defense was "Everybody does it." It is a defense that was not accepted. It was a defense that was not acceptable when the higher moral consciousness of the age— a consciousness often expressed by Bacon himself in his own essays—regarded bribe-taking by a judge as evil.

It turned out on examination that Bacon had a lawful income of 3,000 pounds a year (one of the highest in England in an age when 30 pounds a year was that of an ordinary worker) and in bribes he was taking somewhere between 12,000 and 16,000 a year from litigants in chancery. A regular machine existed to sell chancery judgments, to pay the Chancellor and his henchmen, and to use lawyers as bagmen. Bacon had a whole system working to produce bribes.

Bacon's conviction is the only recorded instance of an English secular judge being convicted of bribe-taking. It was a turning point. Apparently it was such a shocking and traumatic event that English judges from that day until this have had a just reputation for honesty in office. It was a signal moment in the history of the concept of the bribe that it was applied and applied in particular against such a powerful official.

Up to this point almost all the legal focus had been on bribe-taking by judges. It took a major intellectual effort to extend the idea beyond judges. It took an effort because the biblical paradigm was that of God as judge. God was not presented by the Bible as an administrator nor as a member of a legislature. It was hard to extend the paradigm to administrators and to legislators. Reflection eventually achieved the extension.

The diary of Samuel Pepys is illustrative. Sixty years after Bacon, he was the highest civil administrator in the British Navy, the highest person in the Navy not in a political post. He is regarded by many as the founder of the modern British Navy and even of the modern British civil service. He was also a bribe-taker on a grand scale and is perhaps unique among bribe-takers in recording his bribes. Pepys had a salary of 350 pounds a year. He started his office possessing 25 pounds. Seven years later he had 7,000 pounds put away. Pepys in the diary shows a dim consciousness that what he is doing is wrong. He records the bribes with a sense of semi-guilt. Here is Pepys' diary for April 3, 1663:

Thence, going out of Whitehall I met Captain Grove who did give me a letter, directed to myself from himself. I discerned money to be in it and took it, knowing as I found it to be, the proceeds from the place I have got him—to have the taking up of vessels for Tangiers. But I did not open it until I came home to my office and there I broke it open, not looking into it until all the money was out, that I might say, "I saw no money in the paper" if ever I should be questioned about it. There was a piece of gold and four pounds in silver.

That is the consciousness of a high civil servant of the period. He knows that he has to cover himself. He is contented with a fig leaf for cover.

The idea expands slowly in England. The high point for attempted enforcement in the civil service is the trial of Warren Hastings in the eighteenth century. Edmund Burke led the prosecution against Hastings for his bribe-taking as Governor General of Bengal. The House of Lords could not bring itself to convict him. The standards laid down by Burke nonetheless became the standards honored and, to a substantial extent, observed by later civil servants of the British Empire.

The Constitution of the United States puts bribery along with treason as one of the two specific crimes justifying the impeachment of the President. From the beginning, the United States had a legal tradition that bribery on the part of judges was wrong. It took a long while to establish anything as to legislators. Throughout the nineteenth century, state legislators were notoriously corrupt. Not until 1853 was any statute enacted making it a crime for a congressman to accept a bribe. The statute was not enforced for the remainder of the century, although there was a political penalty to pay. In the aftermath of the Civil War the Republican leadership of the House was found, in the famous Credit Mobilier Affair, to have been bribed by the promoters of the Union Pacific Railroad. A political price was exacted. The Republicans suffered at the polls for their involvement. But speaking as a legal realist, one may say that there was no criminal law against bribery on the part of the President, Vice President, members of the Cabinet, Federal Judges, Senators, or Congressmen. Throughout the nineteenth century no criminal sanction existed as to bribe-taking in any of these positions; the worst penalty was retirement from office.

Lincoln Steffens, a journalist who was an expert on bribery at the beginning of the twentieth century, chronicled the story of American corruption that he found then present throughout the country. Time after time he found bribery was how business worked. Every

American enterprise got its franchises or licenses from state or city governments by paying off officeholders. Bribery was a way of life in this country. To pay off officeholders was a way of life.

In the course of this century, that way of life began to change. The first signs of change occurred in the 1920s after the crash and the Great Depression. Then, for the first time, a Cabinet officer was sent to jail for taking a bribe — Albert Bacon Fall, convicted of taking bribes in the Teapot Dome Affair. In the 1930s a high federal judge, the chief judge of the Court of Appeals for the Second Circuit, Martin Manton, was found to have taken bribes almost as systematically as Francis Bacon. He had been taking bribes for at least ten years and had taken them from a variety of businesses, including the American Tobacco Company. Nothing was done about his bribe-taking until 1939 when he was prosecuted and convicted and sent to prison. Another judge, J. Warren Davis, a court of appeals judge in the Third Circuit, was prosecuted but acquitted by a jury. In civil proceedings to set aside some of his decisions, it was judicially determined that he had been bribed by Chevron and Shell Oil. From the careers of these high federal judges it is plain that well into the 1930s American business was willing to pay off federal judges and that some federal judges were willing to be paid off.

That Fall and Manton were actually sent to jail were straws in the wind that American consciousness on bribery was changing. The real expansion of the criminal law has occurred only in the last twenty-five years. Between 1961 and 1986 there has been an amazing change in the enforcement of criminal law against bribery.

In this period, two things have happened. One has been an immense expansion of statutory law against bribery. The other has been an immense expansion in the prosecution of bribery. For the first time in history, there have been many serious prosecutions carried out either under the bribery laws or under related statutes that reach bribery. That approach has reached its height in the United States with the statutes against wire fraud, mail fraud, income tax evasion, conspiracy, and racketeering being used as major tools to reach bribe-takers.

As a result of the combination of statutes and prosecution, a development has occurred that would have amazed earlier stages of our civilization. Several thousand American officeholders have been prosecuted and sent to jail for taking bribes. Five governors have been sent to prison for taking bribes. Federal judges have been convicted of taking bribes. For the first time in history, a Senator and six Congressmen have been convicted of taking bribes. The American standard has now by statute been made effective throughout the world for Americans by enactment of the Foreign Corrupt Practices Act.

Through the combination of divine example and instruction and the enlistment of professional interest, particularly that of lawyers, there has evolved an elaboration of the concept of the bribe. That elaboration has been partly in the direction of purity, and it has partly been based on hard experience.

How seriously will the concept of the bribe be taken in the future? Substantial reasons exist for objecting to the present emphasis the concept is receiving. When the standards are applied outside the United States, familiar arguments are raised to support the objections: "Everybody does it in that country." "It has to be done." Of course, along with these slogans goes the implication that if everybody does it and you have to do it, it really cannot be wrong. Then the thought is advanced, "After all, life is shot through with reciprocities. You cannot eliminate them all. Why eliminate this particular type of reciprocity you call a bribe?"

In fact it is difficult to draw a line between what is a good reciprocity and what is a bad one. The most striking example in the American context is the campaign contribution. Most people who have written about campaign contributions have had difficulty showing the difference between a campaign contribution and a bribe.

Finally, a common cry is "After all, what harm does a bribe do?" Economically the effect may be trivial. The bribe may not cause as much economic harm as waste or as bureaucratic delay. Why not accept bribery as a fairly small cost of doing business in countries where it is a way of life?

These are some of the objections advanced to the present criminal law on bribery. A reply is possible. The arguments that "Everybody does it" and "It is necessary to do it" are not persuasive arguments on a moral level. No moral progress would ever occur if those arguments were good arguments. Every part of the world once practiced slavery. Slavery was thought essential to the maintenance of civilization. If the argument had held that slavery was necessary in every culture that practiced it, the advance would never have been made to the moral level which repudiated slavery.

The argument that "It does no harm or only trivial harm" is morally obtuse. This kind of argument often surfaces in the area of sexual morals. It is an argument that implicitly assumes that the only recognizable harm is that which can be quantified. In this case, the assumption as to quantification makes the arguments two-faced. Bribery cannot be quantified and so no one can say that it does no harm or only trivial harm. Data does not exist to support the claim made. More fundamentally, to rest the argument on quantified data is to reduce the moral argument to too narrow limits. The argument based on economic harm totally overlooks the central importance of fidelity in office. Thinking in crude economic terms of quantity overlooks the essential: civilized governments depend on the keeping of trust in office.

The difficulty of making distinctions is the most challenging objection. The difficulty can be met only by an understanding of the spectrum. There is a pure gift and a pure bribe. In between there is a substantial gray area. One can distinguish grades of gray only by knowing the white and the black. Black is a bribe, white is a gift, and in between there are a number of things that lean one way or another, where exact discrimination can be achieved only by positive law.

Christianity makes possible an appreciation of the spectrum. At the black end, a bribe is secret, shameful, manipulative. The briber regards the person he bribes as a thing. In the pure bribe, the briber has no thought of identifying with the recipient. At the white end of the spectrum is the gift. Christians understand the gift through the Redemption. The pure gift is openly given. It is not shameful. Above all, it is an expression of love. It is an effort on the part of the donor to identify with the donee. The only completely pure gift, perhaps, is the Redemption, where God identifies with human beings. In the light of the pure gift we can understand the range along the spectrum.

The concept of the bribe has a future. The concept may not live in the way it now lives, enforced by the criminal law, but it is likely that the concept will be observed and developed among persons who partake of the Jewish and Christian traditions. The concept depends for us on the example presented in the Hebrew Bible of God as one who does not take offerings to influence his decision. It depends on the ideal presented in the New Testament that what you have received freely you must give freely. On the level of earthly interest, the concept is fundamental to a sound understanding of politics for a bribe is a breach of the fidelity that alone distinguishes public office from raw power.

Response

Discussion of Judge Noonan's paper focused on two issues: universalism versus relativism, and the moral difference between extortion and bribery.

Dennis McCann pointed to the fact that all of our work on the multinational corporate interaction with governments is based on the knowledge that cultures are sufficiently different to warrant actions tailored to each specific people, yet, with the Foreign Corrupt Practices Act[1] the United States is practicing cultural universalism. McCann noted that Noonan's position on bribery, particularly the distinction between a bribe and a gift, is drawn from Judeo-Christian tradition. He asked, first, how this view of bribery can be imposed on a secular, pluralistic society and, second, how it can be extended to the whole international context through the Foreign Corrupt Practices Act.

Noonan responded,

The concept of imposing a Christian vision on a secular society I find to be of great interest. Bribery is one of the few remaining moral concepts with deep religious roots that has not been challenged in our society as a whole, which is still a common bond with people who are strongly secular, and where I would assume that the very strong rational reasons for avoiding a bribe-taking society are still quite persuasive. On the other hand, I consider it more than a straw in the wind that a whole range of social scientists have attacked the idea of bribery. They really would like to relativize it to the point of triviality and their reasoning has appeared almost universally in terms of Third World countries where they will rationalize any practice. Of course, the trick is that any practice that exists in a society can be found to have a function. If it didn't have a function, it wouldn't exist. So any social scientist can look at a country and say, "Well, this is a function of the society." That kind of reasoning would justify anything from slavery to cannibalism. I am not sanguine that our society will continue to accept the concept of bribery. It may not; it may well reject it.

As to universalizing it, I think there are two things to be said. I do believe that Christian ideals have permeated cultures that are not themselves Christian, and that one way or another, Christian ideals percolate though non-Christian cultures. And then, of course, I do believe that there are good, strong earthly reasons for rejecting bribe-taking. I am perfectly willing on that point to be a cultural imperialist and say that it is more rational to have a society where high officials do not take bribes than one where they do take bribes. I think, given the chance, societies will see that.

Of course, legally, what is bribery depends upon the laws of a particular country and that is going to vary from country to country. Morally, you have a kind of core concept and the expansion of that concept is a contested area—how far are you going to carry it? And in this gray area, you get many situations which can be analyzed in terms of that classic moral principle, double effect. The question is, Does the good effect outweigh the bad effect as you are simultaneously achieving them?

Undoubtedly, there may be times when the law will be so aware of the bad effects that a given act will be proscribed, it may be occasionally so harmless that there is no moral problem. I think it is something that will vary from culture to culture and from law to law. People in different contexts will make different judgments.

As to whether the United States has the right to universalize standards under the Foreign Corrupt Practices Act, Noonan commented:

There are, of course, countries in which our standards appear far more stringent than those of the country. The argument is, "We are entitled to do that because we are applying it to our citizens, we expect our citizens to live by our rules. They cannot do business in another country if they are going to violate our rules." I think there is an argument for saying, "Yes, we can make these standards universal as far as Americans go even though there is going to be a secondary impact on a foreign country."

A second issue had to do with the difference between extortion and bribery. Noonan stated:

There is a clear distinction between extortion and bribery. There are cases where people are subject to extortion. I think actually that is the reason why the person making the payment historically has been treated more leniently than the official taking it. The usual assumption has been that the official is more powerful and therefore is able to demand payment for something to which the person paying has a right. And so, going back to the Hebrew Bible, the payor is not condemned; going right up to modern times, usually it is the high official who is subject to criminal prosecution rather than the person paying. The Foreign Corrupt Practices Act is almost unique in making the payor the guilty party alone and not the recipient. So there is a difference to be made. Medieval theology had a great phrase for it, "To buy back your harassment." If you were being harassed, it was permissible to buy it back and that was different from paying an immoral bribe. And, of course that distinction has to be recognized.

Note

1. The Foreign Corrupt Practices Act (FCPA) was enacted in 1977 as an amendment (Section 30A) to the Securities Exchange Act of 1934. The FCPA can be summarized as follows:

> It prohibits public companies from using any means or instrumentality of interstate commerce in furtherance of any offer, payment or gift of any money or other item of value to a foreign official, foreign political party or candidate for foreign political office for the "corrupt" purpose of obtaining, retaining or directing business to any person. Section 30A also proscribes the promise or authorization of such payments or gifts by public companies and prohibits any officer, director, employee, or agent of such a company, and any natural person in control of such a company, from authorizing, ordering or carrying out any act or practice constituting a violation of the foregoing prohibitions.

Statement of Commission policy concerning Section 30A of the Securities Exchange Act of 1934. 45 Fed. Reg. 59001-02 (1980).

PART IV

Case Studies: Korea and Mexico

National development strategies and the regulation of multinational firms have been the subject of extensive research. Few observers, however, have studied the *process* of how that interaction takes place. The interaction itself is subject to a confluence of factors that are difficult to measure, closely interrelated, and elusive. Field interviews in comparative case studies were selected as the technique to provide insight into the process.

The results of the Korean field work are presented by Kwan Kim and those of Mexico by Kenneth Jameson and Juan Rivera. Two panels were selected to comment on these findings. One group comments on the similarities and differences of the situation in the two countries: William Glade from the perspective of a development social scientist, Ernesto Marcos from that of a senior Third World governmental official, and George Suter as a multinational manager. The second panel was asked to speak directly to the bribery issue: John Collins from an international accounting perspective, Michael Shannon from a multinational corporate view, John Noonan from that of a lawyer, and José Antonio Fernandez-Arena as a previous senior member of a Third World host government.

The Korean Case:
Culturally Dominated Interactions

*KWAN S. KIM**

Multinational corporations (MNCs) often run into conflicts with host governments or their local partners. Among the myriad sources of the conflict that affect the success or failure of international ventures, a common cause has to do with the differences in motives and interests as perceived by foreign companies and the nation-state. Moreover, perceived national and corporate interests are both evolving and changing to reflect changing circumstances and environment.

Even when conflicting interests are worked out for mutual benefits, effective functioning of international ventures can still be affected by structures of power[1] relations and the emerging patterns of interaction involving the foreign enterprise and the institutions in the host nation. Thus, a proper understanding of the nature of power relations as well as the dynamics of the interactions involved will be helpful in managing the conflict resolution. In particular, it seems that more serious conflicts occur in business ventures where the cross-cultural differences between the host country and the investing country are striking.

The focus of this paper is less on the understanding of the myriad sources of conflict that MNCs experience in the host country and more on the understanding of structures of power relations and interactions involving the tripartite participants of the host government, the MNC,

*Kwan S. Kim is an economics professor and a faculty fellow of the Helen Kellogg Institute for International Studies at the University of Notre Dame. He formerly was senior economist at the Agency for International Development and at Nacional Financiera, Mexico City, and has taught at Delft Institute for Industrial Management, Holland; Universidad Autonoma de Nuevo Leon, Monterrey, Mexico; University of Dar es Salaam, Tanzania; and University of Nairobi, Kenya.

and the domestic business partner. This will help us to explore further the implications for resolving social conflicts that affect functioning of MNC ventures abroad. To do so we chose to look closely at the recent experience of South Korea (henceforth called Korea). The Korean case is interesting not only because the multinational issues involved are new but because it highlights the added dimension of cross-cultural differences.

The findings in this paper are based on the field work in Korea carried out by a Notre Dame project team in the summer of 1985.[2] Interviews were held with several Korean government officials involved in the management of foreign investment and with a score of the senior executives—both Koreans and Americans—in charge of joint venture projects or foreign subsidiaries. Official documents and other relevant information were also procured.

The organization of the paper is as follows: The first section surveys the evolution of Korea's foreign investment objectives and the attendant policies for implementing these objectives from a recent historical perspective. Next, the nature of power relations between the state and the local business community in general are examined in the context of Korean society. Based on this background information, the discussion then turns to the more specific case of MNC-government relations, followed by an analysis of interaction structures involving the host government and both the local foreign partners in the joint venture. The next section focuses on the patterns of interaction, as well as the problems in the relationships, between the business partners, exploring at the same time their implications for the resolution of partner conflicts in joint ventures. This is followed in the concluding section by a summary of the main findings and the discussion of strategy implications for MNCs.

NATIONAL INTERESTS AND POLICIES IN FOREIGN INVESTMENT

Direct foreign investment is a relatively recent phenomenon for Korea. Throughout the 1960s foreign capital inflows in Korea were largely in the form of grants and loans rather than in the form of direct investment.[3] The rapid economic growth coupled with sustained political stability in Korea attracted highly competitive loan capital from international financial markets. During the early stages of Korea's export-oriented development in which main exports consisted of labor-intensive, traditional manufacturing goods, Korea managed to avoid dependence on the resources and technologies of multinationals by relying more on non-equity foreign capital.

Dependence on the foreign loans extended to all sectors of the economy during the 1960s[4] gradually led to a sizable accumulation of debt. Starting from the position of virtually no outstanding debt in 1965, Korea's debt servicing and amortization rose to over 30 percent of export earnings by 1971.[5] New borrowing leveled off as the authorities struggled with debt-management problems. At this point, direct foreign investment began to play a more important role as a source of financing developmental projects. Direct investment increased from $45 million in 1971 in $110 million in 1972 and to $265 million in 1973, registering increases from about 10 percent of total capital inflow to 20 to 27 percent, respectively.[6]

Coupled with the emergence of debt-management problems, the Korean economy after one decade of energetic growth began to show, around the same period as the debt crisis, certain syndromes of economic slow-down, such as the declining growth rates of GNP and exports and the increasing rate of inflation. The policy response of the government was the restructuring of industry. In order to reduce the economy's import dependency on intermediate and capital goods, the government quickly saw the need for the vertical integration of the economy by establishing systematic linkages in industrial production and technology. Specifically, the development of heavy and chemical industries was given top priority. At the same time, the government made a drastic swing from its past policy of severe restrictions on direct foreign investment to a more selective stance.

In 1973 the Foreign Capital Inducement Act (FCIA) was enacted, which essentially endorsed the selective policy that encouraged only those foreign investments in congruence with the developmental aims of the country, limiting foreign participation in new enterprises. At the same time, the government established a technically sophisticated, bureaucratic apparatus for dealing with foreign investment (see Appendix A).

Beginning in the late 1970s, the Korean economy faced the need of another transition from the traditional basic smokestack industries to higher value-added, sophisticated high technology endeavors. With rising wages in Korea and competition from other Asian developing countries in the more labor-intensive industrial goods, sustained economic growth in Korea would require development of these technology-intensive industries.[7] This transition would have to come through foreign technology and investment inducements rather than through foreign loan capital. MNCs could offer technologies, foreign exchange, and organizational and managerial skills, and moreover, an access to international markets.

To this end, the government adopted a new policy to actively induce direct foreign investment, particularly in the manufacturing sector. The basic guidelines of direct foreign investment were stipulated by the revised FCIA of 1981. The provisions generally contained much less severe restrictions on foreign investment:

- Direct investment was to be allowed in about a half of the nation's industries. The manufacturing sector accounted for 75 percent of all investment-authorized industries.
- A foreign equity share of up to 100 percent is permitted in the category of "priority" industries as defined by the government, and a foreign share of up to 50 percent in others.
- Excluding those foreign-invested firms not covered by the FCIA, full repatriation of the original investment as well as the remittance of profits are guaranteed.[8]

In addition, certain categories of foreign investment qualify for subsidies and other forms of incentives that include exemptions on corporate income,[9] acquisition, and property taxes, accelerated depreciation allowances, or exemptions from duties on capital goods imports. To qualify, foreign-invested projects must substantially contribute to improving Korea's balance of payments,[10] involve highly advanced technology[11] or large amounts of capital,[12] or be located inside export zones. These investment guidelines reflect the national interest criterion: Investment will be acceptable only if it promotes Korea's interests in matters such as foreign exchange acquisition or the transfer of technology.

An interesting aspect of Korea's foreign investment management is that the government has a broad framework of administrative control over foreign investment. The rules stipulated in the guidelines have been applied flexibly so that the government can have extensive discretionary power in determining the merits of projects. For instance, if projects are deemed consistent with the national interests in such matters as the development of the national economy, social welfare, or the strengthening of international competitiveness, the Ministry of Finance is authorized to approve these projects on a case-by-case basis, even though they may not be specifically covered by the guidelines. At the same time, the government has judged incentives as necessary for ventures of special merits; for instance, considerable flexibility has been exercised in approving projects without due regard to the equity share of the domestic partner if they are viewed as facilitating the transfer of technologies. The complex maze of regulations also leaves government officials with considerable room to extend eligibility for tax holidays. Foreign companies forming joint ventures with small and medium-sized Korean firms have recently benefited from such privilege.

Despite the government's open attitude toward foreign investment, investments were slow in coming due largely to the tight international financial market during the early 1980s. To accelerate the capital inflow, the government implemented a further revised FCIA in 1984, which actively solicits foreign direct investment, preferably in the form of joint ventures, by easing approval procedures and by providing more tax holidays to foreign capital. The key provision includes the widening of foreign investment opportunities. For the first time, the "negative" list system is introduced in which applications for investment in industries outside the negative list will automatically be approved. The projects that are specifically prohibited or restricted for foreign investment include those considered harmful to public health, environmental preservation, public order, or social morality as well as public works.[13] In addition, the government is actively studying ways to strengthen the protection of industrial property rights of foreign firms. The existing laws have been inadequate in this area, which has deterred the inducement of higher technology.

Undoubtedly, the ongoing liberalization of foreign investment will greatly enhance possibilities of joint ventures in Korea. Korea will continue to offer a widening range of opportunities for investment. Foreign investors, given Korea's impressive economic growth and adequate production infrastructure,[14] are likely to find Korea an attractive source for investment.

There remains a caveat, however. The overreliance on MNCs will not be considered in the best long-term interests of Korea. It is well to note that the recent move toward liberalization is really part of government efforts to defuse the mounting sentiments of protectionism overseas. Given the government's discretionary power over the business community, which will be examined in the next section, it will continue to monitor whether MNC operations are consistent with the national interests.[15]

A case in point is foreign firms competing in the domestic consumer market. Typically at an initial stage, foreign competition would be welcomed in the attempt to control inflation and improve product quality. As soon as the government feels that competition is excessive, opportunities for new investments will be denied. Foreign firms initially favored for entry to the domestic market are likely to be deprived of access to all incentives.[16]

On the other hand, the key factor in MNC investment-supporting access to incentives is technology. The Korean government attempts to obtain foreign technology to develop industry even by ceding to foreign ownership. The long-term national interest in economic development through absorption of advanced technologies as a way to expedite entry into the ranks of advanced industrialized countries has been the most important policy objective sought in foreign investment.

GOVERNMENT — BUSINESS RELATIONS WITHIN THE NATION-STATE

Perhaps the best way of characterizing the South Korean government is to borrow Myrdal's description of a "hard state" regime.[17] A "hard state" has a highly centralized political system, which is able to quickly formulate decisions and achieve a given social goal by cajoling and coercing the wills of subordinate social units. In a "hard state," policies decided on are effectively enforced.

In the Korean political system, the executive branch has dominated over other branches of the government. The check-and-balance role of the legislature has been virtually emasculated by virtue of the dominance of the ruling party (Liberal Justice Party) in the National Assembly. In the Korean legal tradition, the formal laws, often couched in broad and general terms, only provide guidelines. In particular, legal rules relating to economic and business affairs have been applied with substantial administrative discretion. In practice, the "rule of discretion" rather than the "rule of law" has prevailed in implementing economic policies.

Within the executive branch, the ultimate power resides in the

President, who makes major decisions, aided by a small but competent group of advisors. The process of decision making is highly centralized with virtually all decisions of any importance made by the highly centralized bureaucracy. In this connection, it is worth noting that all the regulatory agencies are organized under the Executive Branch, which allows stronger executive control of the private sector. Once a decision is made, the hierarchical bureaucratic structure reinforces speedy execution. Within the Korean bureaucracy there is a well-established hierarchical direction for enforcing implementation of policy decisions made at the highest tier of government by all the tiers below it. Normally, this takes the form of the assignment of a specific, targeted task to each individual bureaucrat at all the tiers of the hierarchy. The target goal is enforced by expectations of rewards for good performance and penalties for non-compliance.

The centralized structure enables the regime to quickly reach decisions in order to attain the perceived benefits. Its position can be modified as the situation evolves. Such an approach is quite appropriate in the context of an open economy exposed to rapidly changing international economic situations where the costs of inaction can be substantial. New disequilibria brought about by changes in international economic relations outdate earlier policies and require quick adjustments. Tightly defined laws can be viewed as a handicap in a rapidly changing economy where special cases requiring ad hoc decisions, with a low level of generality to be applicable even to a single firm, abound. This is one of the important reasons why competent technocrats in Korea have been allowed substantial flexibility in dealing with investment projects.

In passing, it is worth noting that Korea's Confucian cultural heritage also makes the hierarchical bureaucracy operate efficaciously. The traditional value system inculcated by Confucianism underscores status hierarchy in social relations. The highest prestige is attached to the scholar-government official class and has induced the best talents to work for the government, ensuring civil service quality in Korea. There is also a cultural undercurrent of social sanction of hierarchical organizational structures in Korean society. Collectively, these features provide aspects of cultural compatibility with efficiently functioning centralized bureaucracy.

The "hard state" character of the regime is markedly evident in government-business relations. The government has been especially effective in coercing ultimate business collaboration on matters considered of vital national interest. For instance, evidence of government domination can be found in the recent intervention in the automobile industry. In the early 1980s as the automobile industry started to develop excess capacity for limited local markets, the government decided to reduce competition for a more rational use of resources by dividing up the market among the designated major producers in the industry. In a single stroke, the government ordered Kia Motors to shut down its auto line, but gave Kia a monopoly over vans and small trucks. Daewoo Motors and Hyundai were allowed to share the national market for passenger cars. It turned out that domestic and international demands increased to take a larger share of productive capacity in subsequent years and the competitive restriction was modified. Although the government's restructuring plan proved to be timely, and as a result, a blessing for everyone, such a heavy-handed measure would certainly have provoked strong resistance in a more democratic society.

One of the potent instruments used by the government for influencing local business has been control of bank credit and foreign borrowing. Selective credit policies were used as a popular instrument to enforce a centralized capitalist system in which the government dominated allocative decisions. With access to low-cost foreign loans in the 1960s and 1970s, the Korean government was able to play the role of an arbiter, deciding which local business groups could expand. Indeed, the government's preferred method of supporting business was to make credit available on favorable terms to specific borrowers.[18] Years of access to easy credit and bank-lending have made many large companies in Korea today accustomed to depend heavily on (and certainly vulnerable to) the external financing through government intervention.[19]

The government has other means of prevailing on the private sector to comply with its policies. In addition to various types of material incentives given to firms following the direction of government policies, there is bureaucratic intervention in the form of administrative measures to punish those firms unwilling to comply. Such measures include denial of the approval for joint ventures and technology licenses involving foreign investors, denial of credit flow, or frequent inspection of tax returns. Thus, availability of a wide range of discretionary intervention possibilities has been the key element of state dominance in government-business relations. The state charts basic courses and directions of development which the business community simply cannot afford to take lightly. The state could precipitate the failure of any business, should it choose to do so.

There are two important features of the Korean government in dealing with the business community that must be noted. First, Korean policy makers are in general goal-oriented. Policy makers have tossed out any textbook models of development and concentrate on what works. In order to achieve a desired goal, they would be willing to experiment with any available policy instruments without ideological predilections. The results that have been seen in Korean economic policy are the liberal intermingling of public ownership and private capitalism, coercion and incentives, or reliance on market forces and intervention in Korean economic policy. This pragmatic approach to decision making is often coupled with the practice of fine-tuning policies to apply to a specific industry or firm at a particular time. The combined results give great scope and flexibility for discretion in government intervention in economic affairs.[20]

Another noteworthy aspect of government-business relations in Korea is "openness" in the dialogue for economic policy formulation. Within the realm of economic issues, the process of governmental decision making is open to a wide range of opinion inputs with virtually unlimited freedom of expression and dissent. Although the government exercises great discretion in final decisions, it is unlikely that they run directly counter to the views commonly shared by the business community. There were many instances in which business inputs were incorporated into governmental economic policy making. Business and trade associations largely provide a major vehicle for transmission of business views.[21] Personal contacts, usually evolved from the close ties bonded by family, school, or region, are another frequent means of informing governmental officials of individual needs as well as of business concerns in general. Korean businessmen frequently rely on direct personal appeals to influence officials. Indirect appeals through the intervention of politicians or political parties, with the possible exception of using the intermediation of business associations, are not popular.

The extensive interaction in the process of policy formulation, which interestingly excludes participation of labor, reflects the need for a harmony of, and the mutuality of, interest between government and business in Korea. Historically, Korea's strategies for industrialization favored the support given to large-scale companies with cost efficiency. Such policies were viewed necessary in the late 1960s as Korea was preparing to move into advanced sectors and to face competitive international markets. Size of the firm was also considered an important factor in joint ventures with foreign partners to reduce the risk of being taken over by foreign multinationals. The peculiarity of the Korean situation is that the legitimacy of the regime itself depends on the success of business. Although the Korean government's power base since 1961 was the military, in the course of rapid economic growth it gradually shifted to the broad-based popularity derived mainly from Korea's economic success. Thus, economic success provides the legitimating argument for an authoritarian regime. For this, the government is compelled to work closely with the business community and must listen to its problems, framing policies that are in the best interest of business. The "openness" to the business community in Korea must be understood in this light. Thus, aside from the question of state supremacy, what really held together a close government-business cooperation in Korea was the shared sense of interest in a strong and prosperous economy from which all could benefit.

To summarize: The harsh geopolitics South Korea faces promotes a kind of patriotic alliance between government and business. They have been supportive of each other's role in the pursuit of the common goal for economic development. Thus, the business community is allowed to participate in an interactive process for decision making on vital economic issues. The state has, however, been ad hoc interventionist by enforcing or cajoling enterprise compliance with government policy. Indeed, the salient feature of government-business relations in Korea is the capacity of the state to induce effective compliance from the local business community.

MNC—Host Government Relations

In the previous discussion, the Korean government as the dominant partner in its relationship with the business community was seen as charting the detailed path for the economy with the set of mechanisms by which individual enterprise compliance is stimulated, forced, or cajoled. The influence of the local business community is very much limited to providing opinion inputs to government's economic policy

making. In this section, the relationship between the government and
MNCs, as a subgroup of the local business community in the host nation, will be examined.[22]

Unlike their local counterparts, MNCs as an alien legal entity stand
in a special power relationship vis-à-vis the host state. To begin with,
the bargaining leverage of the host government derives from the value
of economic opportunities the host economy can offer to MNCs and
the controls it commands. Multinational firms are generally interested
in establishing and maintaining a viable position in foreign markets
to assure for themselves adequate returns on investments. The host
government can, however, control a number of factors affecting the
economic performance of the firm—taxes and foreign exchange, imports, and prices. In particular, for countries such as Korea where extensive economic planning and controls are exercised, it is accurate to
characterize a private firm as being more at the mercy of the government. The profitability of the firm's operations would depend in a
large measure on the decisions of bureaucrats. Therein lies an important source of the host government's power.

On the other hand, while foreign corporations may be constrained
in their assertiveness by a need for caution in an unfamiliar setting,
they can obtain assistance from their home government. Also, multinationals can exercise bargaining leverage and show a significant power
advantage through a degree of indispensability, that is, by possessing
something unique to offer to suit national interests.

In Korea, the bureaucratic-authoritarian regimes had already
emerged by the time foreign investors began to arrive in numbers.
Unlike other parts of the developing world (Latin America and Africa)
where foreign capital is considered a structure of control over the host
economy, the centralized bureaucracy in Korea kept the level of dependence on multinationals low, and therefore was, from the beginning, in a better position to dictate the role to be played by MNCs.
Multinational corporations, in a position similar to that faced by the
local business community, must deal with a strong state apparatus,
which insists on conformity in the firm's operations with the national
policy objectives.

There is also a particular reason for the Korean government's hard
stance toward foreign investors. The Korean society is essentially xeno-
phobic, stemming from a long history of foreign invasions and occu-
pations of the country. In comparison to other developing countries,

MNCs find themselves in Korea with a less attentive government, particularly when the issue deals with national policy. MNC influence on the host government is one step further removed than the influence from domestic corporations. The Korean government may be receptive to the views of foreign investors but has been sensitized to the issue of foreign intervention. The point here is not that the state apparatus has an absolute supremacy over MNCs. To the contrary, the foreign enterprise gains in leverage from limitations in the ability of the host government to elicit compulsion in MNC behavior. Unlike the domestic counterpart, the multinational corporation has also an option for a pullout and to solicit assistance from its own government.

In the case of Korea, the determination of the Korean government to exert its influence over foreign investors is implemented with the realities of the relative balance of negotiating power between the government and the MNC. Here, the United States MNC has two sources of support: (1) Korea's geopolitical position, and (2) the importance of the MNC contribution to the local society. First of all, the government's bargaining position is limited by the country's geopolitical situation—South Korea militarily depends on the security umbrella of the United States. A visitor to Seoul is immediately struck by the size of the U.S. military base in the middle of the city, the proximity to the northern border, and the continual media attention to the threat from the North. The Korean government could ill-afford to antagonize the American business community. Multinationals as a group can seek, as they have done in the past, assistance from their home institutions, such as the U.S. Embassy and American Chamber of Commerce in Seoul, to effectively lobby against government policies considered deleterious to their interests. This option provides forceful bargaining leverage.

Moreover, MNCs, unlike their domestic counterparts, can enjoy a special "leveraging" power because of the importance of the resources they bring to the host nation. For instance, MNCs' investments in Korea at present are mostly associated with production for export markets or with activities conducive to promoting advanced technologies. These investment activities coincide with Korea's national interests as defined by the government. Beginning in the late 1970s, as Korea needed to rely increasingly on foreign capital and technology for restructuring the economy from labor-intensive to technology-intensive industrialization, the relative power shifted to some extent in favor of MNCs. In particular, the companies that could offer new technologies needed by the country could negotiate from a position of greater strength. The power of the MNC will be underscored in cases where the initiative comes from the host government, that is, when the host country actively seeks licensing agreements from an MNC because it lacks certain technical and managerial competence or the productive capacity at its command.

On the other hand, the foreign corporations that made the investment mainly to supply the domestic market have been losing the bargaining leverage they previously enjoyed as the domestic market becomes saturated by local competition[23] and the technologies they imparted on Koreans become obsolete. The government will maintain its active role in managing industrial development, particularly in sectors regarded as saturated with domestic producers. Pharmaceutical MNCs are the case in point. The Korean government is not likely to consider approval for majority ownership in this instance.[24] More recently, the government decided not to approve the joint-venture plan by the Samsung Group with Chrysler Corporation for production of passenger cars. The government instituted a policy to restrict passenger car production in two companies (Daewoo Motor Co. in a 50-50 joint venture with General Motors and Hyundai Motor Co.) based on the consideration of the minimum capacity needed to compete internationally. The case of the petrochemical industry provides another fitting illustration. In the early 1970s the Korean government planned the petrochemical complex and set the terms on which foreign investors could participate in downstream ventures.[25] As the plan was being implemented, the government pushed for increased indigenous control of the technology. The market conditions soon no longer justified the continued role of foreign capital. Foreign partners began to lose their leveraging power and were gradually bought out by domestic interests.

To summarize, in a triangle alliance in Korea that involves the government, foreign, and domestic capital, the government has clearly been the dominant partner over the domestic business. There is no clear-cut evidence, however, that the government could exercise a similar extent of dominance over foreign investors. The state's interventions in multinationals have been ad hoc and opportunistic in nature, varying from one firm to another. They depended on the specific firm's leveraging power and own characteristics.

The Structure of Interaction

The Korean government seeks to promote the influx of foreign investment by encouraging joint ventures with Korean firms. There are several reasons for promoting joint ventures. First, with the recent move toward relaxation of the highly centralized structure of the Korean economy, foreign capital is sought out for buttressing the private sector to spearhead the sustained industrialization, in particular in technology-intensive industries. The government views joint ventures as the most fertile ground for absorbing advanced technologies. Second, a joint operation seems the only effective way for Westerners to work in a cross-cultural environment. We found in our interviews that many Korean governmental officials, particularly at low echelons, felt uncomfortable and were reluctant to deal directly with foreigners. There was a sense that in addition to the language barrier, communication gaps would be serious due to the cultural differences. Westerners would have enormous difficulty in understanding the workings of the Korean system. Third, through the intermediation of local partners, the government can avoid unnecessary, direct confrontation with foreign investors, while it can still bring pressure on them to comply with national policies.

On many occasions, the local partner plays the dual role of an agent of the government as well as representing the foreign interest. First, the local partner serves a role instrumental in facilitating approvals of investment and the contacts with government for MNCs.[26] We found it striking that there was very little direct dialogue with governmental officials, particularly on matters of general policy issues.[27] Most of the foreign executives interviewed did not care to develop any personal relationship with governmental officials. There was the tendency to leave most negotiations with government in the hands of their local partners. In one case, a foreign senior executive, during his thirteen years in Korea, met only once with a high-ranking official to discuss the policy issue of common concern.

The local partner, on the other hand, bears direct pressures from government to see to it that there is compliance with government policies. The Korean government adheres to cohesive industrialization strategies and is clear about what it wants from foreign participation. The government can bring pressure on the local partner in a joint operation whenever joint activities are viewed as deviating from the national interest. The company avoiding compliance would subject itself to a wide range of administrative measures, including such inconveniences as frequent tax-auditing or inspections for safety and health standards. The local partner often finds himself caught in a dilemma; while held liable for compliance with government policies, he also has to reconcile with the foreign partner's independent demands. The point was confirmed by our interviews with Korean executives of joint-investment companies. One Korean senior executive long involved in a number of joint operations with MNCs summarized the sentiments of Korean policy makers:

> The Korean partner is presumed to take into account the national interests in a joint operation. The government has confidence in the collaboration of the private sector and relies on us to modify the behavior of foreign investors.

It is worth pointing out that effective enforcement in insuring compliance with governmental instructions is matched by governmental paternalism toward the local business. In particular, small and medium-sized firms are generally viewed as underdogs in their dealings with large foreign corporations. The recently enacted "Fair Trade" laws were aimed specifically at insuring a free and open market for small and medium firms and at enforcing fair trade practices in the joint operation.

The structure of the MNC's interactions with the government and the local partner is illustrated in figure 1. The overlapping area

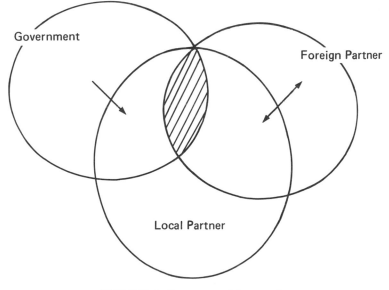

FIGURE 1: Structure of interactions

represents opportunities of direct interactions between different social units, and the arrow suggests the dominance-subordinance relationship. Since the government-MNC interactions are indirect in nature with communications flowing through intermediation of the local partner, the overlapping area between the government and the foreign partner is included in the set of the domestic partner.

In Korea, MNCs interact with the government with different intensity during two distinct phases: original entry and continuing operations. Generally, the first step for MNC entry is to find a Korean partner and to allow the partner to conduct the negotiations with the government. Exceptions exist, however, where U.S. firms have negotiated directly for entry with the Korean government. As indicated before, the governmental requirements for this initial stage have been clarified in recent years, and approval for the projects not on the negative list is almost automatic. But that is only the starting point. As one multinational executive noted:

> The initial approval is the easy part. The government doesn't seem to make many judgments at that stage. Once you proceed with your entry and operations, that's when myriad necessary approvals begin to surface.

These requirements emanate from the various ministries. In the pharmaceutical industry, for example, the Ministry of Health must approve virtually every phase of the product — introduction, production, and marketing. These approvals take place at all bureaucratic levels.

This regulatory operating interaction is almost always conducted by the Korean joint-venture partner. The Koreans have managers and staff interacting on a continuous — in many cases, daily — basis up and down the bureaucratic structure. Those U.S. executives who have attempted to deal with the Korean bureaucracy for operating issues have experienced real problems. One noted:

> A "yes" and a "no" just doesn't come out that way. If it is "yes," you will see it in implementations; and if "no," nothing happens. In business-government interactions, there is one role reserved for the U.S. executive. When *confrontation* with the government is deemed necessary, the American is designated.

Most American senior executives interviewed felt that after the entry the cost of efforts to interact directly with the government would outweigh the benefits. Only a few felt they needed very effective government relations from the beginning and began to organize for the task.

Finally, our survey of field managers of multinational corporations in Korea revealed that they had a mixed feeling about the intermediation of their local partners. In principle, they preferred to have their partners handle govenmental relations, since the latter were obviously more knowledgeable in financial guidelines and local laws and could more effectively negotiate with their government using personal contacts. On the negative side, a few expressed the fear that the local partners could easily conspire with their government against foreign entities in order to protect their own interests. In fact, there has been a tendency for the local partners to take advantage of flexibility and complexity of government rules and regulations in order to press more demands on foreign counterparts.[28] Written regulations are often inadequate to cover specific details. Flexibility in interpretation of the rules can be used to the advantage of either partner by the government. An American senior manager even suspected that his partner had accepted the terms of their joint-venture agreement only because he expected the government to nullify part of the provisions during the phase of actual operations. In a few instances, there was a feeling of frustration over the drawn-out process of negotiations with the government because of the involvement of the local partner. It was suspected that the bargaining periods, which in these instances ranged from a few months to five years, could have been much shorter had direct negotiations with the government taken place.

One lesson that emerged from our findings is that MNCs in Korea must consider the implications of governmental relations seriously. Effective governmental relations would be tantamount to the augmentation of complementary factors in the production process. The Korean government does not necessarily operate by the book, as it is involved, directly and indirectly, in a wide range of individual enterprises' operations that include financing, production, marketing, and international trade. The regulatory environment can change overnight even without consulting the companies.[29] It thus becomes important to find ways of maintaining close communications with the government.

PARTNER INTERACTIONS, CONFLICTS, AND RESOLUTION

As a general rule, South Korea requires joint ventures for entry of foreign firms. Because of the need to cope with a different social and business environment, going the joint-venture route is considered the most effective means to take advantage of recently expanded opportunities for foreign investment. When an MNC was considered capable of providing modern technology and assistance in designing a worldwide complex for Korean industry, the government did not hesitate to offer liberal incentive schemes to induce foreign entry for joint ventures.[30] Joint ownership requirements were waived only in exceptional cases where comparable domestic firms did not exist.

With the government's progressive easing of foreign investment control since the late 1970s, an increasing number of foreign companies have begun to create joint ventures with Korean companies. While a number of these joint ventures have thrived in Korea, from our interviews the majority of them were found to have experienced some sort of partner conflicts, and, in a few cases, on a recurrent basis. The critical factor affecting effective functioning of the joint venture in Korea appeared to stem from differences in the Korean and Western cultures. They were reflected in partners' differences in the perception of business objectives as well as in approaches to management. Specifically, the most common sources of conflict have been differences in perceived business interest, managerial control, the perception of legal contracts, and communication problems.

Business Interests

Almost all interviewed executives, including both Koreans and Americans, agreed that the single, important cause of partner conflicts was the difference in the partner perception of business goals. The American executive attaches importance to profits with a guarantee for reasonable rates of repatriation. The Korean counterpart is concerned more with longer-term goals, such as sales growth and the market share. Dividend return generally ranks a lower priority in Korea. Korean businessmen seek from an association with a foreign company a sustained relation in which status and recognition become important in the hierarchical social structure of Korean society. For the owner of the large company, current income is less important in relation to their massive wealth. They, and in particular the small companies, want sustained growth, development of export capability as well as a larger market share through the introduction of foreign products, technology, and capital. Thus, disagreement often emerges when profit retention decisions have to be made. The government's policy also discourages large dividend declarations by imposing a heavy tax on dividend income.

The Korean bias against repatriated profits puts great pressure on U.S. subsidiaries, accustomed to carrying their own weight in earnings. One mutually agreeable solution is to take U.S. returns through transfer prices for those firms importing components to Korea or exporting them to other parts of the multinational production or marketing system.

Differences in business orientation essentially reflect difference in the mode of business organization. The companies in Korea—large or small—are generally owned by, and operate within the network of, "family groups." The head of the family chairs the business conglomerate with sons and sons-in-law heading the affiliated firms. The family interest tends to be vested in growth and stability of the company. This contrasts with the American corporation representing the general stockholders' interests. There is also an element of uncertainty and risk with foreign investment, and it is natural that foreign investors seek the security of early payoffs from investments.

Perception of Legal Contracts

The legal system in Korea is patterned on continental "civil law" countries as in Latin America with essentially the same structural differences from the common law of the United States. Also, the role of the law in the Korean society is different from that in the American tradition. A clear signal is the number of practicing lawyers in relation to the population. In the United States, there is one lawyer per 800 inhabitants, while in Korea there is one per 35,000 inhabitants.

In Korea, formal laws are often overridden by the moral force of interpersonal relationship. To Korean business partners, a joint-venture agreement may be compared to a marriage contract. It represents a symbol of commitment to a business relationship rather than a working document. A change in circumstances warrants a change in terms of the agreement. Since the future can never be known with certainty, a contract should not be expected to rigidly apply. That is, the local partner likely takes it for granted that the written agreements can be modified on the basis of personal relationships developed, as circumstances change. The personal relationship in Korea is the bond, and not the "written word" as expressed in the document. The agreement is made between people, not between institutions. As people change, so does the agreement.

A scene outlined repeatedly to us was that of the U.S. negotiators surrounded by lawyers and accountants, with stacks of proposed legal documents, sitting down with a Korean manager, his small staff, and a single sheet of paper. In our interviews, Korean senior executives tended to deemphasize the importance of legal contracts, and felt uncomfortable to see Americans walk in, surrounded by lawyers. Indeed, seldom is there a corporate legal department in a Korean firm, and few lawyers to hire.

Universally, all of the executives interviewed stated: "If a conflict ever gets to the courts, both parties are viewed as failures, and neither can win." Litigation is frowned upon socially and considered to be terminal in terms of business relations. Reliance on recourse to the law in Korea is not an advisable alternative. This is in clear contrast with Western cultures, where problems tend to be brought into an open confrontation for resolution, including litigation in the courts of law.

Detailed contractural provisions are considered unnecessary, and even insulting, since a distrustful partner relationship is presumed. They can only contribute to the climate for disagreement over the specifics in the future. In this regard, an American official experienced in Korean affairs remarked: "In Korea, from the date a contract is signed, it is going to be renegotiated. Everything is negotiable, including the tax amount in this country. Korea is not really ruled by law in the way the U.S. is ruled."

Communications

The related cause for the partner conflict is the communication problems rooted in cultural differences, which seems more serious in hampering effective collaboration in joint ventures than the language barrier. In the Sino cultural society, business relations would be defined by a careful maintenance of personal relations. The basic moral codes in Korean business relations are mutual trust and harmony of conflicting interests. For a successful business relationship, it is often more important to cultivate personal relations than to promote immediate business interests. For example, in the Korean culture, gift-giving as a token of appreciation is generally accepted as an appropriate etiquette. The tradition is that government officials are to be honored through the support of others. Gift-giving is a part of the respect indicated in engendering a close personal relationship. It is important to note that this is a general respect and support. Seldom would a specific gift in a conspicuous amount be given for a specific favor. This could easily be interpreted as bribery. The support is on a general, continuing basis. Also, open confrontation tends to be widely avoided. In a dispute, for example, the one who raises his voice would be regarded as having "lost face" as he or she could not exist harmoniously with others. Hence, a conflict tends to be resolved beneath the surface by friendly argument over a drink or by intermediation of good friends.

The contrasting manners of communication by the two partners of different cultures are depicted in a caricatured illustration of figure 2.[31] In an American environment, partnership agreement is generally

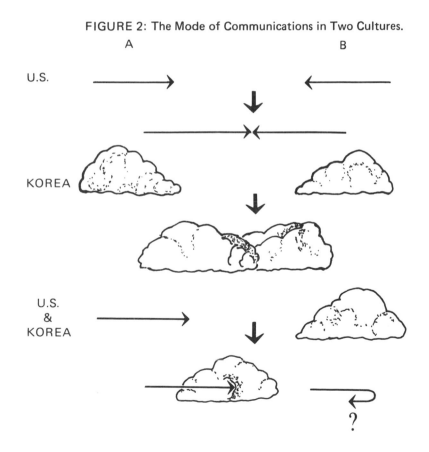

FIGURE 2: The Mode of Communications in Two Cultures.

worked out on the "tit" for "tat" basis; the rights and obligation of
each partner as well as the exact nature of the working relationship
are negotiated in detail. Compatibility in personal relations would be
helpful but not indispensable as a trait for success in partnership. This
environment is compared to two arrows meeting each other head-on.
The Korean style in the working relations is depicted by a "cloudy"
environment. The presumption for a successful business relationship
is that the interflow of confidence and understanding must precede
any formal agreement. The Korean approach to doing business together
is often casual, based on the broadly framed work plans rather than
on the detailed plans of action. Changes in circumstances of business
are always expected. To Koreans, the detailed agreement cannot define
the business relationship, it can only be based on the personal bond.

Incompatibility in personal relations can lead to serious conflicts.
The striking observation from our field interviews was that both Korean
and American managers alike pointed out cross-cultural communication problems as the most serious barrier to a joint operation. The
Korean executive generally prefers to work with a Korean-American
counterpart, if given a choice. For one thing, it seems imperative for
the effective functioning of a joint venture, that continuous, mutual
efforts be made to cultivate a close, interpersonal relationship by maintaining sincere, open lines of communication to each other.

Given the differences in culture, these communications among
joint-venture partners have, however, been surprisingly open. At one
point, for instance, we sat with a bilingual American and a bilingual
Korean, discussing the problem of communications as they existed in
the executive office with the American in English and the Korean in
his native tongue.

Managerial Control

Management right is another common cause of partner conflict
in Korea. It is usually contested at the time of the initial contact. The
contest usually results in an agreement for a joint ownership shared
equally between the multinational and the local Korean partner. Currently a 50-50 ownership-sharing arrangement accounts for about 90
percent of all joint ventures. Management control must thus be established on a basis other than ownership rights. Control is usually determined, initially, in some form of managerial agreement, and then

worked out within the framework of the legal structure and the culturally influenced communications between the partners as outlined above. As an early step in the relationship, it is often the subject of the scene of legal hoards from the United States facing a handful of Korean executives.

Not surprisingly, the determination of control can start all over again as the operation gets underway. In a culture steeped in the respect for age and position, the older, organizationally senior Korean executive will assume what he sees as his determined role as the decision maker with responsibility for the younger, U.S. executive layered well below, and a great distance from, the top management of the U.S. corporate structure.

The Koreans generally assume that only they can understand and effectively deal with the complex process of conducting business in Korea. They perceive the inevitable handicaps facing foreigners in dealing with the bureaucracy. This contrasts to the attitudes of a number of foreign executives toward the natives, which, often tinged with a superiority complex, show a subconscious distrust in the ability and integrity of the local partners.

Finally, the Korean xenophobia, replete with experience of foreign domination, has made them sensitive about their national identity. This deep-seated emotion is prominent in the national psychology.

The final, negotiated outcome in Korea can vary greatly. The titled president of the joint-venture company is usually a Korean. He generally bears the responsibility for governmental relations. Typically, his involvement with day-to-day management issues is, however, limited. The position of vice president empowered to deal with corporate finance invariably belongs to the U.S. multinational.

Other Areas of Conflict

Judging from our interviews, another frequent cause of partner conflicts was disagreements in the following policy issues:

- Technology licensing agreement versus sale of technologies.[32]
- Marketing strategy concerning domestic-market emphasis versus export promotion.
- The management style of personnel policies, and marketing and selling practices.

Korean partners seem to prefer an outright purchase of technology to licensing agreements, and attached much importance to enhancing export capabilites based on the MNC's marketing network abroad. With no coincidence, these business priorities are generally congruent with the directions of governmental policies. The government pursues a policy of adapting Western technology, viewing the future of the country in the role of technological intermediary between the West and the developing countries. Domestic enterprises generally look to the government to provide directions and guidance, and to receive assistance from government by complying with its policy as well.

Foreign investors, on the other hand, seem more concerned with such issues as the protection of technology patents and the securing of a foothold in domestic markets. On the whole, given the well-developed production infrastructure in Korea, the policy issues disputed have been concerned more with the forward linkages of investment: the Korean partners appear to be conservative in their marketing strategy and more interested in protecting and consolidating the extant market share rather than expanding the scale of operations. Unlike multinationals, most Korean venture partners cannot well afford the expenditure that would be necessary for expanded operations. Multinationals have often been accused of using the expansionary tactic as a device to take over ownership rights of the joint-investment company.

It was also striking that neither labor interests nor the issues concerning development ethics, such as alleviation of poverty and the role of women, were given much consideration in negotiations between the partners. In several instances, the local partners accused their counterparts of practicing "transfer pricing"; the typical situation was overinvoicing of imported inputs, which was claimed to have afflicted the financial health of the joint operation.

SUMMARY AND CONCLUSIONS

In interacting with the Korean government, foreign investors must recognize that they are dealing with an effectively functioning "hard-state" bureaucracy. The Korean government has assumed a larger and dominant role in government-business relations, and is assertive in regard to the activities of foreign investors. The government accepts foreign investment essentially on its own terms only when the clear advantages are foreseen. Foreign activities will continue to be controlled and regulated in ways consistent with government-perceived national interests. Extensive provisions for acquiring business permits and licenses as well as broad possibilities for discretionary administrative measures in monitoring foreign investment provide an example of intervention mechanisms the government has at its disposal. MNC's *insensitive* attitudes toward government policies would likely bring on the retaliatory response from the government.

Another dimension in the tripartite relations in Korea that is important to consider relates to partner relations in the joint venture. Many foreign investors in Korea consider joint ventures with reliable local partners as the most effective and the only possible way of doing business in Korea. In addition to sharing those economic benefits usually received from a joint venture, foreign firms can rely on the contacts of the local partner to avoid the need of wading through the bureaucracy.

In interacting with the local partner, however, there are serious problems of coping with a different cultural and business environment. In Korea, which is perhaps the most Confucian nation in East Asia, person-to-person relational considerations often supercede formal institutional structures. It behooves Western investors to assume likely possibilities of the cross-cultural partner conflict, and to make prudent inquiry about the manner of conducting business from traditional and cultural perspectives.

These handicaps for foreign investors to invest in Korea can, however, be more than offset by other clear advantages of doing business in a rapidly developing country with a favorable investment climate that includes sizable markets, well-developed productive infrastructure, and an efficient and disciplined labor force. Unlike many Latin American countries, the development in Korea has been achieved with a degree of relatively even income distribution. Excluding the political tensions stemming from repressive governmental policies, there are no extensive problems of unemployment and poverty that foreign investors may feel apprehensive about. On the other hand, foreign business can achieve results quicker in an efficiently run "hard-state." Foreign investors can clearly see where the national interests lie and need not be unduly concerned about the government's ability to implement policies, which should enable them to take a more long-term view in the interests of themselves and of the host state alike.

The Korean government is also pragmatic and flexible in actual implementation of its policies. For policy makers, foreign capital and technology are considered a vital link to Korea's sustained development, and the government is prepared to negotiate pragmatically with foreign investors to acquire these benefits. Moreover, the wide scope of authority and discretion exercised by the Korean government implies that many of the handicaps and conflicts in dealing with the host state can be avoided by efforts for improved communications built on more open, person-to-person relational considerations. Thus, the task of managing relations with the host government must be considered an important and vital one for MNCs, and must not be assumed as a simple nuisance to be dealt with as expeditiously as possible.[33]

APPENDIX A

The Rules and Procedures Governing the Entry

Administrative Structure in Foreign Investment

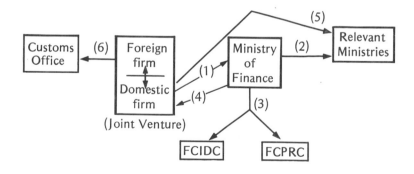

The administrative structures and procedures involved in foreign investment[35] are depicted in the diagram at the left:

(1) The prospective foreign investor must submit a project proposal to the Ministry of Finance[36] in order to obtain authorization of investment.

(2) The Ministry of Finance may refer to the relevant ministries for economic and feasibility studies of the proposed project. The relevant ministries return their evaluations to the Ministry of Finance.

(3) The Ministry of Finance forwards details of the project along with the opinions of other ministries concerned either to the Foreign Capital Inducement Deliberation Committee (FCIDC) or the Foreign Capital Project Review Committee (FCPRC).[37]

(4) After approval from the FCIDC or the FCPRC, the Minister of Finance authorizes the proposed foreign investment.

(5) After obtaining the authorization from the Minister of Finance, the foreign investor must submit an application for confirmation of the specification of capital goods to be imported to the relevant ministries, which then confirm the specification for imports.

(6) The ministries' confirmation must be submitted to the customs office for clearance of imports.

APPENDIX B

The List of Interviews

American Chamber of Commerce in Korea, Seoul.
Caterpillar Americas, Peoria, Illinois.
Chase Manhattan Bank, Seoul.
The Coca-Cola Company, Seoul.
Daewoo Corporation, Seoul.
Daewoo Shipbuilding Industries, Ltd., Seoul.
Daewoong-Eli Lilly Co., Seoul.
Economic Planning Board, Seoul.
Hanchang Textile, Inc., Seoul.
International Business Machinery, Inc., Seoul.
Johnson & Johnson Co., Seoul.
J. O. Kim Investment Lawyers Group, Seoul.

Kirin Computer Consulting Co., Seoul.
Ministry of Commerce and Industry, Seoul.
Ministry of Finance, Seoul.
Pfizer Korean Ltd., Seoul.
Price Waterhouse & Co., Seoul.
Samjin Electric Co., Seoul.
Samsung-Hewlett Packard, Inc., Seoul.

NOTES

1. In this paper the term "power" is used in a broad context of one social unit's capacity to control the actions of other units.

2. The field study was conducted by Professor Kwan S. Kim, Department of Economics and Kellogg Institute; Sung H. Kim, an MBA graduate; and Professor Lee A. Tavis, Department of Finance—all of the University of Notre Dame. A list of organizations in which interviews were conducted is included in Appendix B.

3. The proportion of total investment supplied by foreign capital was over 50 percent in the early 1960s, which declined to 11 percent by 1983. In 1983 equity capital accounted for 5.7 percent of the total with Korea's outstanding debt amounting to $40.6 billion. The debt-service ratio in 1983 was 14.2 percent, an acceptable level by international standards. S. Korea has been rated as possessing a very favorable investment climate for foreign investment, among the developing countries.

4. Within manufacturing, foreign loans in such sectors as textiles, chemicals, and petroleum accounted for as much as 57 percent of manufacturing commercial borrowing in the period of 1959–1975.

5. Anne O. Krueger, *The Developmental Role of the Foreign Sector and Aid*, (Cambridge, Mass.: Harvard University Press, 1979), Tables 41–42.

6. Ibid.

7. For the impact of transferred technologies on industrial development in Korea, see Chung, Kun-Mo, et al., "Technology and Industrial Development in Korea," Final Report of the Korean Science and Technology Policy Instruments Project (Seoul: Korea Advanced Institution of Science, 1977, mimeo. Also, see Economic Planning Board, *Current State of Technology Imports* (in Korean) (Seoul: 1980).

8. When a foreign investment is not made in accordance with the FCIA, repatriation is subject to the more restrictive Foreign Exchange Control Law. In any event, foreign subsidiaries will become eligible for approval of repatriation of the earnings by the Central Bank of Korea three years from the date of the subsidiary establishment. The amount repatriable is restricted to 20 percent of the total operating funds each year for five years commencing from the first repatriation.

9. Income taxes are exempted or reduced in proportion to the percentage of stocks or shares owned by foreign investors for five years. These taxes are reduced by 50 percent for the ensuing three years. Also, payments to the suppliers of technology under a technology inducement contract are exempted from income taxes for five years and are reduced by 50 percent for the ensuing three years.

10. The minimum level of exports necessary to qualify for incentives is determined by the ratio of raw materials imports to annual sales, plus 30 percentage points. Or a foreign-invested firm must satisfy three conditions: (1) Domestic production of the item in question should be less than 30 percent of the total domestic demand for that item; (2) Imported raw materials for production should be less than 30 percent and (3) The items produced should be on the automatic approval list and account for more than 50 percent of the total output.

11. High technology projects require involvement of technical expertise that local industries may not be expected to develop on their own. High-technology industries in Korea include machinery (industrial robots, aircraft manufacture, and repair of auto parts and components), electronics, genetic engineering, and new materials in iron, steel, and chemicals.

12. The qualifying projects comprise ventures with an initial foreign investment of more than US$ 10 million that will manufacture items imported freely and subject to duties of less than 10 percent or hotel projects with a US$ 5-million-plus foreign investment that meet certain earning criteria.

13. On the other hand, investment projects that meet the following criteria will automatically be approved: (1) The foreign equity share is 50 percent or less; (2) When it exceeds 50 percent, a certain percentage (expected to be 70 percent) of production is to be exported, or the item produced is open to import at a tariff rate lower than the percentage to be set in the implementation decree accompanying the FCIA (perhaps around 10 percent); and (3) Tax concessions are not sought. All other investment applications will be subject to the Ministry of Finance review in consultation with other relevant ministries or the interministerial Foreign Capital Inducement Deliberation Committee.

14. The average Korean worker is well-disciplined, efficient, low paid, and on the job 50 hours a week. Korea's infrastructure is well developed, and is being upgraded continuously with the latest technology. Along with development of industrial estates throughout the country, this development makes Korea well-poised for continuing economic progress.

15. It is important to observe that the recent foreign investment liberalization measures are advocated mainly by high-ranking policy makers. Low-level bureaucrats working at an actual implement level may generally disagree with this official policy. The pronounced policy must not be interpreted as leading to an immediate process of easing controls over foreign investors.

16. Recently, the Nestlé Co. along with many pharmaceutical multinationals were denied tax holidays and other incentives, for officials felt that they would compete with local firms in a saturated domestic market.

17. Gunnar Myrdal, *Asian Drama: An Inquiry Into the Poverty of Nations* (New York: Pantheon Press, 1968). Also L. Jones and I. Sakong, *Government, Business, and Entrepreneurship in Economic Development: The Korean Case* (Cambridge, Mass.: Harvard University Press, 1980), p. 133.

18. For discussions on government-business relations, see Kwan S. Kim, "Industrial Policy and Industrialization in South Korea: 1961–1982—Lessons on Industrial Policies for Other Developing Countries," Helen Kellogg Institute for International Studies Working Paper 39, University of Notre Dame, January 1985.

19. According to a 1981 survey (Hankook Ilbo, September 27, 1981), external

funds—those borrowed from domestic banks and foreigners—for the top fifty conglomerates in Korea accounted for as much as 85 percent of the total.

20. For details of the characterization of the Korean government, see L. P. Jones and I. Sakong, *Government Business and Entrepreneurship in Economic Development: The Korean Case.*

21. The Federation of Korean Industries, the Korean Traders Association, and the Cooperative Association of Small and Medium Firms are examples of institutionalized forums through which business input can be transmitted to the government. For example, in 1974 the Korean Traders Association alone (the largest and most influential of all trade associations in Korea) made 167 formal recommendations to the government and 76 percent were adopted by the government, at least in part (L. P. Jones & I. Sakong, *Government Business and Entrepreneurship*, pp. 70–74).

22. For a discussion of MNC-state relations, see J. J. Boddywyn and A. Kapoor, *International Business-Government Relations* (New York: American Management Association, 1973). Also, J. Fayerweather and A. Kapoor, *Strategies and Negotiation for the International Corporation* (Cambridge, Mass.: Ballinger Publishing Co., 1976).

23. The Korean government generally insists on export commitment for a certain percentage of the output or a commitment for the transfer of technologies to Koreans, should the MNC hold out for a majority position.

24. Several U.S. representatives of the pharmaceutical firms in Korea complained about requirements imposed on them by the Ministry of Health, which tended to be "overly protective of the interests of local competitors."

25. Gulf + Western and Dow Chemical participated in those ventures.

26. We found that the Korean executive of a large joint-venture company on average spent 30 to 35 percent of his working time on matters dealing with the government. A Korean top executive of a large joint company observed, "In appearance, the government has no control over business. In reality, however, negotiations with government have been continuous and intense."

27. A few foreign executives, well acculturated to Korean society, have been able to use personal contacts to deal directly with the government with a greater degree of success. By and large, these are rather exceptional cases.

28. This point was acknowledged during our interviews by a number of Korean executives involved in joint ventures.

29. An American top executive of a large pharmaceutical company pointed out that one of the important reasons for his expending personal effort to interact with government was just to keep him updated on new regulations. The difficulty he runs into is the lack of coordination between ministries in implementing government policies. Thus, for foreign investors, the interaction with government has to be with specific offices on a case-by-case basis.

30. In one case, the South Korean government sent government representatives to the United States to seek out possible investors to become involved in a major chemical complex. Initially, a 50-50 ownership deal with a government-owned company was made under the proviso that the government equity would be put into a holding company and eventually spun off to private sectors. Later, the government even conceded to 100 percent foreign ownership with market protection. The govern-

ment motive was to secure advanced technology and assistance in building a large-scale industrial complex for Korea.

31. This illustration was kindly provided by George Cobb of Hewlett Packard Co. in Korea.

32. Licensing agreement refers to the case of renting technologies, whereas sale of technologies involves transfer of technology patent.

33. In this context, an American senior executive observed: "The government bureaucracy is basically rigid, but can be very flexible in trying to accommodate your demands, provided that you use the right channels of contact with a certain ability of persuasion."

34. For details, see *Investment Guide to Korea* (Seoul: Ministry of Finance, 1985).

35. These procedures do not apply to those projects that fall within the categories of the Automatic Approval System.

36. Among the documents required for submission is a joint-venture agreement in which the foreign counterpart must pledge subscription of stocks or shares.

37. The FCIDC deliberates on investment projects only when requested by the Ministry of Finance. The Ministry forwards those projects considered of importance to the economy. The FCPRC is an advisory body of the Ministry, which reviews those projects considered relatively unimportant or involving small amounts of money.

The Mexican Case:
Communication under State Capitalism

KENNETH P. JAMESON
*AND JUAN M. RIVERA**

There is a continual ebb and flow in the relations between multinational corporations and governments, based upon changing goals of governments or of corporate strategies, upon changes in the structures which guide such relations, and upon the domestic and international contexts. These factors manifest themselves most clearly in the process of communication between the multinational corporation and the host government. The difficulty of obtaining information at this level has hampered the success of most efforts to understand and explain this central element in the role of multinational corporations in Third World countries. Because of the access provided by the Notre Dame seminar on "Multinational Corporations and Third World Development," this paper can focus on the actual process of communication between multinational corporations and the Mexican government, and thereby provide an understanding of that process, how it has developed over time, the key factors which affect it, and some insights into its likely future development.

*Kenneth P. Jameson is a professor of economics and faculty fellow of the Helen Kellogg Institute for International Studies at the University of Notre Dame. He has worked on governmental policy toward investment with the Ministry of Industry in Peru, the Ministry of Commerce in Panama, and on projects with the World Bank, the Inter-American Foundation, and the Agency for International Development.

Juan M. Rivera is a member of the accountancy faculty at the University of Notre Dame, and formerly taught accounting at the Instituto Tecnologico in Monterrey and Mexico City. Previously he was a financial analyst for Latin America for Eli Lilly and Company and the financial manager of the company's Venezuelan affiliate.

The ebb and flow of relations is mirrored by our understanding. It is clear today that the traditional view of multinationals as exploiters and all-powerful predators is outdated and irrelevant to the realities of the day. We have moved beyond the period in which "sovereignty at bay" seemed an apt characterization of the relationship. Nation-states have developed and applied a series of mechanisms which aid them in maintaining their sovereignty and in harnessing the multinational corporation to the goals of the country. A later view of the early 1980s that saw an ever-increasing control by the state is also outdated. No longer could one agree with Das that "the competitive advantage which the MNCs have had as a result of their worldwide integration of resources will greatly decrease as a result of the regulatory controls that are being imposed on MNC operations in host countries."[1]

A more correct rendition of the present situation is Moran's: "a decade in which developing countries try to grow out of the debt crisis . . . an era in which Third World societies need foreign direct investment more than ever to create jobs and generate exports to help relieve the pressures from paying off their loans."[2] This new reality has again changed the balance between nations and multinational corporations, and it is clear that such changes will be seen earliest and most clearly in the communication process between multinational corporations and host governments. A static approach to understanding these questions is misguided. Rather, the focus must be on the dynamics of negotiation and communication. These will change over time, and will vary substantially from country to country. Hence, a comparative perspective over time and across countries is essential.

The material for this study of multinational corporation–government communication in Mexico has been drawn from documents and secondary studies, but most heavily from a series of interviews with government policymakers, executives of multinational corporations, Mexican business executives, lobbyists, and analysts of the Mexican scene. Much of the information was gathered during interviews carried out in Mexico during January 1986 by three researchers from Notre Dame.[3]

The interviews were for the most part open-ended and were designed to provide coverage of all the major actors in the communication process. Particular interviews were arranged to ensure the inclusion of key informants. The cooperation was excellent in all cases, facilitated by prior experience with the Notre Dame seminar and with the type of communication it fosters.

The paper is organized as follows. The first section gives a review of the general climate toward foreign investment during the industrialization process in Mexico, particularly since the presidency of Ávila Camacho (1940–46). Any analysis which ignores this historical policy context would be misleading. The next section examines briefly the performance of the Mexican economy, focusing on the role of foreign investment, while the third section provides specific consideration of the characteristics of the Mexican political system and of the possible means of representation of business interests within the government policies and plans. The regulatory structures which influence the relation between the MNCs and the Mexican government are the topic of the next section, which closely examines this process of interaction and communication, in both cases based on material drawn from the interviews. The fifth section offers some observations and findings on a sensitive subject, that of influencing the decisions of Mexican government officials. Section six raises the questions of what direction multinational corporation–host government communication can and should take in the future, while the last section returns again to the context which the seminar provides for considering these issues.

FOREIGN INVESTMENT AND INDUSTRIALIZATION POLICY IN MEXICO

The initial conscious efforts toward industrialization in Mexico were undertaken in the Ávila Camacho administration. From the start the model of industrialization and development was based on directed government policies emphasizing import substitution and local protection. Within this framework, foreign investment was allowed to enter, although always on a limited and controlled basis. From those initial years, foreigners were permitted only a minority interest in many industries. Their participation was allowed only on Mexican terms.

The one constant of Mexican policy toward foreign investment has been to treat it with suspicion and to permit it on Mexican terms[4] and as a necessary evil. The reasons behind this general attitude are geographic as well as historic. Mexicans are keenly aware of the 3,000 kilometer border which they share with the most powerful country in the world, and of the myriad possibilities for U.S. influence or interference. There is ample historical precedent for their concern going back to the 1846 Mexican American War. The current policy-making apparatus evolved after the Revolution of 1910, a movement initiated to replace the dictatorship of Porfirio Díaz and any vestiges of its influence. During his 30-year rule, Díaz allowed foreigners, especially North Americans, to own 25 percent of the Mexican land, 75 percent of the mines, and more than half of the other productive assets. Large segments of Mexico were owned by foreigners, and the future development of the country would depend upon their decisions. It was from the time of Díaz that the incipient railroads crossed the country north to south and were viewed by many as veins to bleed the country of its important raw materials and minerals for the benefit of the colossus of the North.

The Evolution of Government Foreign Investment Policies

The occasional flashes of an invisible hand "à-la-Adam Smith" in the operation of the Mexican economy have certainly been much less evident than the visible and pervading presence of a Mexican government hand in shaping the Mexican industrial system. The Depression and World War II provided the initial impulses to industrial development through import substitution and some export growth.

Industrialization of the country was pushed by the regime of Alemán (1946–52).[5] The key policy was a program for import permits for manufactured goods, and it became the cornerstone of Mexico's import substitution industrialization. The program significantly prevented the importation of many goods, providing an incentive for foreign firms to establish manufacturing facilities in Mexico, and it provided the protected domestic market which would make such operations profitable.

Alemán was amicable to foreign investment, and his approach initiated a pattern of oscillation between nationalistic social reform and industrial growth with foreign involvement. Attitudes toward foreign capital changed according to the political preferences of the President. Still, a common thread in the fabric of the political regimes persisted, the intention of the governments to have the final say and to keep sovereign control in their dealings with foreign capital.

Thus, the administration of Ruiz Cortines (1952–58) wished to push industrialization more rapidly and instituted a series of incentives in the form of reduced taxes for foreign companies which would enter new industries or those which could not be adequately supplied by Mexican firms. Domínguez indicates that this policy generated pressures from domestic Mexican capital which saw its own interests threatened.[6] Later the López Mateos (1958–64) administration, characterized by a more populist flavor, favored prohibitions on foreign capital in certain industries and decreed a number of nationalizations (with compensation). It was at this juncture that the outlines of the state capitalist system of Mexico began to emerge. In the name of nationalism and of development, the government would not hesitate to take a leading role both as a regulator of local and foreign capital and as entrepreneur in state enterprises.

There were other legacies of this administration as well. Outlines for the development of the automotive industry were established, a forerunner of Mexico's industrial planning which relies upon detailed sectoral analysis and policy. On the other side, the López Mateos policies led to a significant flight of international capital, and so it showed the limits to nationalist policies, or at least the costs which they might involve. Of most long-term significance was the growth in government expertise and experience, the human resource base for the policies which would be subsequently followed.

The administration of Díaz Ordaz (1964–70) was much less antagonistic to foreign capital, and its accommodative stance generated domestic pressure from business and political forces for more stringent controls. Later, as a typical swing of the pendulum in the Mexican political arena, the Echeverría government (1970–76) took a very hard position on foreign investment and laid the legal framework for present policies. Two key pieces of legislation were enacted under Echeverría, the Law to Promote Mexican Investment and Regulate Foreign Investment of 1973 and the Law for the Control and Registration of the Transfer of Technology and the Use and Exploitation of Patents and Trademarks of 1972. Those laws continue to be the basis for policy vis-à-vis foreign investment, and they established a specific procedure and structure to guide decision making in the area.

The initial years of the López Portillo (1976–82) administration saw a much softer attitude toward foreign capital, seen clearly in the administrative interpretation of existing laws. In the domestic sphere, the government undertook a very aggressive program of expanding state capitalism, using the ballooning oil revenues as the basis for its entrepreneurial role. The logic of this position led it to nationalize the banking system at the end of López Portillo's six-year term as a means of dealing with a severe internal financial crisis.

Due more to the precarious recent conditions of the Mexican economy than to a fundamental switch in philosophical beliefs, the de la Madrid (1982–88) administration has demonstrated a generally favorable stance toward foreign investment. There are, of course, exceptions to this recent trend, for example the 1982 decree on the pharmaceutical industry. However, there is certainly no return to the days of Echeverría. The shift has been in how to operate the state capitalist system. The expansion of government into new areas of the economy has now been halted and there have been some efforts to sell to the private sector some government parastatals or the government's share in certain joint ventures.

Legal Delimiters of Government–MNC Communication

The Law for the Control and Registration of the Transfer of Technology and the Use and Exploitation of Patents and Trademarks (amended in 1982) and the 1973 Law to Promote Mexican Investment and Regulate Foreign Investments set the legal framework for MNC and Mexican host government interaction.[7] In broader terms they specified the realm of communication between multinational corporations and the government in all cases where multinational corporations would propose a majority-owned project.

The Law to Regulate Foreign Investments generally restricts entrance of foreign capital to a ceiling of 49 percent control in those fields not reserved for the government or for full Mexican participation. However—and here is where the element of official discretion is introduced—the act permits acceptance of higher than 49 percent of capital "in the interest of the country's economy." The Commission on Foreign Investment, an ad-hoc organization composed of the heads of several governmental ministries, is vested with the application of this law. To implement it, a series of thirteen general resolutions are currently in effect (Appendix A), which serve as guidelines or criteria for the Commission in deciding individual cases. There is a formal and technical decision-making process. However, so much flexibility is written into the law that the authorities' case-by-case application is the key to the actual communication. The casuistic nature of the process encourages extensive give-and-take negotiations between government and participating foreign capital.

The Law on Technology Transfer and Use of Patents and Trademarks is another powerful instrument for the government to control operations of a foreign-owned firm. It requires all agreements dealing with patents, trademarks, and technological assistance to be filed in a National Registry in order to be enforceable. A governmental unit within the Secretary of Commerce and Industrial Development reviews each contract and authorizes the level of royalties adjudicated to the foreign supplier of the technology or patent. The individual merits of the transfer agreements are also judged on a case-by-case basis by the governmental agency.

Another potential factor that could influence the legal framework for government and business relations is the possible decision by the Mexican government to join the General Agreement on Tariffs and Trade (GATT).[8] It is widely agreed that there will be no precipitate change in policy, although the direction will necessarily be toward a liberalization of the economy over a longer period of time. Joining the GATT will be a tangible restraint on any steps toward further regulations and protection, and a continuous stimulus for less regulation.

In spite of this liberalization, the basic suspicion of foreign investment, its treatment as a necessary evil, and the clear commitment to accepting it only on Mexican terms are unlikely to change nor are the formal legal delimiters. The reality of the United States and the influence of the historical relations will not disappear. Any Mexican government which ignored that would unleash significant internal forces leading to its demise.

THE ECONOMIC PERFORMANCE OF MEXICO

In most important respects, Mexico's economic performance in the post–World War II period must be judged at least a relative success.[9] Until recent years, it has been able to maintain a good performance, avoiding the stagnation of high-income countries such as Uruguay and Argentina, and this has allowed it to continue to incorporate more of its citizens into a domestic market economy.

Economic performance can be measured in terms of (1) growth of the gross national product which has been quite good by world standards until the last three years; (2) industrialization which advanced steadily until recent years; and (3) the ability to attract foreign investment. There is one important area where performance has not been good. Even though the government can receive high marks for industrialization and economic growth, the income distribution has not improved from its patterns of 20 or 30 years ago, and it probably has worsened in the last decade.[10]

Favorable Economic Growth

The World Bank's *World Development Report* indicates clearly that Mexico has been among the most successful of the world economies in terms of growth. Its annual growth rate of GDP was 7.9 percent from 1965–73 and 5.6 percent from 1973–83.[11] Particular countries may have grown more rapidly at times, but Mexico's is far higher than the world average, the average of countries with comparable incomes, except the high-income oil exporters such as Saudi Arabia. In the late 1970s and early 1980s, real per capita growth rates were over 5 percent. Of course this was largely a result of oil revenues and debt increases, but it continued a pattern of growth which was interrupted only in exceptional years, 1976 being one case in point. As a result, Mexico attained a per capita gross national product of $2240 in 1983.

Decadal annual growth rates of gross domestic product were over 5.5 percent from 1950 through 1979. The growth of manufacturing output was greater by approximately .5 percent in every case. For the most part, the demand for these manufactured goods was in the domestic market, which represented over 70 million Mexican citizens in 1980.

The crisis of 1982 altered this pattern. Gross domestic product fell one half of a percent in 1982 and 5.3 percent in 1983, while 1984 showed a rather anemic recovery with 3.7 percent growth. Manufacturing output fell by 2.9 percent, then by a dramatic 7.3 percent in 1983, and grew by 4.8 percent in 1984, thus following the world economic cycle.[12]

Increasing Industrialization

The goal of the Mexican government has been to make Mexico one of the most important Third World industrial countries. In 1980, Mexico accounted for 10.8 percent of the value added in industry in Third World countries, surpassed only by Brazil's 22.7 percent, but having surpassed both Argentina and India. Similarly it had a relatively high proportion of its production in capital and intermediate goods, 35 percent and 20 percent respectively.[13]

The one clear area in which Mexico's industrial development lags behind other countries is in its exports. Kim has observed that Korea, India, and Brazil have greater exports of industrial projects, technology licenses, civil construction, capital goods, and general direct investment than Mexico.[14] This is one argument of the Mexican government's clear desire to rejuvenate its industrial machine to enter the competitive but attractive international markets.

Ability to Attract Foreign Investment

The final question is how Mexico fared with respect to foreign investment — Has the environment of economic policy and domestic demand creation attracted foreign investment in a significant manner? The answer again is yes. Newfarmer and Mueller found that 32 percent of the 300 largest Mexican manufacturing firms were owned by U.S. capital.[15] Grindle reports a series of indicators on the growth and importance of foreign investment in Mexico.[16] Since 1955 the share of U.S. Latin American investment in Mexico has increased almost continually, reaching close to 19 percent by 1979. In the same year, Mexico ranked seventh in terms of countries with U.S. manufacturing investment. Of the U.S. investment in Mexico, 74 percent was in industry, compared with 7 percent in 1940. However, the difficulties encountered by Mexico in paying its fixed debt in 1982 had a significant chilling effect on additional investment. The $2.5 billion of new investment in 1981 became a slushy $1.65 billion in 1982 and a glacier-like $391 million in 1984.

In summary, in terms of its own policies and goals, the Mexican model has been successful. The success has been tarnished by the major downturn of 1982–83, and it is not clear that the previous approaches are likely to meet with the same success in the future. Still, to this point, the balance is on the favorable side and indicates the significant resourcefulness of Mexico in attaining its economic goals.

As we turn to the way in which the Mexican government guides the private sector and its foreign investment component toward development, we should recognize that industrialization and growth are not synonymous with development. The bottom line of development is what happens to the people of a country. In Mexico, the income distribution remains skewed and has probably become more so during the last decade. At the low end of the scale are large numbers of unemployed or subemployed, and many whose poverty is a tragedy.

Perhaps the greatest failure of Mexico, as of most of Latin America, has been in agriculture. Non-export agricultural incomes are generally low and stagnant, and rural productivity is similarly low and unchanging. This is a central factor in the continuing migration to urban areas, even though there is much uncultivated land in the Mexican countryside. These problems will have to be dealt with in the future.

GOVERNMENT AND THE PRIVATE SECTOR

Political power in Mexico has traditionally been exercised by the President, with Congress acting as a rubber-stamp for executive decrees and legislative initiative emanating from the executive branch. The President comes from the one official party in power, the Partido Revolucionario Institucional (PRI). Indirectly, his influence extends beyond his six-year term of office since he is a major force behind the selection of his successor.

The Mexican Political System

The political system in Mexico can be understood as a one-party, corporatist state. Since its consolidation in the late 1920s, it has been uniquely successful when viewed from the Latin American context. The PRI and the government support each other and often the lines of distinction between the two organisms are blurred. Six other parties contest elections, though some of these parties are in fact government-encouraged through a limited "apertura" (opening) that functions as an escape valve in the tight political machine. Of the six other parties, the only viable opponent is the Partido de Acción Nacional (PAN). It can dispute the PRI at the local and sometimes the state level, but it is clear that the PRI will cede miniscule ground only grudgingly. The structure is corporatist in that the party incorporates various interest groups, some with formal mechanisms to express their views and exercise their power. The PRI has been described as the most "opaque" controlling political party in the hemisphere, precisely because there is a spectrum of political philosophies allowed within the organization, all competing for power; and this is often reflected in the government as well. It is difficult to establish what group or individual is consolidating its position within the party and the government. The traditional sectors of the party are the unionized workers, the farmers, the government bureaucracy, and some independent professionals. There is no formal representation for the private business sector in the PRI.

Most of the important members of the bureaucracy are active members of the PRI, or certainly collaborators, and thus responsive to the interest group representation. They are, for the most part, career governmental employees. There is relatively little of the flow between business and government which characterizes the United States today.

Private Sector Representation

Even though business interests are not directly represented in the PRI, they are represented to the government, often forcefully. This process operates at three different levels. The first is the public debate forum. There is an active press in Mexico, and although it generally knows its limits, the opinion of business is channeled through the press, allowing it to force a public debate on important policies and their implementation.

The second level of action is through a series of well-organized business associations. Most are nationwide and obligatory, in that every company is required by law to join its corresponding industrial group. Others are voluntary. All of these associations are represented at the summit by the Consejo Coordinador Empresarial (CCE) (Private Sector Coordinating Council). The Consejo is an umbrella organization created in 1975 as a mechanism to present to the government the business position on issues perceived as affecting private business interest.[17] The Consejo has the most access and rapport with the government. Although there is no established formal channel of influence, the head of the CCE deals directly with the President and with his cabinet members, and can quite clearly provide an excellent representation of business ideas. As one interviewee put it, "Going to see the head of the CCE is like going to see God."

Among other active independent associations, one with a recognized status and relevance is the Confederación Patronal de la República Mexicana (COPARMEX) (Federation of Mexican Employers) encompassing approximately 25,000 employers from all industries and firm sizes. This association acts as a voice of business and formally participates in a Commission with government and labor sectors for the periodic revision and approval of minimum wages.

The last of the relevant business associations in Mexico is the American Chamber of Commerce. It is the largest AmCham in the world with 3,000 members — of which two-thirds are Mexican-owned firms. This association works more as a provider of information than as a lobbyist. Its policy is never to represent an individual member's position or claim before the government, but rather to convey feelings or complaints of an industry or group before the government.

The final channel for interaction is the personal. There is a Mexican elite which went to the same schools, knows the same people, and frequents the same places as the successful government employees. There is a good deal of informal communication, lobbying, and general reality-checking which goes on. This pattern is seen quite clearly in interviews with government authorities who deal with industry policy and who often mention the projects they are involved in with the private sector.

The corporatist structure of this socio-political apparatus has served Mexico well in the past. It has provided space for new groups to express opinions and needs and has allowed them to become incorporated into the society and the economy. It has forced a responsiveness from government not observable in most Latin governments. As a result Mexican government policy has resorted to much less repression than in other countries of Latin America.

There are some indications that the resilience of the system has lessened, that the views of many groups are no longer heard. While it is difficult to assess these claims, their importance is fundamental, for the stability of the country is at stake. It may ultimately define the success of the development efforts in Mexico.

This is not unrelated to the ascendancy of a technocracy in the Mexican government. Since the adoption of state capitalism, the responsibilities, confidence, and the standard of living for senior officials in the government has dramatically improved. As one of them pointed out, "The time of government by politicians with horses and pistols is long gone." It is now a government of technicians, which may be another factor in the loss of political contact. To prove the point, one government official took out the biography of government employees, opened it at random, and read the education of the officials on one page. Stanford, Harvard, Notre Dame, and MIT appeared as frequently as the National University of Mexico. All of the officials had advanced degrees.

General Patterns of Business and Government Interaction

Although the corporate structure has long been in place, interaction between business and government in Mexico has changed significantly over the past quarter-century in part because of the technification of the government. In the 1950s and 1960s, there was a free and informal communication between the private sector and government authorities. This was described by one respondent as "an easy relationship where both sides understood each other. Business leaders were treated as elder statesmen. Conversations were frequent and informal."

According to some observers, in the past two decades, communication between the business sector and the Mexican government has deteriorated. Mexican government technocrats have become more and more sophisticated, more determined to direct the economy independent of influence from the business groups, especially the foreign multinational corporate component. There are now fewer spontaneous personal contacts between business and government, particularly between MNC managers and governmental officials. The government technocrat has become more and more distant. This might well be due to the status and expertise of the senior official in the government which has improved dramatically, especially since the adoption of state capitalism.

As for businesses, the contact is increasingly the result of petitions by the business side and bargaining and concession-granting by the government actors, all within the framework of a competitive business game. Often many of the contacts are between the business association and the government. In this process, there has been a loss in communication. As one executive noted, "One side does not understand the other. In my attempts to convince the government of the importance of confidence among local and foreign investors, the ministry could simply not understand my point. We were speaking different languages, both in Spanish." The interaction can now best be described as one of "unilateral indicative planning."

There is the possibility for a new type of interaction to develop.

As Mexico moves into the GATT, a third kind of interaction might result—"delegated market planning." Here, government policymakers could rely more on market mechanisms rather than government regulations to allocate resources.

The debt crisis of the past five years, and even the tragic earthquake of 1985, has not served to bring the business and government communities together. Still, the process of interaction does not seem to be working to the detriment of the MNC operating in Mexico. No respondent could recall a multinational that had left Mexico because its subsidiary was no longer viable or because the business conditions in Mexico were inhospitable.

Ultimately the power of decision resides with the government, and there are enough instruments at its disposal to ensure that its will prevails over the opposition which could be mounted by the private sector. In modern state capitalism, however, the private sector and the state are dependent upon one another. There is little likelihood that any issue will go all the way to a major confrontation. It will be negotiated so that each side will come away with some gains from the resolution.

The private sector does have one other defense from the government executive, and this is the court system. However, the infrequency of its use in any major policy dispute indicates that other mechanisms are more successful in reaching an accord between the two.

REGULATION OF MULTINATIONAL INVESTMENT

The interaction between the government and MNCs is highly conditioned by two key factors: first, the mode under which the MNC chooses to enter the Mexican economy, i.e. as minority partner with other Mexican private enterprises, as a wholly owned subsidiary (or more than 49 percent owned), or as minority partner with government majority participation; second, the industry in which the firm chooses to operate. In the latter case, there are certain industries in which it is clear that foreign capital will be highly controlled and limited, for example, the mining industry, the petroleum or petrochemical industries. In others, there will be a highly structured effort to control the firms so they fit within an overall industrial plan. The three main cases are the automotive, the electronic, and the pharmaceutical industries. Other industries provide a good deal more flexibility in the dealings with the government.

In this section the concentration will be on the first of these factors, the form of entry of the firm, and the three cases will be treated separately. It then moves on to consider cases in which the rules of the game are changed and finally to examine the day-to-day regulation of firms.

Differentiation by Mode of Entry

1. Ventures with Mexican Majority Ownership: MNC minority partners in joint ventures with Mexican firms provide the greatest ease of entry. This form of organization is prescribed in the 1973 Law on Foreign Investment. For those firms entering during the 1970s, the stipulations were generally enforced.

There are a number of advantages for these "Mexicanized firms." Many of stipulations and controls of the foreign investment law do not apply once the firm is formed, thus providing greater agility in making decisions without the burden of governmental permission and approval. In addition, a joint-venture partner, if chosen well, will have excellent contacts within the government and can use that influence to gain favorable decisions for the firm, a process which is far more difficult for a wholly owned foreign firm. The joint-venture partners are generally drawn from a relatively small number of influential Mexican economic groups.[18]

These Mexican entrepreneurs have an advantage in dealing with the day-to-day requirements of the government. Mexican firms expect to be treated with more understanding on a whole range of governmental policies such as price controls, expansion of product lines, purchases of real estate, channeling of credit, etc. Subsidies, such as tax incentives or favorable interest rates, are more readily available to wholly or partially owned Mexican firms.[19]

Success in this area can have a substantial effect on firm performance. Indeed one manager indicated he was very happy the firm's Mexican name made it seem like a very common Mexican undertaking, for he felt this protected them from some pressure and made their own efforts more successful. The other potential advantage is in sales to the government sector, for in many industries the government is a major purchaser of goods and services. Again success in selling to the government — and in collecting payment — can have a substantial effect on financial returns, and a Mexicanized firm may perform better.

Another potential benefit of a Mexican joint venture is access to the capabilities of the Mexican business people. They generally drew highly favorable comments from MNC managers. "They are bright, hard-working [12–16 hour days], and savvy about their own reality. Mexican business firms are less structured than their North American counterparts, though they press for clear and excellent results. They are also a source of key information on Mexican business conditions, government policy decisions or initiatives, and industry trends, as a result of their range of contacts across the major sectors of the economy."

There are potential difficulties for joint ventures with Mexican firms. The first is loss of managerial control by the multinational corporation. By law, managerial control is tied to ownership in Mexico. In practice, it does not work out that way. In most joint ventures the control of managerial decisions reside with the U.S. partner. They are typically more experienced in the industry, are recognized by their Mexican partners as excelling in managerial capabilities, and are more effective in tying the Mexican operation to the parent marketing and sales organization for imports and exports.

Loss of control does not appear to have been a major problem. We asked for any examples of joint ventures which had gone sour and none were forthcoming, although some managers knew of examples in other countries such as Taiwan. Moreover, there are often a number of Mexican joint-venture partners which again ensures MNC dominance.

A second problem is the control over technology. There may be cases of joint ventures where the U.S. partner provides new and sophisticated technology, but our respondents indicated that there would be a great reluctance to provide the newest technology in a joint-venture relationship because of the difficulty in maintaining control of that technology and preventing it from being copied by the Mexican partner. There is general agreement that the Law on Patents and Trademarks does not strongly protect intellectual property. One of the ironies of the Mexican case may be that in providing a variety of modes of entry into the Mexican market, the government provides an incentive to the high-tech firm to hold out for 100 percent ownership and complete control over the technology which the government of Mexico is attempting to have transferred into its own economy.

The third problem is that the Mexican partners are likely to be directly affected by the difficulties of the Mexican economy, and their resources may indeed be stretched very thinly, making it difficult for them to aid in recapitalizing an enterprise or even in generating the resources necessary to get the joint venture off the ground.

2. Joint Ventures with the Government: Joint ventures with the Mexican government are normally undertaken with Nacional Financiera (NAFINSA) the Mexican development bank. With this form of organization, the same advantages as Mexican ownership would be expected — greater ability to deal with day-to-day business demands in Mexico and a greater ability to sell to the Mexican government in its state enterprises.[20]

The other advantage during the 1970s was NAFINSA's access to international capital markets. In addition NAFINSA has developed a reputation for carefully monitoring firms' management practices. Managers see this as an advantage, particularly as it applies to their Mexican partners. A possible problem for the foreign partner is the right reserved and exercised by Nacional Financiera to name the general manager and the financial director of the companies in which it participates.

Also, NAFINSA represents the Mexican government and could easily sacrifice the interests of its U.S. joint-venture partner, or indeed of the entire joint venture, in pursuit of macro-economic or political governmental policies. Although a possibility, we found no evidence that this had occurred.

On balance, most U.S. multinationals strive for 100 percent ownership in Mexico, so we can conclude that they see the benefit scales tipped in that direction.

3. Wholly Owned U.S. Subsidiaries: For a new project or a new investment, the National Commission of Foreign Investments has the final say on whether to grant approval. Its decision is based on the work provided by the technicians, office directors, and subsecretaries of the various entities. In addition, the decisions are taken within the framework of the Law on Technology Transfer and the Law on Foreign Investment.

The Foreign Investment Law reserves certain industries for governmental parastatals, prohibits foreign capital in some strategic industries, and limits foreign capital to a maximum 49 percent ownership or control in other areas of the economy. When the law was passed, there were many MNCs operating with 100 percent ownership. Those existing operations of MNCs were respected. For these firms, however, all new activities — new facilities and new product lines — were subject to the stipulations of the Foreign Investment Law. In this way, existing entities did not have to sell off a majority to Mexican partners, but neither were they simply grandfathered and exempted from the regulatory process.

Following the requirement for majority Mexican capital, the law goes on to state, "The National Commission on Foreign Investment may decide on the increase or reduction of the percentage . . . when it judges this to be in the interest of the country's economy, and it may establish the conditions under which foreign investment will be accepted in specific cases." It is this paragraph which defines the interaction between the MNCs and the Mexican government. The reality is that "anything is negotiable." The law is simply a starting point. Any final outcome will be a result of a negotiating process between the National Investment Commission, as a representative of Mexico, and the MNC.

Multinationals are still pressing for, and achieving 100 percent ownership. Recent agreements in the automotive and electronic industries show how far this can go.[21] Both of these industries fall within the requirement of Mexican majority ownership, and in both specific sectoral programs have been designed to foster orderly development. Yet, there have been agreements for 100 percent ownership in both industries. In these cases, the governmental desire to increase exports overcame the legal requirement for majority Mexican ownership.

A firm that wants to make an investment in Mexico with majority ownership will have a long process of negotiation. One respondent outlined the effort. "The application is only about seven pages long. However it is quite complex and has within it a series of cross checks which the very savvy technicians can and do use to ask additional sets of questions." In addition, and this is the difficult part, by custom and as a result of previous experience with such negotiations, a large amount of additional technical and analytical information must also be included with the application, perhaps four or five volumes of material. This material is submitted with the application and then discussions are held on it and negotiations are carried out on the elements of the project. This indeed is a very time-consuming process, especially for top management of the MNC seeking entry. One of the interviewees from the interior of the country mentioned that before a final agreement was drafted, a total of 72 business trips trips to confer with Mexican officials in the capital were needed during a span of four years.

The recent expansion of the IBM investment in Mexico is an example of this process. IBM negotiated with the Mexican authorities for a number of years over a proposal to expand their Mexican facilities to build microcomputers. Mexico welcomed the investment but insisted that the additional investment be subject to the stipulation of the Foreign Investment Law limiting foreign capital to 49 percent. The original IBM investment, made before the passage of the law, was wholly owned and IBM insisted on extending that control to the new facilities.

In January 1985 the Mexican government turned down the IBM proposal, noting that other U.S. microcomputer companies had taken minority interests in accordance with the law. Following another year of negotiations, IBM agreed to invest substantially more than they had originally proposed, to create a semiconductor design center, and, most importantly, to export nine-tenths of the new output (making IBM one of the ten largest Mexican exporters) in return for 100 percent ownership of the new facilities.

Once the decision is made to permit the investment, an agreement will be signed with a certain number of specific performance requirements on the part of the multinational corporation. Yearly reports of compliance must be submitted for three to five years, with justifications for shortfalls to avoid the penalities which could be applied.

The government claims that once the project is approved and subject to monitoring for compliance with the agreement, the firm is treated as any other firm. As one government official said, "There are no foreign firms operating in Mexico. They are all Mexican firms."

In actual fact, of course, the situation is somewhat different. First, the Mexican authorities make decisions on a case-by-case basis, using as general criteria those guidelines contained in the Thirteen General Resolutions to Administer the Application of Foreign Investment Regulations. A type of case law is built in the process, but the official interpretation of the legal precedent is final. There is no viable appeal to the courts. Each new project is subject to a protracted and extensive negotiation on all aspects. The approvals are very detailed agreements with specific requirements of performance. It is in these negotiations, primarily at the Office-Director level, that the main contact between multinational corporations and government occurs and where the most intensive contact and communication takes place.

After entry, the same approval process is required for new projects, for new lines of business, or for plant expansion. In these cases, the process is burdensome but the outcome generally foreordained. Once the basic rules of the game have been established, the firm is unlikely to make any proposal which would fall outside existing "case law." There may be exceptions, but for the most part, the relations are much less difficult and complicated after the initial entry interaction.

The case law which is created is constantly changing in response to shifting governmental objectives. These are presented most specifically in the National Development Plan of 1983–88 and in the National Program for Industrial Development and Foreign Trade of 1984–88.

Although not a component of the 1973 Law on Foreign Investment, or of the present implementing regulations, the pressure for exports is a central element of all governmental negotiations, with technology transfer running second. At the present time, corporate negotiating strength depends upon the firm's ability to generate a positive hard currency balance in its export and import activities. For relief from other requirements, such as negotiating Mexican ownership, firms must commit to generate positive balance. The Mexican government is upgrading its computerized monitoring of these balances.

In the cases surveyed, these positive hard currency balances are guaranteed by locational shifts in the multinational firm's production and marketing networks. Mexican components or products are given preference over those produced in other locations. The government's emphasis on technology as well as exports will, of course, enhance productivity and thus export capability.[22]

From the governmental standpoint, the 1973 law clearly specifies the rules of the game and, in their minds, clearly indicates to a foreign firm the context within which it will operate in Mexico. It is a political fact that no Mexican government is in a position to change the law. Thus, the informal changes in regulatory implementation are used to accomplish this objective. The law provides the umbrella under which governmental officials can pursue changing policies.

However, the flexibility in the application of Mexican law is particularly frustrating for U.S. managers. An exception today may not hold tomorrow. As governmental objectives change, different multinational performance will be demanded as an offset to the 100 percent ownership allowed. Still, the managers in Mexico seemed perfectly able and willing to operate in this environment. Their problem was in making parent firms understand the situation—its constraints and its possibilities.

Changing the Rules of the Game

For the most part the initial agreement reached is one which both sides are expected to keep. There were some indications that continuing disputes about interpretations could occur. Given the great flexibility of legal interpretation and the changing development strategies on the part of the government, these would be expected. But, for the most part, the initial agreements provided a firm basis on which to do business.

As noted above, the key current consideration for the Mexican government is the export capacity of the project and the transmission of technology, with local content, location, and capital flow following. Five years ago local content and technology would have headed the list. Along the way, other traditional concerns such as plant location, complementarity to local investment, the displacement of local investment, external financing, non-monopoly, environmental impact, and employment creation have all taken a secondary role.

Once a firm is in the Mexican economy, it is in its interest to settle disputes amicably within the normal bounds. The interviews give the impression that Mexico is much less prone to apply specific pressure to individual firms after they have begun their operations than is Brazil, for example. Also when the rules of the game are changed, there are enough adjustments made that the interests of the multinational corporations are protected. Of course it is also costly for firms to close operations.

There have been some cases in which the agreed rules of the game have been altered in a significant manner by governmental decree. The two prime examples are the automotive industry and the pharmaceutical industry. In the first case, a 1983 decision effectively forced the U.S. automakers out of the medium-sized truck production business by mandating dieselization and limiting the number of producers.[23]

Reflecting again the general framework of accommodation and

bargaining, the resolution was flexed to find new niches for the U.S. automakers, for example, one company will enter a joint production venture with a Mexican firm and another will be the major distributor for the other producer. Although the state capitalist rules have changed, the corporatist approach ensures that the firms' interests will not be completely neglected.

In the pharmaceutical industry, a sectoral decree published in 1982 threatened the operations of the foreign pharmaceutical firms. The financial crisis brought a general scarcity of foreign currency and the government limited import permits and price increases. This affected operations of the pharmaceutical plants. Empty shelves started to be common in some pharmacies. A very concerned Mexican government, realizing then that the country was perhaps too dependent on foreign suppliers, came up with a sectoral pharmaceutical decree which was received with strong opposition by those companies affected. The decree contemplated the generalized use of generics, equal prices for similar products, the creation of a national laboratory, and the mass distribution of medicines by a government agency. The joint reaction of the foreign firms was to obtain an injunction. They believed that this decree would give the market to Mexican firms and drive the multinationals out of Mexico.

Even though the decree was never rescinded, neither was it ever enforced. The implementation rules were much more flexible and acceptable to MNC pharmaceuticals. In essence, this case was resolved by softening greatly the final implementation of the sectoral program. Some respondents indicated that in this instance great pressure was brought to bear on the Mexican government by the Mexican Pharmaceutical Association, by its American counterpart—the Pharmaceutical Manufacturing Association (PNA)—and even by the U.S. government. Pressure was applied at the ambassadorial level and above. The final chip in the negotiation was a trade agreement between the two countries, one of whose key elements was the application of more stringent criteria—proof of injury by the affected American manufacturer—before Mexican goods could be subjected to countervailing duties on the basis of dumping claims. This development presented a significant change in the communication process which would have been inconceivable in the mid-1970s. It remains to be seen whether it signals a long lasting change.

Continuing Operational Regulation as Part of the Private Sector

Following entry, the majority-owned multinational subsidiary is subject to continuing requirements of the Foreign Investment Law, and beyond that, there are a welter of controls that apply to the Mexican private sector such as price controls, registration of technology, sanitary and health approvals, zoning permits, import approvals, or the channeling of credit. There is also the reality that for many products the Mexican government is a major purchaser.

Price controls are probably the most important. Food items and those considered basic for family requirements such as drugs and paper products are generally controlled at the retail level. Beyond that, firms in other industries such as cement or aluminum are required to register price increases, and to defend them if called upon by the Department of Commerce Price Commission.

Price increases are approved on a case-by-case basis. Since these decisions are firm specific, they can have a great impact on the profits of individual subsidiaries. Controlled prices vary within the same industry and among the specific products for a given firm. In practice, there can be dramatic differences in allowed increases, and so this becomes a key issue in ensuring successful performance.

There are a series of clear business requirements before a price increase is granted. Respondents agreed that the essence of the process is to make a good economic case, with evidence to support the request, and framed in the terms of the Ministry. Without that technical backing, there will be no success in the effort.

With the size of the Mexican food distribution system, the Social Security system, and the Mexican parastatals, the government represents an important consumer. According to a number of interviews, the role of government as consumer in the economy may have increased with the economic strain in the past three years. The choice of vendor resides solely in the government, generally at the level of the Office Director, occasionally at the sub-secretary level.

On these matters as well as the entry questions, there is assured access to the government decision-makers, though if the political winds are blowing against multinational corporations or against a particular request, the success of the effort will be affected. But doors are never closed. As one person put it, "The Mexican government officials are always quite polite and gracious; what changes is the effectiveness of the effort." Once the technical case is made, cleverness, persistence, and generally the working of the personal system will affect the outcome. Many respondents noted that a Mexican partner could be very helpful in some of these areas.

Summary

It is clear that the communication and negotiation process is a long one for most decisions, and many managers indicated that the home office had a difficult time understanding and accepting that. Nevertheless, in the long run, it is the most effective way to operate in Mexico. Confrontation and standing on the rights of the matter or pushing for a clear-cut solution would ultimately be counterproductive. There was a general feeling that the outcomes are fair, and that the interests of the multinational corporation could be quite well-protected in this operational environment. Indeed several managers noted that their profit rates were higher than those of the overall corporation, and that even though the overall economy had been quite buffered by the international disruptions, they had been able to increase their profits, in dollar terms, despite the domestic problems and the major devaluations of the peso. An interesting note was the uniform desire to keep a "low profile."

Thus, underneath the formal clarity of the relation between multinational corporations and governments, there is a highly complex and variable relationship, but one which in operation is not arbitrary. It is a reflection of Mexico's state capitalist economic structure and its inclusive corporatism.

THE NATURE OF COMMUNICATIONS

There are three levels of interaction between multinationals and the Mexican government: interactions between individual firms and specific ministries; through associations; or through U.S. governmental pressure.

Mexico has a reputation, probably well earned, of *la mordida*. The great discretion allowable within the law for both entry and continuing operations, the applications of specific requirements on a firm-by-firm and product-by-product basis as in price controls, combined with the protected, imperfect Mexican markets surely present the opportunities for influence and discretionary treatment. In this kind of environment, the multinational manager can resort to any of three approaches: documented technical arguments, personal contacts, the passing of monies.

In today's Mexico, documented technical arguments are increasingly a necessary condition for discussions with the government. Any involvement with the Foreign Investment Commission or the Department of Commerce pricing authorities, for example, must be exhaustively documented. This is especially true in the de la Madrid government which is regarded as a technical, as opposed to a political, regime.

As with any society, however, careful analysis does not always carry the day. Personal relationships and trust or other influences can play a significant role. Many U.S. firms employ Mexican nationals in senior management. They are technically competent and well-prepared in a variety of managerial positions within the multinational organization. They have an understanding of the Mexican system as well as personal contacts within the government. Beyond that, some firms rely on formal public relations offices, others on well-connected consultants.

Most of our respondents concluded that bribery of governmental officials was not a viable alternative in Mexico. They observed that there was an efficient communications network among those in the government with an eye toward extra rewards, and that a bribe in one case led to demands in others. A favor for an inspector on the plant floor simply led to more frequent inspections from more inspectors, even from different agencies. The general conclusion was that the cost/benefit tradeoff, at least for low-level bureaucratic payments, led to a cost greater than the gain.

When extortion becomes an issue, U.S. multinational corporate managers tend to use the Foreign Corrupt Practices Act as a shield. The requirements of this legislation are well known in Mexico. The situation is more difficult for corporations with 100 percent Mexican capital, since the FCPA does not apply. This is obviously a field more open to the possibility of bribery. According to one of the respondents, this "influencing" could be left out of the accounting trace, typically when the owner-manager uses segregated secret funds or his personal assets. Another possibility is to record these bribes or commissions as part of "confidential" expenses which are not deductible for tax purposes. For the case of Mexican companies the practice is observable and disclosure by the company's auditors should occur if the amounts involved are material. However, since these disclosures do not normally circulate beyond the owner-managers of closely held corporations, any attempt to quantify the degree and extent of these illegal payments is impossible.

For the case of foreign-owned corporations, a strategy followed by a number of respondents has been to "wait them out." It is traditional that a change in the presidency of Mexico carries along changes in ministerial appointments down through the fifth level. Exceptions are the Treasury Department, the Bank of Mexico, and the Foreign Ministry where senior technocrats tend to have greater tenure. One manager noted, "Our company has been here for fifty years; if we run into a block in a ministry, we just wait for the next election." In one case he waited four years for a new face in one Mexican agency.

In Mexico, a policy not to initiate a bribe or to resist extortion will generally slow the process of approval, but not necessarily cancel it. In a number of cases, the multinational management was unable to assess the exact cause of the painfully slow approval process. Others knew of specific circumstances where approval was slowed but not denied as management stepped behind the FCPA shield.

In some areas such as bidding on government contracts, the waiting strategy makes no sense and refusal to participate in extra "commissions" leaves one out of the bidding. This is a particularly difficult area. Here, there is a suggestion that unincorporated subsidiaries with shadow partners may be used as a device to channel funds. In two cases, however, we encountered strong, principled, effective action on the part of senior Mexican officials to eliminate this kind of corruption.

An area which invites corruption in every country, import and export licenses, has recently been changed in Mexico. Under President de la Madrid, import and export licenses have been largely replaced with tariffs.

The second level of communication is through business associations such as the Consejo Cordinador Empresarial, COPARMEX, the American Chamber of Commerce, or specific trade groups. With this mechanism, the contact can be made on the highest levels regarding the proposed policies. However, the influence of these associations on the government policies is only limited. They can be heard and the Mexican officials, even the President, are open to receive their arguments. However, this process never guarantees that their propositions or arguments would be followed.

The final level of contact can be through out-and-out political pressure as outlined in the pharmaceuticals. An interesting question is the effect that such communications will have on the overall process of relations of multinational corporations and the Mexican government. Will it cause Mexico to be more pliable, more open to the needs of U.S. business firms? Will it, on the other hand, cause resentment in the government and spark a recalcitrance that will make agreements more difficult to reach?

DIRECTIONS FOR THE FUTURE

The interviews in Mexico provided a snapshot of the relation between multinational corporations and the Mexican government. Multinational corporations have indeed found a niche in the corporatist structure of the country. Their niche is assured by their technology, by their capital, by their network of contacts and friends, by their contribution to the output and employment of the country. And as befits an element of the inclusive corporatist structure which has historically been Mexico's, their interests are generally taken into account in decision making. In this sense, it is correct to say, as do the government authorities, that there are no foreign firms operating in Mexico. All are Mexican firms. Everybody accommodates and all players benefit. As a Mexican manager graciously put it, "Being in Mexico is like being on a roller coaster. Things might go down but you know they will go up again. As a whole, you end up having a nice ride."

Of course, there have been changes over time, at least partly as a reflection of the external conditions which provide a context for these interactions. The period of the 1970s seemed to provide an opportunity to ensure the dominance of national needs in the relationship, while the economic difficulties and the debt overhang have clearly given the owners of foreign capital a stronger negotiating position. Yet it is clear that all of the power is not on one side. The Mexican government will continue to assess proposals and to choose those which it estimates are beneficial to the country. In part, this reflects the continuity of the stance toward foreign investment as a necessary evil. In part, it reflects the secondary role which foreign investment plays in the overall capital structure of the economy, accounting for between 4 percent and 5 percent of the total investment. Thus, foreign investment comes to be important mainly at the strategic margin.

At issue is the question of what in the international context might affect this role and this relation. On the one side, the pharmaceutical sectoral plan and the pressure which the U.S. government brought to bear may indicate a return to times of increased pressure in favor of foreign investors and foreign investment. On the other side, the government's willingness to undertake the steps to enter the GATT indicates that there is also an internal pressure toward improving the treatment of foreign investors, toward removing some of the restrictions on capital flows and some of the deviations from patent treatment. Of course the question is how far this process will be allowed to continue. It is possible that a subsequent Presidential sexenio could reverse these tendencies and go back to a much more nationalistic stance along the lines of Peru or even of Brazil. In part, this will depend upon internal definitions of whether the nation state is being jeopardized by the current treatment of foreign capital.

ENDNOTE

This series of seminars began by considering the role of multinationals in development, particularly the question of the relation of multinational managers and poverty in the Third World.

It is clear that in the Mexican case, the multinational corporations have been responsive and creative in developing and maintaining their niche in that corporatist structure. Although subject to extensive debate and interpretation, the usual positive and negative elements of their role can be found.[24] On the positive side, they have brought more technology, jobs, capital, and managerial expertise. On the negative side, they have resulted in some outflow of capital, probably more than was permitted because of flexibility in transfer prices. The capability to create technology has not been transferred, and they have generally geared their production to the upper end of the income distribution.

Still in a real sense, the positive or negative impact of the multinational is secondary to the fundamental reality that these firms have, to a large extent, adjusted their activities to fit the objectives of the

Mexican government. To the extent that the Mexican approach is developmental, the multinational corporations can be said to contribute to development.

Multinationals will be pressured by the government to provide increases in capital which Mexico needs, and we believe that it is in their best interest to respond. In our view, however, the present drive for exports and the associated emphasis on new technology will diminish the multinational corporate contribution to the poor. The necessary enhancements to productivity must come at the cost of less labor-intensive production techniques. Also, GATT will pressure local managers and strip away margins that could otherwise flow to developmentally responsive uses.

Governmental pressures for MNC contributions to the "popular sectors" seem to have declined. In past years, multinational managers have felt pressure from the government, real or imagined, to be more responsive to the broader elements of development. We encountered none of this ingredient in the demands of the present administration. Again, MNC efforts mirror governmental preference.

The fundamental question as to whether the policies of the Mexican government are developmental in its broadest sense is left unaddressed. In the future, this issue must remain subject to continuing debate, examining the role of politicians and of technicians in the ruling government, as well as of the growth in the role of the technicians.

APPENDIX A

General Resolutions

The National Commission on Foreign Investments approved a regrouping of General Resolutions under attributions conferred upon it by Articles 5, 12, and 14 of the Law to Promote Mexican Investment and Regulate Foreign Investment and those of its Regulations, as well as based on the "Accord that concrete acts of dependencies and entities of the Federal Public Administration should seek an administrative simplification, to speed up and provide transparency to procedures and transactions therein."

The Resolutions were approved by the National Commission on Foreign Investments in its session of July 25, 1984, and published in the *Diario Oficial de la Federación* (Official Daily Journal of the Constitutional Government of the United Mexican States) issue of August 30, 1984.

These Resolutions, in effect since August 31, 1984, are as follows:

1. General Resolutions such as, 1, 2, 4, 5, 6, 7, 8, 14, 15, 18, and 19 by the National Commission on Foreign Investments, published in the Official Gazettes of the Federation dated November 5, 1975, July 27, 1977, and October 11, 1982 are to be abrogated.
2. General Resolutions No. 3, 9, 10, 11, 12, 13, 16, and 17 by the National Commission on Foreign Investments, published in the Official Gazettes dated November 5, 1977, January 15, 1976, July 27 and September 6, 1977, March 4, 1980, November 19, 1984, and December 9, 1981, are still in force. Numerals are modified to the following:

GENERAL RESOLUTION NO. 1

Criteria to approve applications addressed to the National Commission on Foreign Investments and the Executive Secretary thereof.

GENERAL RESOLUTION NO. 2

Foreign investments in in-Bond companies.

GENERAL RESOLUTION NO. 3

Foreign investment in company management.

GENERAL RESOLUTION NO. 4

Criteria applicable to Article 8 of the Law to Promote Mexican Investment and Regulate Foreign Investment.

GENERAL RESOLUTION NO. 5

Foreign investments in capital stock of companies.

GENERAL RESOLUTION NO. 6

Authorizing trust funds.

GENERAL RESOLUTION NO. 7

Purchase of bearer stocks in Stock Exchange.

GENERAL RESOLUTION NO. 8

Authorizing and underwriting stock quoted in the Mexican Stock Exchange.

GENERAL RESOLUTION NO. 9

Expanding foreign investments.

GENERAL RESOLUTION NO. 10

Closing new establishments.

GENERAL RESOLUTION NO. 11

Tranferring stocks or assets among foreign investors pertaining to a group of the same interest.

GENERAL RESOLUTION NO. 12

Agreements on real estate sales operations published abroad.

GENERAL RESOLUTION NO. 13

New field of economic activity and lines of new products.

APPENDIX B

The List of Interviews

Aluminum Company of America
American Chamber of Commerce
Anderson Clayton & Co.
Baker & McKenzie — Mexico
Banco de México, S.A.
Banco Mexicano Somex, S.N.C. ·
Cementos Mexicanos, S.A.
Centro Universitario de Ciencias Humanas, A.C.
Chase Manhattan Bank, N.A.
Cía. Minera Autlán, S.A. de C.V.
Coca-Cola Export Corporation
Conek, S.A. de C.V.
Confederación Patronal de la República Mexicana
Coopers & Lybrand — México
Corporación Industrial San Luis, S.A. de C.V.
Eli Lilly de México, S.A. de C.V.
Escuela de Graduados en Administración — ITESM
General Electric de México, S.A.
General Motors de México, S.A. de C.V.
Hewlett Packard de México, S.A. de C.V.
Index, Economía Aplicada, S.A.
Johnson & Johnson de México, S.A. de C.V.
Nacional Financera, S.N.C.
Pfizer de México, S.A. de C.V.
Productos de Maíz, S.A.
Searle de México, S.A. de C.V.
Secretaría de Comercio y Fomento Industrial

NOTES

1. Ranjan Das, "Impact of Host Government Regulations on MNC Operation: Learning from Third World Countries," *Columbia Journal of World Business* (Spring 1981): p. 89.

2. Theodore Moran, "Conclusions and Policy Implications," in *Multinational Corporations: The Political Economy of Foreign Direct Investment*, ed. Theodore H. Moran (New York: Lexington Books, 1985), pp. 267–268.

3. The field study was conducted by Professors Kenneth Jameson, Department of Economics and Kellogg Institute; Juan Rivera, Department of Accountancy; and Lee Tavis, Department of Finance — all of the University of Notre Dame. A list of organizations in which interviews were conducted is included in Appendix B.

4. Business International, *Mexico: New Look at a Maturing Market* (New York: Business International Corporation, 1978), p. 75.

5. There are a number of excellent studies of Mexican industrial policy and of the Mexican stance toward foreign investment. See, for example, Merilee Grindle, "Public Policy, Foreign Investment, and Implementation Style in Mexico" in *Economic Issues and Political Conflict: U.S. Latin American Relations*, ed. Jorge Dominguez (New York: Butterworth, 1982) or Gary Gereffi, "The Renegotiation of Dependency and the Limits of State Autonomy in Mexico (1975–1982)," in *Multinational Corporations: The Political Economy of Foreign Direct Investment*, ed. Theodore Moran (New York: Lexington Books, 1985).

6. See Jorge Dominguez, *Economic Issues and Political Conflict: U.S. Latin American Relations* (New York: Butterworth, 1982).

7. National Commission of Foreign Investments, *Foreign Investments*: Juridical Framework and its Applications (Mexico Comisión Nacional de Inversiones Extranjeras, 1984), pp. 48–64, 95–111.

8. Flirtations with the GATT organization are not new to Mexico. During 1979–80, Mexico had negotiated very favorable terms with GATT and its entrance was imminent. However, by political decision, the proposal was rejected and shelved. See Robert G. Newell and Luis F. Rubio, *Mexico's Dilemma: The Political Origins of Economic Crisis* (Boulder, Col.: Westview Press, 1984), p. 199, and George W. Grayson, *The United States and Mexico, Patterns of Influence* (New York: Praeger, 1984), pp. 121–138.

9. For an excellent review of recent economic conditions of the Mexican economy and its perspectives for the future, see *Mexico and United States*, ed. Peggy B. Musgrave (Boulder, Col.: Westview Press, 1985) especially Francisco Gil Diaz, "Investments and Debt," pp. 3–32, and Thomas T. Trebat, "Mexico's Foreign Financing," pp. 33–70.

10. See Pedro Aspe and Paul E. Sigmund, eds., *The Political Economy of Income Distribution in Mexico* (New York: Holmes and Meier, 1984).

11. IBRD, World Development Report 1985 (New York: Oxford University Press, 1985).

12. Recent statistical data are from those published by Banco de Mexico, "Indicadores Economicos," various issues of the monthly bulletin prepared by the Subdirección de Investigación Económica.

13. See Kwan S. Kim, "Industrial Development in Mexico: Problems, Policy Issues, and Perspectives," in *Debt and Development in Latin America*, ed. Kwan S. Kim and David F. Ruccio (Notre Dame, Ind.: University of Notre Dame Press, 1985).

14. Ibid.

15. Richard Newfarmer and Willard Mueller, *Multinational Corporations in Brazil and Mexico: Structural Sources of Economic and Noneconomic Powers*, Report to the Subcommittee on Multinational Corporations of the Committee on Foreign Relations, August 1975, p. 54.

16. Grindle, "Public Policy, Foreign Investment, and Implementation Style in Mexico."

17. Newell and Rubio, *Mexico's Dilemma: The Political Origins of Economic Crisis*, p. 199.

18. Although our evidence must make any conclusions highly tentative, it was claimed, and we had no counter-examples, that MNCs would tend to enter joint ventures only with members of the "Consejo Mexicano de Hombres de Negocios" (Mexican Council of Businessmen). This is an association of the thirty-odd most important Mexican economic groups and it has separate representation as one of the six organizations which constitute the CCE, the highest business association in the country.

19. It is difficult to discern the impact of the Mexican bank nationalization that took place September 1, 1982 at the close of the López Portillo presidency. Among foreign investors there has been a loss in confidence in the Mexican banking system. One executive observed that the bank nationalization was the greatest barrier to the future rekindling of development in Mexico.

There is little evidence, however, that the National Credit Societies are serving a different function than they did as private banks before 1982. The present illiquidity in the economy and high reserve requirements (90 percent) are a result of economic conditions, not administrative caprices of the nationalized banks.

The Mexican banking system has always been closely controlled by the Banco de Mexico — interest rate ceilings, required lending allocation, and high reserve requirements. In this institutionally controlled environment, their impact on the flow of funds in the economy in the passage from private to public will be mitigated.

Over time inefficiences are likely to grow as with industrial parastatals. Chief executive officers, some of whom have no banking experience, are appointed, and banks are not allowed to fail. One clear change which may be beneficial has been the separation of banks from their previously associated industrial groups. This had been a largely unachieved objective of Mexican banking regulation for many years and it may provide MNCs with more access to domestic capital markets.

20. This section is drawn from interviews with Nacional Financiera and secondary sources.

21. A general analysis of the decrees affecting the automotive, textile, and steel industrial sector is presented in Sidney Weintraub, "Trade and Structural Change," in *Mexico and the United States*, ed. Peggy B. Musgrave (Boulder, Col.: Westview Press, 1985).

22. The export requirement for most multinationals is associated with a loss in overall systemic returns. Some respondents indicated that the Mexican components or products were replacing those produced at a lower cost elsewhere in the multina-

tional system. Others noted that Mexican productivity was comparable to other locations but the multinational had preferred to deliver Mexican products to Mexican markets because of the high markups available in the protected domestic markets.

23. The automotive sectoral decrees provide a good example of how regulation has changed over time. For example, just in the area of lines of vehicles and engines, General Motors of Mexico has seen the following changes.

1962 GMM was authorized to produce Chevrolet standard size models, the Opel line, and commercial trucks.

1972 Companies producing compact, standard, and sporty automobiles could not produce popular-type cars. (Using this premise, GMM was able to incorporate the Chevy Nova and drop the Opel line), 60 percent of any new engine authorized for production must be exported.

1977 Only companies with majority Mexican ownership may be authorized to produce different vehicle lines than those already approved. However, authorization may be obtained to produce different models, when significant technological changes are involved. Diesel engines for the original equipment market can be incorporated on trucks, trailer trucks, and integral buses only by companies with majority Mexican ownership. (Diesel engines for passenger care are not restricted.)

1983 Starting with 1984, the government will authorize only 3 lines and 7 models; 1985/86, 2 lines and 5 models; and 1987, one line and 5 models. It will be possible to obtain additional lines authorization based on a self-sufficient balance of trade.

There have been similar developments in regulations on engine size, exports, local integration, local content, optional equipment, and vehicle selling prices.

On this topic, see also Douglas C. Bennett and Kennth E. Sharpe, *Transnational Corporation Versus the State: The Political Economy of the Mexican Auto Industry* (Princeton, N.J.: Princeton University Press, 1985).

24. See Michael J. Francis and Cecilia G. Manrique, "Clarifying the Debate" in the first volume of this series, pp. 68–89.

Patterns of Similarity and Difference

ERNESTO MARCOS*

The most striking effect of the Korean paper was that I thought I was reading the Mexican paper. Many of the descriptions of how multinationals have to cooperate with a democracy would still be valid if the name were changed from "Korea" to "Mexico." Perhaps Americans who come to Mexico and find that almost everyone can speak English and looks occidental don't realize that in the basic social culture we are much more similar to Asian than to Western countries. On the other hand these cultural similarities contrast with economic dissimilarities, and in our two countries, multinational corporations serve different roles.

CULTURAL SIMILARITIES

Like Korea, Mexico is a hierarchical society in which status and recognition are very important. We, too, have an authoritarian bureaucracy with extensive discretionary power to determine the merits of projects. Xenophobia stemming from a long history of foreign invasions is also very valid for Mexico—we lost half of our territory last century to the United States. Most Mexican corporations, large and small, are run as family groups. The attitude toward the law is also similar to that in Korea. In Mexico, we see contracts more as symbols of commitment to a business relationship rather than as working con-

*Ernesto G. Marcos is director general of Nacional Financiera, the National Development Bank of Mexico. He was formerly head officer of the Department of Economic Programing of the General Direction for Economic and Social Programing in the Ministry of the Mexican Presidency.

239

tracts, and we almost never go to the courts to solve a problem. These cultural characteristics that we share with Asian countries must be considered in understanding the interaction between multinational corporations and host governments.[1]

DIFFERENT ECONOMIC STRUCTURES

Although we are culturally similar, some statistics will illustrate the differences between Mexico and Korea, both in development strategies and in the involvement of multinational corporations. These statistical comparisons must be understood in the light of two important differences. First, the Mexican economy is slightly more than twice the size of the Korean economy. This is a significant difference. Also, unlike Korea, where the role of multinationals has been marginal (and their participation in that economy is more recent), in Mexico those corporations have had a leading role for a long time. When the investment law was passed in 1973, almost all of the 500 largest American firms were already there. It is clear, therefore, that the regulations are necessarily different from those in Korea.

In Mexico, foreign affiliates are responsible for more than 35 percent of total manufacturing production, compared to less than 15 percent in Korea, reflecting the important differences in the level of participation by MNCs. Mexico's growth strategy has been import-oriented; Korea's, export-oriented. In Mexico, we export less than 10 percent of our manufacturing production, whereas Korea exports more than 30 percent. These two basic facts—level of participation by MNCs and the countries' development strategies—can explain almost all the differences in approach to regulation of the foreign investor that were outlined in the two field research reports.

Of course, one need go only a little deeper to find even more fundamental differences. Korea has been far more successful than Mexico in competing for international markets. In 1984, Mexican exports of manufactured products amounted to 2.5 billion dollars, compared to 20 billion for Korea. The ratio of manufacturing exports to total exports is 11 percent in Mexico and 85 percent in Korea. It is a fact that most of our exports continue to be raw materials, mainly minerals and oil. It is also true that Korea invests three times as much as Mexico in research and development. It is then not surprising that in 1982 the Mexican ratio of imports of capital goods to total imports was 31 percent, whereas in Korea it was less than 10 percent.

Mexico, of course, has a greater public sector participation. Public expenditures in Mexico represent 32 percent of GNP, and only 20 percent in Korea. Korea has a much better record in terms of income distribution. The lower 40 percent of the population gets 17 percent of the total income in Korea, but less than 10 percent in Mexico. Of the newly industrialized countries, only Brazil has a lower share of income flowing to the poor than Mexico.

A very important difference is that the Mexican consumer resembles a consumer in the United States. This is not the case in Korea. Consider a striking statistic: in Korea there is one car for every 105 inhabitants; in Mexico, one for every 15. It is not easy to refrain from consumption in Mexico because of the 3,000-kilometer northern border shared with the United States.

GOVERNMENT REGULATION

To understand the Mexican regulation of multinationals the central role of these firms in the Mexican economy must be recognized. To say that the magnitude of foreign investment in Mexico does not exceed 7 percent of total fixed assets might be misleading. When one looks at specific markets, the leadership of multinational firms becomes very clear. By focusing on the three or four most important enterprises in each specific market, foreign investment is found to be quite pervasive. These three or four companies will dominate that market with a coverage as high as 80 or 85 percent. Of almost 70,000 firms in Mexico that have foreign stockholders, more than 3,000 are majority or totally foreign-owned. More than 70 percent of foreign investment is of U.S. origin. And multinationals accounted for almost 30 percent of ongoing exports last year.

Given these facts, I cannot agree with the paper's contention that the Mexican government considers multinationals a necessary evil. Rather, I would characterize our approach as "high threshold," setting very stict conditions for entry which then are negotiated to more favorable terms on an individual basis. The rule of Mexican majority ownership is not intended for general application; it is only an initial position from which the government wants to enter into further negotiations for each specific case. In some other countries, the opposite approach prevails: "Let them in and squeeze them later." That is, very easy entry conditions can be followed by domestic operating controls and restrictive profit repatriation.

What was not clearly stated in the Mexican paper is that the Mexican government prefers the joint-venture approach for the same reasons argued in the Korean paper. The government sees joint ventures as the most fertile ground for absorbing advanced technologies, as the most effective way for Westerners to work in a cross-cultural environment, and also as an effective way for the government to force compliance with national policies without directly confronting the foreign investors.

Difficulties with joint ventures were overstated in the paper. It was said, for example, that potential loss of managerial control by the multinational corporation or joint ventures with state-owned agencies impose specific problems because they can sacrifice the interests of the U.S. partner in pursuit of macro-economic or political governmental policies. It also was said that the Mexican partners are likely to be directly affected by difficulties in the Mexican economy, seriously jeopardizing their resources. We have found no evidence, however, that any of these possibilities have occurred. Perhaps Steinberg's phrase, it is not Asia that is inscrutable, it is our lack of understanding that makes it seem so, also applies to Mexico.

Another perceived difficulty might also be eased by better understanding of cultural considerations. The paper described the flexibility in application of Mexican law as particularly frustrating to U.S. managers, although managers in Mexico seem perfectly able and willing to operate in this environment. Their problem, the paper stated, is in making parent firms understand the situation — its constraints and its possibilities. I understand that many U.S. companies assign the monitoring of the Mexican operation, like the Canadian operation, to their domestic division rather than to the international division. People in charge of the domestic divisions are not sensitive to cultural difference.

A significant issue is the well-documented case of the U.S. government intervention with the Mexican government regarding the sectoral pharmaceutical degree of 1982. We no longer have a trilateral relation between local partners, the Mexican government, and foreign partners. We now must somehow include the foreign company's government. This can significantly change the negotiating positions. Perhaps the U.S. government also assigns operations in Mexico to domestic representatives.

SUMMARY

The Mexican paper offers a significant advance in understanding the actual process of communication between multinationals and the Mexican government. Multinationals have indeed found a niche in the structure of this country's economy. In fact, unlike the Korean situation, multinationals operate as part of the business system in Mexico, even though they don't have a position in the Institutional Revolutionary Party (PRI). Unlike other countries, direct communication between managers of multinational corporations and governmental officials is very effective in Mexico. Perhaps this strong relationship at the personal level opens the potential for multinational managers to participate in the developmental responsibility. It also obviously implies a certain degree of influence in designing rules and strategies for development[2].

Finally, I strongly support the conclusion of the study, that in the foreseeable future, Third World societies, particularly Mexico, will need direct foreign investment more than ever to help relieve the pressures of paying off their foreign debt. The role of multinationals in the development process of these countries clearly points in the direction of larger and more selective participation and responsibilities.

NOTES

1. It would be very interesting to analyze how U.S. corporations operate in Mexico compared to how Japanese and European corporations operate there. A number of interesting differences in approach will become apparent.

2. For example, the American Chamber of Commerce in Mexico, which is the largest American Chamber in the world, has instituted an annual award among its members. It is called Teponaztli, a Mexican-Indian name, in recognition of outstanding contributions of American companies to programs geared to social or community development in Mexico.

Patterns of Similarity and Difference

WILLIAM P. GLADE*

The influence of culture[1] on enterprise organization and business behavior has engaged the interest of a modest band of scholars over the years, yet the results of this culturological approach are, to say the least, inconclusive. Many are the times that the lakes of Notre Dame have frozen over since Fayerweather published his *The Executive Overseas*[2] and Hall's *The Silent Language*[3] first appeared, but we are still skating on thin ice when it comes to generating a systematic set of propositions in this field. For the most part, efforts to relate culture to business have tended toward the anecdotal or have simply catalogued the kinds of behavior traits of which tourists or diplomats commonly want to be aware.[4] Works of the quality of Benedict's examination of family and firm in Africa[5] or Abegglen's look into the Japanese factory[6] have been more the exception than the rule, though the seminar on entrepreneurship that was organized a number of years ago by Greenfield, Strickon, and Aubey[7] must also be reckoned among the more serious and successful efforts along this line. Entrepreneurial research, in fact, has been the area of business studies in which culture as an explanatory variable has been most frequently, if not always profitably, used.[8]

On the other hand, the systematic cross-national examination of various government-business relations has been undertaken much more often and, on the whole, with relatively greater success. Specialists from a variety of fields — economics, law, political science, and so on — have

*William P. Glade is a professor of economics and past director of the Institute of Latin American Studies at the University of Texas at Austin. A recognized authority on economic development, he is a member of Notre Dame's Helen Kellogg Institute for International Studies Advisory Council.

mined this area to advantage. Nevertheless, explicit attention to the influence of culture on government-business interaction is still in its infancy, not unlike the study of the cultural underpinnings of enterprise generally. Hence, the work of this seminar in pushing a path through what, analytically speaking, is poorly charted territory is especially to be appreciated.

COMMON FACTORS IN DEVELOPMENT

As it happens, one of the most interesting findings supports the views held by many in the development field that trans-cultural structural factors may be more important than distinctively cultural ones in shaping policy response to problems. Both Korea and Mexico, for example, are late industrializers and have successfully launched their respective programs in the shadow of a large neighbor that ranks among the major industrial powers. Both have, though in very different circumstances, been exposed to strong cultural, political, and economic influences from the neighbors, and both have been suppliers of labor to the large expanding economies next door. Interestingly, too, in Korea as in Mexico, industrial development was predicated on a comprehensive agrarian reform, albeit the programs were of very different design, and policy implementation took place in very different contexts. "Hardstate authoritarian" could be the descriptor of the political system in either country, to round out the parallels. While situational differences abound, no less than cultural ones, one cannot fail to be struck by the fact that in both countries govenment has played a major role in propelling the economy forward. This is, of course, exactly what one might expect in the light of the structuralist analysis of Eckstein, Gerschenkron, Mark, and others.[9]

It has been popular in recent years to contrast the export-oriented industrial success of Asia's four "Little Tigers" with the more problematic record of Latin America's import-substituting route, a contrast that is certainly valid as a characterization of the dominant strategy in each set of cases. What is questionable is the tendency of some to go beyond this and associate the Asian policy preference with market economics, in contrast to Latin America's clear predilection for interventionism. As the papers we have heard indicate, however, the visible hand of the entrepreneurial state has, in Korea quite as much as in Mexico, been employed in lieu of the invisible hand of the market. (In Taiwan, too, consciously active government policy has been one of the main ingredients in the recipe for growth.)

If the papers have dispelled the popular myth that devotion to market magic is a differentiating factor, they have at the same time invited us to direct our attention to several factors that are possibly culture-based and that play a role in accounting for inter-country differences. Such differences, in turn, could conceivably tell us something useful about the relative efficacy of development policy and different patterns of government-business interaction. At best, it is these factors, rather than whether the public sector plays second fiddle to private enterprise or vice versa, that may yield more understanding of the nuances of contemporary economic experience.

The papers suggest several promising possibilities for closer scrutiny. One, for example, is the greater readiness of the Koreans to adopt an ethic of population control. This factor does not seem to be attributable to the degree of urbanization or the average per capita income level, for Korea ranks lower than Mexico in these respects (though in literacy it is somewhat higher). Surely here lies part of the explanation for the fact that from 1960 through 1981, the average annual rate of growth in per capita income was 6.9 percent in Korea compared with 3.8 percent in Mexico. Suggestive, too, is the seemingly greater measure of social discipline that prevails in Korea — a disciplined work ethic, driven by ambition and a value on performance that has, possibly, more parallels in northern Europe than in Mediterranean cultures. It would appear, further, that there is a marked disparity between the two in the socially tolerable levels of public corruption. The evidence is hardly the kind that would withstand rigorous testing, but despite the fact that widespread gift-giving is institutionalized in Korea, Mexico seems to outdo the Asian country in the prevasiveness of payoffs and bribes and in the diversion of public funds to private use, to say nothing of favoritism in the allocation of resources and official privilege. It is in Mexico, after all, that recent presidents, ostensibly committed to cleaning up, have ended their terms by mopping up instead.

More measurable are the income differentials that are judged to be socially acceptable, among different classes as well as between rural and urban segments of society. By all indications Korea comes out as the country with significantly smaller disparities among income classes and between urban and rural people. Whereas, for instance, the bottom two quintiles in Mexico receive 9.9 percent of household income, in Korea the corresponding figure is 16.9 percent. The third quintile in Mexico takes in 12 percent of the household income; in Korea, 15.4 percent. Health and other statistics also tend to bear out the contention that dualism is less pronounced in Korea than in Mexico.

Social organization reflects cultural variables in other ways as well. The decisional process in both Mexico and Korea looks woolly to North Americans. However, in Korea this process seems to go hand-in-hand with a greater sense of direction and a greater application in following up on objectives—which may, of course, relate to the factor of social discipline. Alternatively, it could also be said that policy goals are, in Korea, more sharply defined to begin with, and ordered in priority, whereas in Mexico there is a tendency—born, perhaps, of the process of consensus building—to enunciate so many and diffused development objectives that concerted action over a sustained interval proves difficult if not impossible. (However, there may well be political circumstances in which mumbling is preferable to clear enunciation.) In this respect there is a curious parallel in the policy style of the two countries' influential neighbors. The industrial targeting Korea has borrowed from Japan contrasts sharply with Mexico's shopping-list approach which rather resembles the sprawling policy agenda of the United States.

From all the foregoing, it could be argued that in policy implementation there is notably less slippage and goal displacement in Korea than in Mexico and that there is, in addition, greater overall policy coherence and consistency. It is not easy to trace this slippage because in many fields the repercussions may be fairly indirect. In one area, however, there are some fairly good indicators. World Bank figures show the Mexican government spending substantially more per capita than Korea on health and education, from a per capita income level that is also somewhat higher than Korea's. Yet, Korea comes out generally ahead of Mexico on various health and education indicators. Discrepancies of this sort provide at least an indirect measure of routine administrative efficiency and policy effectiveness.

On the other hand, the ambiguity and policy slack in the Mexican system could also be interpreted as providing a political cushion through which intergroup conflicts are blunted a well as room for a pragmatic adaptation to changing circumstances. Though uncertainty can be a problem in business calculations, in Mexico it would seem to have its use as a mechanism of system maintenance on the political side. So, too, may the corruption. By all odds, the political structure of the country has become shakier than it used to be, and the once vaunted revolutionary consensus has tended to fray. Nevertheless, like the famous wooden cathedral of St. George in Guyana, the Institutional Revolutionary Party (PRI) may be tottering, but it is still a rather magnificent wreck — and, arguably, not yet quite beyond all hope of repair. It may well be, as liberalization moves ahead that the Korean government will wish that it were so lucky as to have such a structure to renovate.

Still other variations in cultural patterns prompt reflection on the different operation of the two societies. A case in point might be welfare expenditures in Mexico, which are much higher than in Korea, though apparently less efficacious. While this suggests that to some extent public consensus is an item for hire, it could also mean that the Western norms generated by the industrialized North Atlantic societies have been earlier and more pervasively incorporated into Latin American public expectations and preferences than has yet been the case in Asia. In contrast, Korean military spending is far higher than are Mexican outlays. Although much of this doubtlessly reflects the proximity of an aggressively hostile regime in North Korea, recent tensions lead one to wonder if there may not also be a connection between armed coercion and the maintenance of domestic discipline. The Korean social compact, in other words, may to some extent be an enforced consensus and not just something that arises spontaneously from a common agreement on the background values provided by Confucianism. If this is so, then the resources spent on the Korean military are partly a functional counterpart to the resources spent in Mexico on various welfare programs, or those "lost" through corruption and assorted policy contradictions and inconsistencies, all of which represent ways of appeasing contending groups and managing conflict.

Interestingly, several other contributions to this project shed corroborating light on the cultural basis of policy slippage and goal displacement in Mexico. Archbishop McGrath notes how certain normative teachings in Latin American culture have been formally acknowledged but little observed in practice, a lapse that applies to the secular belief system of the Mexican Revolution no less than to the religious belief system the Archbishop explores. Exactly the same disparity carries over into the operations of Latin American legal systems, as Rosenn tellingly illustrates. Both observations are fully consistent with the policy behavior and expectations ascribed to Mexico. By the same token, Steinberg's interpretation does much to buttress Kim's characterization of the more goal-focused policy process in Korea.

In this brief survey of the suggested explanatory elements of a cultural nature, one other clue of possible significance lies buried in Kim's brief discussion of joint ventures. Not uncommonly, he reports, foreign investors find themselves in conflict with their local partners, the former preferring more short-range goals of high profits and the latter inclining toward longer-range goals and payoffs. Interestingly, this divergence in preferences seems to run almost exactly counter to the nature of the time-horizon conflicts reported for joint ventures in other parts of the world, particularly Latin America. Does this suggest the operation of a stronger reality principle (i.e., a preference for deferred gratification) in Asia than in Latin America and, possibly, a higher savings function?

BUSINESS GOVERNMENT INTERFACE

In the last analysis, our interest is in how all of this affects the rather ample interface between business and government in the two societies, particularly the relations of multinationals with their hosts. As the papers demonstrate, a cultural influence can plausibly be posited, but the variations on the relationships do not sort themselves out into neat categories. From what is reported, it would seem that, despite the presence of informal connections between business and government in both countries, the Korean government-business interactions may be more likely structured on a basis of more-or-less continuing consultation through regular institutional channels and perhaps more likely suffused with technocratic considerations, though Jameson and Rivera show that these have gained ground in Mexico in recent years. On the other hand, some institutionalized communication is also found in the corporate structure of Mexico, as Jameson and Rivera make plain, and in both countries multinational corporations may find many of their contacts with the state mediated by local interests, whether partners or associations. For our puposes, regular consultation may be assumed to result in a richer exchange of information, to the benefit of decisional processes, while the influence of technocratic norms would operate to reduce the risk of goal displacement or substitution and, presumably, lead to a preference for instrumental-universalistic over affective-particularistic criteria in decision making—to lapse into the Weberian-Parsonian language that was so popular some years ago. The papers give us some reason to believe that a technocratic centering on stated goals has been less likely to be deflected by instrumentally extraneous factors (*mordidas*, political trading, etc.) in Korea than in Mexico, but the differences are possibly narrowing over time.

CULTURAL CONVERGENCE AND POLICY

If it is reasonable to suppose that cultural differences bear on the nature of contemporary business-government interactions in each country, the distinctiveness that this implies may, for structural reasons, tend to diminish in the future. Three factors lie behind this convergence. In first place stand the socialization and recruitment of leadership. Over the past decade or so, public-sector staffing in Mexico has brought into the upper and middle echelons of the state a growing number of more technocratically trained functionaries, who are, in addition, much more likely than were their predecessors in public office to have been educated in private schools or abroad. Recruitment processes, therefore, would seem to favor the emergence in Mexico of a more technically adept officialdom—one which, moreover, will increasingly share ties of family, friendship, and professional formation with private business leaders, whatever the communications gap at present. In this, the relationship may eventually resemble the Korean one.

Second, the collapse of the petroleum market and the Mexican decision to enter the General Agreement on Tariffs and Trade (GATT) will almost certainly constrain that country's policy, moving it in a direction that bears greater similarity to that of Korea. Systematic and consistent attention will have to be given to diversifying and expanding exports of nontraditional character, and this is likely to move the country toward some form of industrial targeting and a clearer identification of priorities. What is more, the shift from a "sheltered workshop" manufacturing sector to one more exposed to the winds of international competition should force the cost structure of traded goods, if not of nontraded goods, to conform to internationally competitive standards. With the movement, in turn, there will be less and less room in the economy for absorbing the costs of corruption and those associated with a too casual policy management.

Third, there is a dawning awareness that multinational corporations in particular are gatekeepers for a whole range of information inputs to which Mexican policymakers need fuller access: information on product design, production methods, research and development, overseas marketing channels, etc. Both policy design and implementation, in other words, should favor the development of a greater institutional porosity vis-à-vis foreign enterprise than the county has hitherto managed to put together. If the drastic fall in export earnings has not sufficed to bring this to pass, the concurrent throttling down of access to external lenders would clearly have done so. Together the two adversities, along with entry into GATT, have foreclosed a number of the policy options of the past by radically restructuring the opportunity costs of alternative courses of action.

All of this, finally, revolves to the point mentioned near the outset: the structuring impact of circumstances (or environment) on public policy and institutional behavior today. Cultural factors remain helpful in understanding many inter-country differences in business and government behavior, as well as relations between the two sets of institutions, for social solutions to particular problems are culture traits quite as much as are attitudes, values, and beliefs. Yet as time progresses, the likelihood is that structural exigencies will operate increasingly to conform behavior and policy to an underlying set of technical-organizational patterns. Differences between Korea and Mexico may, therefore, be smaller in the future than they are today, though, as the example of Japan indicates, there is no reason to expect that cultural distinctiveness need wither away, let alone vanish, in response to the spread of a common mode of production.

NOTES

1. Let me make explicit in this comment what seems implicit in the deliberations of this seminar: namely, that we are employing the term "culture" not in the full anthropological sense (which would include material culture) but as a shorthand way of referring to the complex of such things as attitudes, values and preferences, beliefs, systems of cognition, model personality orientations, prevailing behavioral expectations, and expressive traits.

A more anthropological conceptualization of culture as the full range of non-biological needs would also comprehend laws, social organization and relationships, and such like, in which case one could not logically speak of "cultural influences on government or business (or government-business relations)" since the latter would be part and parcel of the culture, helping to give it shape in the first place. Nevertheless, as the more restricted meaning is the one clearly underlying the discussions here, my comments will conform to this usage.

2. John Fayerweather, *The Executive Overseas* (Syracuse, New York: Syracuse University Press, 1959).

3. Edward T. Hall, *The Silent Language* (Garden City, New York: Doubleday, 1959).

4. We are, of course, skirting past the "grand theories" of culture and economic organization as represented by the work of Tawney, Weber, Polanyi, Veblen, and others. More immediately helpful, though there is not space to cite the abundant literature in the field, is the work that Smelser, Moore, Whyte, and others have done on the sociology of economic life, to say nothing of the contributions of Geertz and others in the field of economic anthropology.

5. Burton Benedict, "Family Firms and Economic Development," *Southwestern Journal of Anthropology* 24 (1968): pp. 1–19.

6. James C. Abegglen, *The Japanese Factory* (Glencoe, Illinois: Free Press, 1958).

7. Sidney M. Greenfield, Arnold Strickon, and Robert T. Aubey, editors, *Entrepreneurs in Cultural Context* (Albuquerque, New Mexico: University of New Mexico Press, 1979).

8. One of the more ambitious examples of this genre was Everett Hagen's *On the Theory of Social Change* (Homewood, Illinois: Dorsey Press, 1962), a work which for all its heroic synthesis also illustrates the methodological difficulties of a culturological approach. For a suggestive attempt to relate cultural variables to public-sector entrepreneurship, see Ira Sharkansky's *Whither the State? Politics and Public Enterprise in Three Countries* (Chatham, New Jersey: Chatham House Publishers, 1979).

9. Alexander Eckstein, "Individualism and the Role of the State in Economic Growth," *Economic Development and Cultural Change* 6 (1958): pp. 81–87; Alexander Gerschenkron, "Economic Backwardness in Historical Perspective," in *The Progress of Underdeveloped Countries*, ed. B. F. Hoselitz, (Chicago: University of Chicago Press, 1952); Louis Mark, "The Favored Status of the State Entrepreneur in Economic Development Programs," *Economic Development and Cultural Change*, 7 (1959): pp. 422–430.

Patterns of Similarity and Difference

GEORGE SUTER*

While they have similar objectives, there are also natural different interests among a host government, local entrepreneurs, and multinational corporations. This is an important starting point to better understand the interactions among these groups in Mexico and Korea.

The field studies pointed to the multinational corporate goal to do business in local markets, set against the host government's interests in, for example, promoting exports. This divergence of objectives is particularly important in the pharmaceutical industry. There are few pharmaceutical markets that are not served by local production and essentially saturated. Pfizer has exported from Korea to other Southeast Asian markets in the past, but is now finding that these opportunities are becoming fewer and fewer. This situation exists across Asia. In China, for example, possibilities of a joint venture are limited by the ability to find other markets, outside of China, to which pharmaceuticals could be exported. Exports are necessary in order to generate the foreign exchange necessary to pay for raw materials.

Normally, when a multinational is accepted as an investor in the country, it expects to be accorded what is referred to as "national treatment." Unfortunately, we frequently find that, in the course of events, treatment is not quite so national and may even border on discrimination. In many instances, the multinational is not afforded the same provisions in doing business that a national company would be. The

*George Suter is vice president — administration, Europe, Africa, and Middle East of Pfizer International Inc. He has resided and worked abroad for multinational firms in Thailand, Singapore, Malaysia, and Pakistan throughout most of his professional career, and was president of the American Chamber of Commerce of the Philippines on three separate, non-consecutive occasions.

divergence of interest between multinationals and host governments seems to explain the non-tariff barriers imposed on multinationals or discrimination in operational regulations.

A key point of differences in a number of Third World countries (and for that matter, in some First World countries) is the protection of industrial property rights. Many host governments are convinced that they should have free access to technology on essential products. The pharmaceutical companies, of course, believe that they own that technology and seek a contribution to their product development costs, which often run over $1 million per product.

In spite of the divergent objectives, we have found that the interaction with host governments, involving the operation of the multi-national's subsidiary, can work well. Both papers noted that nothing is ever cast in concrete in Third World countries and that, in reality, everything is negotiable with the host governments. Multinationals are, indeed, treated on a case-by-case basis. Understanding this can be of great managerial benefit. In my experience, a persuasive argument can generally negotiate conditions which enable the business to be managed with reasonable profitability.

Still, the question remains as to how to correctly interact with the host government. A firm can either "go it alone," work through local industry associations, or act through the American Chambers of Commerce. The most appropriate starting point is through the local industry association. These associations include all segments of the industry, not just the foreign investors. Local firms, as well as multi-nationals, face many of the same problems associated with regulation of the private sectors. In the pharmaceutical industry, this includes dealing with ministries of health. In many countries, the ministry of health can be the most demanding and inflexible part of the bureaucracy.

Alternatively, there are some issues that are specific to the foreign investors. Here, the American Chamber of Commerce is a good vehicle to interact, as a group, with the host government.

As a last resort, it may be necessary to "go it alone." This is not an easy approach. The Korean paper discussed the problems of ex-patriate managers dealing with senior government officials. As noted, the governmental officials far prefer to deal with the joint-venture partner. While this can be an effective conduit, it does have dangers as outlined in the paper.

In Southeastern Asia, as opposed to the situation in Korea, my experience suggests that governmental officials are more receptive to direct contact and exhibit strong concern to maintain a favorable climate for foreign investors. Still, to "go it alone" can be a rocky, if not treacherous path. In these interactions, particularly if they involve senior corporation officials with senior governmental officials, neither of whom are directly involved with the issue at hand, there is great opportunity for misinformation and misinterpretation. Hence, in my view, associations, particularly host country industrial associations, are surely the safest form of interaction, and can often be effective.

Finally, we should add a fourth party to the interaction among the host government, local entrepreneurs, and multinationals — the United States government. The Trade Act of 1984, Section 301, provides a mechanism for U.S. companies to request governmental intervention on their behalf in situations where the company management believes conditions are adverse to investments. In the past year, the U.S. government under Section 301 of the Trade Act has raised key issues on intellectual property rights with the Korean government.

Coping with Extortion and Bribery*

Any discussion of multinational corporate-host government interaction must address the opportunities for and frequent charges of extortion and bribery. To say that extortion and bribery are immoral and illegal is not to address the issue. Corruption exists in every culture and every country. It involves the structure of the various institutions as well as the attitudes of individuals.

Each country has its own traditions, and each is at its own stage in the cultural and legal evolution of the notion of bribery. Korean gift-giving practices are rooted in the centuries-old tradition of supporting those in high places. Mexico is presently where the United States was a quarter-century ago in its ability to identify and prosecute extortion and bribery.

*John D. Collins is a partner in the firm of Peat, Marwick, Mitchell and Company. He is the partner in charge of the Audit, Long Range Planning, and Research Group in the Department of Professional Practice Accounting and Auditing, the vice chairman of the firm's Auditing Procedures Committee, and a United States representative on the International Auditing Procedures Committee.

José Antonio Fernández-Arena is an associate of Centro Universitario de Ciencias Humanas, A.C. Previously he served in Mexico City as assistant to the General Attorney and advisor to the President, establishing an office of anti-corruption.

John T. Noonan, Jr. is a judge of the U.S. Court of Appeals for the Ninth Circuit and the Robbins Professor Emeritus at the University of California, Berkeley. A recognized scholar in the areas of church history, canon law, and theological development, he has served as a consultant to the Papal Commission on the Family, the Presidential Commission on Population and the American Future, and the United States Catholic Conference. In 1984, Judge Noonan was awarded the Laetare Medal by the University of Notre Dame.

Michael E. Shannon is an executive vice president, chief administrative officer, and chief financial officer with Economics Laboratory, Inc. He was with Republic Steel Corporation for nine years as treasurer, executive vice president, and chief financial officer; and also served in various domestic and international financial positions with Gulf Oil Corporation in Europe, Africa, and the Middle East.

Four panelists were asked to comment on the implications of the Mexican and Korean field findings for strategies of coping with corruption: Michael A. Shannon, a multinational view; John D. Collins, an auditor's view; John T. Noonan, Jr., a moral view; and José Antonio Fernández-Arena, a governmental view. These panelists shared their analyses of how multinationals and host countries might deal with bribery and corruption. Each noted that bribery is a fact of life in all countries and cultures, but it is not quantifiable because people don't talk about it.

Judge Noonan compared bribery to witchcraft.

I often ask people in business about their own experience and that of others with bribery. With few exceptions, they outline the conditions in the various countries and note that, while they do not pay bribes, other people do. As a matter of fact, I have never met anybody who paid a bribe himself. A colleague of mine compared bribery to witchcraft in Africa. There, nobody does witchcraft himself, but everyone knows about someone who does.

If there are opportunities, extortion and bribery will occur. Both multinational corporations and host governments must continually monitor to ensure that they discourage rather than encourage extortion and bribery.

MULTINATIONAL CORPORATE COPING

Michael Shannon crisply outlined a policy which he believes should be adopted by all multinational corporations.

While the subject of corporate bribery is immensely complex and murky, corporate strategy must be universal. The evolution of thought on the question of bribery within our own society is not identical to that of other societies. Yet, the nature of corporate systems demands a simple response to this complex and murky issue because if it isn't simple, it will never be communicated or implemented. We are forced to apply a universal program. It cannot be tailored to each society. The managerial requirement is not the only one, of course, since U.S. multinationals are not only spurred on by the Foreign Corrupt Practices Act but also aided by its existence.

The principle is simple: Don't do it. The question is, "Why don't you do it?" The answer in today's multinational corporate environment is multifaceted but it gets down to something which is fundamental—for American multinational corporations, bribery in any of its forms, whether it works or not, is corrupting. Judge Noonon pointed out how it is morally corrupting. It is also organizationally corrupting.

Corruption is one of the most difficult problems to contain within corporations. To bribe is to pay money to a governmental official, directly or indirectly, to obtain something. The bribe must be funded and the money accounted for in some way. Since bribery is illegal for an American corporation, I can assure you that this funding and accounting will involve those associated with the action in conspiracy if they are part of a well-controlled U.S. multinational. Any corporate control system is designed to prevent people from drawing funds and spending them for their own purposes.

The accounting requirement draws the conspirators into terrible judgments about whom they are going to tell and whom they are not going to tell. Once a manager starts lying, lying becomes the mode of the operation.

Some will say, "There are always ways to handle that. You transfer money to your partners in those countries and they make the payments. You never have to get personally involved." I can tell you right now that most boards of directors know about indirect payments through intermediary partners and they are very aware of their liabilities as directors, especially when they look at the market for liability insurance on directors and officers.

When I must talk to the members of the board's audit committee about illegal payments and compliance with the Foreign Corrupt Practices Act, the first thing they say is, "You have a clean report as far as the code of conduct goes but, tell us, is there anything of which you are aware in our operation, that of our affiliates, or any operation with which we have a connection that involves a payment, not necessarily on our behalf, but perhaps by some other party?" If I have knowledge of such payments, I must either tell them or lie. In our organization, my position is well known. The conspiracy must thus go around me. What kind of situation do you have if you cannot talk to the chief financial and administrative officer of the corporation about serious corporate business?

Bribery is, indeed, corrupting.

Still, when opposing the obvious policy, the response of many managers is that the policy is naive. They say, "Out in the real world, we compete with others who do not follow these rules. They come from jurisdictions that don't have laws like ours." That is true. But anyone in a senior management position spends as much time turning down business as accepting it. One obvious reason is believing that the customer will be unable to pay. Sometimes a company does not have the financial resources to support the growth, and in some cases the amount of money to be made simply does not warrant the risk. Sometimes you just don't want to deal with those people. Turning down business is not automatically bad.

Moreover, refusing to give a bribe does not necessarily mean losing the business.

There are three tests to which any corporate decision must be subjected. Bribery fails all three of them. The first test is obvious and straightforward: Is it legal? The second reflects the appropriate response for multinationals: Does it work? Is it pragmatic? The third is different but equally important: Can you talk about it?

Let me share two examples from my personal experience that strongly reinforce the need for a clear policy and the imposition of these three rules.

The first involves the Gulf Oil Corporation in Korea. I was the treasurer of Gulf Oil's operation in Europe, Africa, and the Middle East at the time, on the other side of the world from Korea, but I have read the McCloy Report[1] and am generally familiar with what happened there. The need for a domestic petroleum operation in the developing South Korean Republic coincided with Gulf's need to find a market for its Kuwait crude because the Kuwaitians were putting pressure on Gulf to produce more and more each year. It looked like a marriage made in heaven. At the same time, the State Department was all in favor of helping our ally to develop and interested in promoting democracy in Korea. So in 1966, when Gulf was about to sink $200 million in Korea, the Korean government suggested that Gulf help finance democracy by putting up a million dollars to fund the election. Now, true, it was funding their party for the election, but it never occurred to them that there was any other party, and indeed, at that time there wasn't. So it seemed to be a compelling case for making a payment. Unfortunately, in 1970 they came back and said, "Your president insists that we have another election. This time we need $10 million." I said these things regenerate. Clearly this was extortion; they were very graphic about what would happen to the company if the contribution were not made. The poor chairman of Gulf was in a real dilemma because by that time he had more than $200 million of assets in Korea. I am sure that he was influenced in making his decision by the senior executive responsible for the Pacific Far East, who was a former diplomat in the State Department. Unfortunately, perhaps he knew too much, because they didn't make a simple decision, they made a very complicated decision taking into account Korean laws and practices, which led them to do two things. One was to make a payment—not $10 million; I think they got it down to $3 million. And, two, because the cultures are so different, they decided not to tell the board of directors because they wouldn't understand the difference in cultures. The decision was the beginning of a corporate disaster.

While I was not directly involved, I saw the web of corruption develop in that company and I saw what it did to very fine people. It is a terrible, terrible position to be in when you are told to compromise your principles or you don't have a job.

My next example happened at almost exactly the same time. There was no bribery, but it happened in a country whose name is associated with bribery, and that is Nigeria. Gulf was one of the first major oil companies into Nigeria. The officer responsible for developing that operation was not an experienced diplomat and he didn't pay much attention to differences in culture. He came right out of West Texas. I knew him well because Nigeria was in my territory. The first time the government said, "We need a payment," he said, "No, no, not only no, but, hell no!" And then he said, "And if you still want to talk about it, I'm leaving right now." Nigerian Gulf Oil Company established a principle that it would not pay bribes. That principle was honored by Nigeria, and Gulf never paid a penny. Yet other oil companies said they couldn't get their boats moved from one end of the harbor to the other if they didn't pay bribes.

Now let's apply the three rules to the Korean situation. Is it legal? It wasn't clearly illegal at the time, but there was sufficient concern about its legality that the board of directors was not told. So I suspect, deep in their hearts, those involved knew the answer was no. Does it work? Well, it didn't work in Korea; in the parallel situation in Nigeria, refusing a bribe did work. If you conclude that you must make a payment to do business, then I think you just turn down the business. Finally, can you talk about it? In Gulf's case, not being able to talk about it meant that a small group of people in the corporation hid from a large group of people in the corporation some terrible secrets that ended up being discussed in the press, to the immense embarrassment of the vast majority of the corporate management. They never forgave the senior management, ever. And I submit that one reason why the tenth largest corporation in this country finally succumbed to T. Boone Pickens and rushed into a shotgun marriage with Chevron Corporation goes right back to the day that the middle management of the corporation lost faith forever in the senior management.

The notion that a company following the Shannon policy might not actually experience a loss in business was generally supported by the group. Judge Noonan noted:

Along those lines, I tried at a conference at the Woodrow Wilson Center to get the business community to substantiate losses they claimed to have suffered because of the Foreign Corrupt Practices Act. Nobody did it. Now I know it was very difficult, that you would have to show that your competitor paid a bribe. But I would say that the showing really didn't come close. It was just rumor, gossip, sort of in the witchcraft category. If there are real losses because of it, and there may be, they have not yet been proved in any fashion that I would recognize as proof.

There are curious and strange analogies between bribery and witchcraft besides that. Witchcraft was usually the explanation as to why something that you couldn't really explain happened to somebody. And similarly bribery: When your competitor gets the business, it is not witchcraft today. It must have been pure bribery.

John Collins supported the Shannon policy in that "bribery will not be tolerated" on the basis that this is the most practical policy.

Multinationals have gone to great lengths to guard against bribery through the statements of clear policies, educational programs, and the extension of both internal and external audits. Still, the key to eliminating bribery is the statement by senior management that "it will not be tolerated."

Bribery is cancerous. It involves circumventing the control system and undertaking activities outside the law. That will eat its way through the complete operation.

There is no question in my mind that American multinationals have lost business when they have refused to participate in this activity. Alternatively, once a firm makes it clear that it will not participate in bribery and will not even discuss the issue, the process becomes easier. American firms have found that they can operate in places where bribery is common. This includes countries where the American firms have themselves been involved in bribery before the passage of the FCPA.

The FCPA has, indeed, influenced the American position. The potential for suit and a jail sentence can have a dramatically deterring effect. Directors and executives join the auditors in eliminating bribery from the corporate organization.

The main problem in implementing a simple policy of nontoleration is distinguishing between facilitating payments and bribes.[2] Judge Noonan believes there is a moral difference between the two.

There is a moral difference between bribery and facilitating payments, both in the gravity of the trust violated and the gravity of the harm to society. St. Augustine made the distinction in the fifth century. He said that a good man would not take low-level payments. A person who has undergone a religious conversion would give the money back. But someone taking such payments would not incur a mortal sin at the same level as a judge or governor who takes a bribe. There is a moral line to be drawn in today's world as well, particularly in countries where clerks and some officials are paid at a subsistence level. There is much to be said in the way of excusing people who take petty amounts. Still, it would be better to eliminate them.

John Collins noted:

There is a distinction between "facilitating" payments and what I would call "enabling" payments. Bribery enables you to do something, the other facilitates the way you do it. You are paying the cop on the beat to let you double-park or you are paying the customs agent to let you get things into the country a little faster. Clearly, then, one practical measure is the level of the official involved. A facilitating payment generally goes to a functionary of some sort. In many cases, these payments, while not strictly legal, are common, and in many cases, they are recorded for what they are, unlike bribery where a significant effort is made to conceal the true nature of the payment — resulting in collusion, circumvention of the control system, and improper records.

Michael Shannon sees facilitating payments as a possible exception to a simple policy of "Don't do it."

Facilitating payments should fit within the general principle that there will be no bribery of any kind. Then, the burden of proof should be placed on those managers who want to circumvent the general policy. For facilitating payments I would extend my three questions to include: 4. Is it legal in that country? 5. Is it commonplace in that it is done all of the time? 6. Can you talk about it in that country?

Finally, we need to ask whether such payments violate the commonly held ethics of our own company. When there are questions, "Don't do it."

HOST GOVERNMENT COPING

Directly or indirectly, all sectors of society are affected by and involved in governmental corruption. In the process, the distinction between extortion and bribery is seldom observable.

Judge Noonan believes that an anticorruption campaign must begin with the judiciary.

It is absolutely imperative that the judges are honest. If they are not, the rest of the society won't be. Assure first that the judiciary will not take bribes and then move from that base.

In this statement I am speaking from our own tradition. It might be much harder in a country where the law is not a separate component of the culture or in a civilization where power is not seen as finite and delegable. Still, the statement would apply to both Mexico and Korea.

John Collins sees bribery as tied to a single-party system.

In my experience, when bribery does occur, it seems to occur most frequently in those countries where there is no effective opposition, and a single party is in power. In these circumstances, there is no system of checks and balances, there is no opportunity for someone new to come in and operate in a different manner. The dominant single party is a problem in both Korea and Mexico.

Antonio Fernández-Arena described two attempts to eliminate corruption in Mexico.

In the United States, there are many jokes about the Mexican "la Mordida." I am reminded of the response of the former head of the Agency for Research and Development in Mexico when he was asked by an English reporter in London about Mexican governmental corruption. "Excellent question," said Mr. Flores. "I believe that corruption in my country is like homosexuality in England. It is an optional act between consenting adults. We cannot say that all English men and women are homosexual, or that all Mexicans are crooks."

There are many reasons for an individual act of bribery. Some have to do with the nature of human beings. Many of the pressures to extort or bribe, however, are tied to bureaucratic structures.

There can be governmental bureaucratic pressures, often unintentional, that press an official to accept, or seek, a bribe.

- The official may be seeking extra income to enhance an inadequate salary.
- Excessive regulatory requirements lead to enormous bureaucracies which develop their own reasons for existence and impede any modernization programs.
- Highly centralized bureaucracies draw the power to the top and make decisions impossible at lower echelon levels. The absence of responsibility at these lower levels creates great pressure to avoid mistakes and the possibility of losing a good position. The concentration of decision-making power at the top attracts bribery.
- New laws and regulations can be passed but without the bureaucratic structure to implement them and an auditing authority to ensure that they are implemented properly, bribery cannot be eliminated.

When political power and governmental control are so closely tied and so concentrated as they are in Mexico, the challenge to eliminate corruption is, indeed, great. Two major anti-corruption programs have been mounted since 1976.

The Anti-Corruption Program of the López Portillo Government

In 1976, the Mexican government under López Portillo initiated an anti-corruption program based on four precise and strictly enforced principles.

- Complete cooperation between the Treasury and the Justice Department. This relationship had not been very effective before 1976 but turned out to be the key to the program's success.
- Full power was given to these departments to complete any investigation they initiated. The program was organized to involve both ministries in each investigation and make it very difficult for a senior official to squelch an investigation.
- A third concern addressed by the program was to prevent unfounded charges and witch hunts. Detailed analysis and careful selection of proofs and dispositions helped to avoid any political vendettas.
- Great emphasis was placed on cooperation with foreign departments of justice. The existence of the United States' Foreign Corrupt Practices Act proved to be very helpful.

The Secretaria de la Contraloria

In 1983 the anti-corruption efforts of the Mexican government were formalized in a cabinet position — the Secretaria de la Contraloria. The new senior governmental position was supported by a large department. This approach brings more prominence to the anti-corruption efforts but has not achieved the interministerial cooperation so necessary for results. Competition rather than cooperation has developed between the new Secretaria de la Contraloria and the Justice Department, whose people do not think that those in the Secretaria have the necessary qualifications and experience. This lack of cooperation makes it easier for an official to impede an investigation. The laws and regulations in place are inadequate to match the formality of the new secretariat. In all cases, it has been a very slow process. According to one observer, there are 10,000 cases pending.

Eliminating corruption is a major challenge in any society. In Mexico, we do not want corruption. We have made strides in eliminating it but much, much more needs to be done in all sectors, public and private.

Our efforts must be directed towards people and structures. Commitment to country, not self, and to the values that we espouse must be prerequisites for appointment to public offices. Bureaucracies, political systems, and legal and regulatory requirements must be structures to discourage rather than allow, or even encourage, corruption. Appointees to public office must be continually subjected to public scrutiny. Businesses — private, public, and multinational — need effective auditing.

NOTES

1. John J. McCloy, Mathan W. Pearson, Beverly Matthews, *The Great Oil Spill* (New York: Chelsea House, 1976).

2. The Foreign Corrupt Practices Act does not set forth clear and comprehensive guidelines. One of the ambiguous areas is the distinction between "facilitating payment" (grease payments) which are not illegal when made abroad, and bribes which are illegal under the Act. A facilitating payment is one made to expedite performance on the part of a minor official who is responsible for that performance without the additional payment.

Facilitating payments are not prescribed in the law. Their distinction revolves around the definition of the recipient of the payment. A bribe is a payment to a foreign official where a foreign official is defined as:

> any officer or employee of a foreign government of any department, agency, or instrumentality thereof, or any person acting in an official capacity for or on behalf of such government or department, agency or instrumentality. Such term does not include any employee of a foreign government or any department, agency, or instrumentality thereof whose duties are essentially ministerial or clerical. (15 U.S.C. paragraph 78 [1982])

The distinction between a "foreign official" and one whose "duties are essentially ministerial or clerical" is ambiguous.

For a good summary of the problems in applying the FCPA, see "The Anti-bribery Provisions of the Foreign Corrupt Practices Act of 1977: Are They Really as Valuable as We Think They Are?" *The Delaware Journal of Corporate Law* 10, 1 (1985): p. 76.

PART V

Moral Standards and Social Realities

In Part 5, the ethical dimension is explicitly separated from the self-interest objectives underlying the discussion to this point. So far, we have assigned objectives to the multinational and the host governments based on self-interest, albeit enlightened self-interest. The earlier discussions of religious tradition in Part 3 were presented as a basis of better understanding the institutional and individual goals and attitudes of host governments as well as the cultural barriers to communications.

At this point, we extend our consideration of religious traditions to include moral responsibilities. Given the statistics presented in Part 1, the moral mandate to break through the economic and social barriers to help the poor in the Third World is clear. The area selected in Part 5 is Latin America, where we have a clearly stated mandate in Catholic social doctrine and its preferential option for the poor, as presented earlier by McGrath and de Avila.

In Part 5, Guillermo Chapman shares the unique experience of a group of Panamanian leaders from all sectors of that society who, over a number of years, attempted to forge a developmental model from the orientation of Catholic social teaching. Their recommendations reflect the potential ties between that doctrine and national strategies. Ernest Bartell, an early participant in that group, generalizes and comments on the tensions of applying a moral standard in today's world. Bartell helps us to understand the Latin American perception of the multinational presence.

An Application of Doctrine to Economic, Political, and Social Policy

GUILLERMO O. CHAPMAN, JR. *

This paper presents the experience of a diverse group of Panamanians who came together to explore ways in which Catholic social doctrine could be applied to a concrete situation.

The group was called together by Archbishop McGrath in an attempt to develop a common diagnosis or interpretation of the economic, social, and political processes of Panama—especially since the advent of a militarily led government in 1968 and the economic crises following the oil shock and the Latin American external debt problems since 1982. We made a serious effort to reconcile different approaches and ideological biases to the question of the application of Catholic social teaching in a concrete situation such as Panama.

The fifteen participants included economists, sociologists, business executives, community leaders, and theologians as well as religious activists. Beginning in 1980, we met a number of times each year, usually in a small town called El Valle (hence the name "El Valle Project"). In 1984, we sensed enough unity among a majority in the group to state our conclusions in writing.[1] The published document is intended to serve as a guideline or basis of discussion for Christians and other concerned parties in Panama as we attempt to orient and guide the efforts of our society in dealing with the country's problems.

In this document, we addressed economic, social, and political areas, analyzed causes, and stated the social principles which we believe

*Guillermo O. Chapman, Jr. is the founder and chairman of the board of Investigacion y Desarrollo, S.A., a firm of economic and financial consultants. He has served as an economist in the planning office of the Presidency of the Republic of Panama and as a member of the Panamanian Canal Treaty Negotiating Mission.

are applicable to the Panamanian situation. Finally, we suggested possible lines of actions which Catholics and other concerned Panamanians might follow in an endeavor to improve the quality of life in Panama. The completed document was then distributed widely to involve as many people as possible in its call to launch an anti-corruption campaign and to begin a process defining a common set of goals and a national strategy.

This article summarizes the principles of Catholic social teaching which guided the discussion, attempts to set them in the perspective of our concrete reality, and outlines our call to action.

Guiding Principles

We started by identifying basic principles in Catholic social teaching that in our judgment had the greatest economic and political implications.

First, we believe that the economy and the economic system should be at the service of the whole person and of all humanity, not the other way around. This reflects the change in emphasis in Catholic social thinking from the traditional concern with the problem of property to the focus on work or employment.

The second element which is common to social thinking but which has been stressed especially in the Latin American case is the preferential option for the poor. This means that all economic or political efforts should aim to improve the conditions of life for everyone but especially for those within our society who have the lowest income levels and living conditions.

As a consequence of this second element, a third principle would be to promote full employment as a direct goal, not as a byproduct or as an indirect consequence of economic growth. Classical development — the trickle down effect — claims that employment is a consequence, an indirect benefit of growth. We conclude that economic growth in a less-developed country does not necessarily lead to full employment and that the emphasis should be on the promotion of employment directly, simultaneously with the promotion of economic growth. If the employment focus requires economic growth, then that growth should be geared to enhancing employment.

The recognition of universally accepted workers' rights is another key principle.

Fifth, the main function of the means of production is to be at the service of men and women and the service of human work.

Principle number six is worker participation in the productive process. This, of course, is subject to a great deal of interpretation and controversy regarding the different sets of specific conditions and status of development of the different countries.

Principle number seven is the so-called principle of subsidiarity, meaning very simply that if a smaller or lower-level organization can do a given task, preference should be given to it rather than to a higher-level. If the private sector, a cooperative, or a lower-level organization can do a job, then the principle states: Let that organization do it rather than a state enterprise or the state itself. The state would be the ultimate level of organization.

The eighth principle says that some degree of economic planning at the national level is necessary. This principle recognizes that neither economic growth nor development occurs spontaneously. The forces of the market, when left to themselves, would not solve most of the social problems, and there are certain areas which require direct and corrective or protective action for society. The obvious cases are monopolies and quasi-monopolies, various forms of collusion, education, health, and pollution, where the forces of the market will not produce a just solution. Moreover, economic development requires the definition of a national strategy and a set of economic policies in areas such as the tax and tariff systems, fiscal incentives, and public investment that would be consistent among themselves vis-á-vis the global strategy. This approach to "planning" does not contradict the principle of subsidiarity, since it does not imply that the state will replace lower-level organizations in performing the basic functions of society.

Principle number nine states that the building of a humane economy which responds to these principles requires a political system which is based on democracy and guarantees fundamental human rights and justice. Ultimately, a humane society will be built on a new person, a person who has responsibility, and who has solidarity.

THE LATIN AMERICAN CONTEXT

To apply these guiding principles in the Latin American context, it is necessary to understand the unique nature of its economic and social order. Common critiques about the imperfections of democracy and capitalism in the United States have little application in Latin America.

First, most of the Latin American countries do not really have fully functioning market economies. Microeconomic policy is characterized by monopolies and oligopolies, many of which take the form of state-owned enterprises. There is a great deal of collusion in these markets, and a large degree of state intervention in market mechanisms such as manipulating prices and other controls. Markets do not function freely in many instances.

On the other hand, macroeconomic policy in Latin America is characterized by three major biases which distort the functioning of the markets. There is or has been a marked preference for external debt as a means of obtaining foreign capital vis-à-vis the possibility of direct investment. Given the choice, almost any Latin American government would go in debt if it could obtain the external credit rather than attract foreign direct investment. A second bias is a tendency to overvalue the national currency, which, in turn, brings about very drastic devaluations from time to time. Probably the outstanding example against this practice would be Brazil with its so-called mini-devaluations. Controls on foreign exchange transactions and multiple exchange rates are also common. On the other side of the coin from this foreign exchange policy is a marked tendency to undervalue interest rates, which means that credit in the economy is often allocated through political preference or other non-economic mechanisms. These factors, when combined, are a very powerful inducement to capital flight. Attempts to pose a moral challenge to the society is especially difficult in the face of ineffective and inefficient economics.

The same kind of comment applies to the political system. Whatever degree of national planning that we may agree is acceptable in a society requires effective democracy, a system of checks and balances, a system of accountability from the public sector, and at least some minimum efficiency in the functioning of the state apparatus. Unfortunately, many of these basic requirements of effective democracy — accountability, and efficiency, or at least effectiveness in some cases — are lacking in most Latin American countries. The priority for political reform in these countries is obvious.

The Panamanian Context

Within this general context, Panama is facing specific problems. Despite a marked and fairly consistent improvement in most social indicators during the past thirty years, we still have large pockets of extreme poverty. Recent studies show that if one-fifth of all Panamanian families were to apply all of their income to the purchase of food, they could not acquire the basic food basket that satisfies the minimum nutritional requirements. By any definition, this is a situation of extreme poverty. Moreover, two-fifth of all families, including the first quintile just mentioned, could not satisfy all of their basic necessities with the level of family income that they get. Thus, one-fifth of our population is presently experiencing a situation of extreme poverty, and two-fifths of the population lives in a condition of poverty. Geographically, this takes the form of tremendous regional imbalance. Most of the modern, market-oriented economic activity takes place in the metropolitan areas of Panama City and Colón, or the area adjacent or parallel to the Canal access. Of course, the result is a wide gulf in the level of income between the urban and rural populations.

There has been little impact on the welfare of the rural population by the leading economic sectors — the dominant export-oriented services, the banking industry, the financial industry, the re-export activity, and, more recently, the oil pipeline. These activities are not labor-intensive. They have few linkages with the rest of the local economy, and, with the exception of the pipeline, they are not major sources of tax revenue. An astute outside observer has pointed out that even though the export services sector is neither detrimental to the country per se, nor does it impose an economic opportunity cost, it does have a psychological opportunity cost in the sense that the relative well-being of the population living in the cities near the Canal makes it easy to forget the plight of the large proportion of rural families in a condition of extreme poverty. The country needs to actively develop additional types of economic activities in order to solve the basic problems of maldistributed income, unemployment, and extreme poverty.

These structural problems have been aggravated by a serious recession in 1983–84 followed by a timid recovery as a consequence of the Latin American debt crisis and the lack of a national strategy and consistent economic policies to rekindle growth and development.

An Action Program

Given the foregoing analysis, the group concluded that in order to get Panama moving again, we need first to start an anti-corruption campaign, since one of the most fundamental problems is the pervasiveness of corruption in public life and in many aspects of private activity, which poses both moral and practical problems. We also need to mobilize the energies of our people to define a set of commonly accepted national goals and to instill a sense of national purpose.

A national development strategy must identify new sources of employment and foreign exchange earnings. We need a new set of ideas — new thinking — about a long-term view for the utilization of our geographic position, which has been the source of a substantial part of our economic activity on a secular time frame. We have to provide for a much more balanced regional distribution of economic activity.

In the social areas, the suggestions made by the group go well beyond traditional public-sector policies. In nutrition, direct effort has to be made immediately to distribute food to the undernourished. In the medium term, we have another program to provide credit to small subsistence-level farmers. Agricultural producers must be provided with food on loan to sustain them over the learning period as they adapt new techniques and become more efficient producers. This is a lending program where the borrower will repay in kind whatever food is advanced.

The same type of approach applies in housing. We found that more than 60 percent of the housing units produced over a ten-year period have come through the informal sector. That is, they do not appear in the housing permits of any of the municipalities and have not been financed by a formal financial institution; the people themselves are providing their own financing and undertaking their own contruction. That initiative needs to be fostered and provided with technical assistance since, over the medium term, close to 50 percent of the families cannot be expected to have sufficient income (both monetary and in kind) to be able to purchase a home in the market even with subsidized credit. This could be achieved. Housing quality can be improved through better designs and better services. Housing could be complemented with small-scale industries producing construction materials in the local communities. Since this housing activity is already there, it would not do away with the formal housing market. There is ample opportunity to apply this principle of subsidiarity to this situation.

In education, we feel that the system in Panama — and this is probably the case in most of Latin America — is geared to the university. The ultimate goal of the system is to have the students earn a university degree. We lack in intermediate professions, in skills, in crafts; and we feel that a more sensible approach within this context would be to de-emphasize the university and provide emphasis on teaching people how to produce, how to be more efficient and effective; a focus on *being*, rather than *having*.

With respect to economic activity in general, we feel that the emphasis should be shifted away from the present dominating sectors of international banking, re-export trade, or the pipeline. The idea is not to punish any of these activities but to promote at the same time those which can do the most to generate employment. There are untapped opportunities in agriculture, mariculture, light industry, construction (especially the self-help approach), and tourism, as well as an improved or new export service which can generate more employment than the traditional ones.

How can this be accomplished? We feel that we have to embark on a process of education and participation. The widespread distribution of the document must be followed by ample discussion of its contents by all groups throughout the country. The keys are participation and integration of all efforts in a set of globally acceptable goals, a national strategy, on which the majority of Panamanians willingly concur.

CONCLUSION

The Church does not have an economic or social model, but rather an orientation in its social teaching and a set of guiding principle These principles can be used to build a model. The purpose of the El Valle process has been to translate these principles to an action plan and, with the participation of all sectors of our society, see it through to implementation.

NOTE

1. A full statement in Spanish on the El Valle project is *Hacia Una Economía Más Humana: Reflexiones Cristianas Para El Desarrollo De Panama Con Prioridad En Los Más Pobres* (Panama: Editorial Litográfica, S. A., 1985).

The Tensions in Applying a
Moral Standard in Today's World

ERNEST J. BARTELL, C.S.C.*

The role of the multinationals in the Third World will be actively debated in Catholic social teaching over the next few years. While the Latin American countries will probably borrow whatever funds they can get, they will not have access to significant credit for the next twenty years. If there is going to be new capital coming back into Latin America, which is a necessary prerequisite for growth, there must be much more attention to direct foreign investment. This means that the dependency literature of the 1950s and 1960s is going to get dusted off again and reexamined as new attempts are made to work out collaborative schemes which will entice the inflow of capital through direct foreign investment. Given the changes in society and the renewed influence of Catholic social teaching in Latin America, the role of the multinational corporation in Latin America will be different in the next decade than it was in the last. That role will be best forged through collaboration within the Latin tradition.

I approach the issue of applying moral standards to economic, social, and political realities with some degree of optimism drawn from the success of the El Valle project.[1] I had the privilege of participating in the very beginning of those discussions. The group, which included widely different perspectives, was able to draw together a document

*Ernest J. Bartell, C.S.C., is a professor of economics and the executive director of the Helen Kellogg Institute for International Studies at the University of Notre Dame. He also serves as overseas mission coordinator for the Congregation of the Holy Cross, Indiana Province (C.S.C.) with missionaries in South America, East Africa, and South Asia.

to which the diverse members could all subscribe, and then to present it to the various social sectors that they represented. It is an amazing accomplishment.

Although Panama is a small society by U.S. standards, it is a microcosm of many larger ones. The problems encountered by the El Valle group in its attempt to apply a moral doctrine to economic, social, or political spheres are like those I have observed in other Latin, African, and Asian countries. Six tensions can be observed.

The Sacred Versus the Secular

In dealing with social teaching, there is a basic tension between the sacred and the secular. As noted by McGrath and de Avila,[2] there is a wide variation between those who take a purely spiritual approach to faith and ignore the social dimension and those who take a more incarnational approach, consistent with our belief in an incarnational God, a redeemed human person, and a redeemed society.

The tension is in evidence in the way we approach our daily life—with a direct involvement with social change or, alternatively, a compartmentalization of one's life. For a number of us in the U.S., a fairly dominant feature is that one does what one has to do in one's career, according to the rules of the career, and then achieves one's larger perspectives on the outside. Business is business. If I am successful there, I can attack my social responsibilities in my free time. Alternatively, many Latin Americans approach the tensions between the sacred and the secular from a very different perspective. They talk about a more integrated life. Dialogue among these two fundamentally different perspectives is strained, even when both are proceeding from the same good will of trying to live in both worlds—the sacred and the secular.

The tension is pervasive. It exists in academic life, the sciences as well as the social sciences. McGrath and de Avila wrote about the autonomy of the secular order, and there certainly is an autonomy of the secular social sciences where each discipline defines itself according to its own criteria. It is not an easy task for the committed believer to respect that autonomy and draw upon the secular sciences for moral ends and moral purposes, particularly when the tools of these sciences are often developed in a positivist methodology that tries to separate the value content from the analytic content. This is a challenge that I personally have found quite difficult to handle.

In its critique of the multinationals, the Church has demonstrated an attempt to bridge the sacred and the secular. The critique is drawn heavily from a secular dependency literature in the social sciences of the 1950s and 1960s. There is, however, an attempt to draw upon that perspective of analysis, and then incorporate it into a larger framework of Christian vision. This immediately involves the Church in the secular order and makes it vulnerable to all the critiques of that same body of literature. If one is going to respect the autonomy of the secular, one has to respect the autonomy of the critiques too, and that is not easy to do. A good deal of the uneasiness that exists between Church people and secular academics is precisely at this point of trying to extend disciplines and tools of analyses that are developed in a secular context to a larger faith context. Business people are uncomfortable with the insertion of moral criteria into market activity. At the same time, U.S. Catholic Bishops wrestle with the integration of social philosophy, biblical theology, and positive analysis in contemporary Catholic social thought.[3]

Another clear example of the secular-sacred tension exists in the analysis of basic Christian communities. These basic Christian communities are analyzed one way by believers, using some of the tools of sociology, but from a different perspective by the academic disciplines. The great success of the basic Christian communities in Brazil and even in places like Nicaragua stimulated the interest of secular social scientists. These analyses helped us understand the conditions that would make those basic communities flourish — the need for grass roots action, the need for participation on the part of people marginalized and excluded from society. This social science analysis helped us strengthen the initial stages of the basic communities.

Once the basic communities developed an autonomy of their own, the secular analysis took its own tack. These same secular social scientists argue that the very success of these basic communities threaten a traditional authority structure. They see the Church as now threatened by a possible loss of its political hegemony over its own people. This fails to capture the reality as understood by the people on the inside who are working toward a continual strengthening of the whole Church community, with the pastors as guides. It is, however, what we must deal with when we are using these same tools of analysis, the tools which actually helped in getting some of these basic communities started.

As a result, we constantly face a challenge of how to relate the methodology of the secular analyst to our own perspective and belief.

THE IDEAL VERSUS THE ACTUAL

There is always a challenge of the ideal versus the actual. As believers, we have a hope that goes beyond the existing order of things. The life of the Spirit is precisely a life of hope in the individual, thus carrying us beyond the actual world. This has been reflected in the earlier Catholic social teaching very much in the way in which the early documents like *Rerum Novarum*[4] and *Quadragesimo Anno*[5] contrasted capitalism and communism. They spoke about ideal forms, that is, mental forms; they talked very little about the actual historical experience. As a result, there was a great deal of discussion during the 1930s about a third way, another abstract, ideal kind of model which was something different than either the capitalism or the communism described by Pius XI and Pius XII. Beginning with *Guadium et Spes*[6] in 1965, there has been a shift to more of a confrontation with the actual circumstances—an attempt to analyze the reality, to look at the real world as it is. This new thrust can lead either to reformist type solutions of the existing reality or possibly even to revolutionary solutions if the conclusion is that the actual reality is irredeemable.

The shift in Catholic social teaching has implications for multinationals. As more attention is paid to the actual world, the behavior of the multinational companies comes under direct scrutiny. The MNC is no longer one of the many enterprises viewed as an idealistic actor in a general equilibrium model of world markets. And, people's perceptions are going to be very different of the same actual reality.

At the heart of the discussion will be the ideal person versus the actual person. As Christians and believers we talk about the new person hopefully and ideally. Many defenders of existing institutions speak of the actual person. Business people live in the world of actual people and give credence to existing institutions as ways to harness the drives of people as they are, not as we would like them to be in a redeemed state. They justify existing institutional structures as the best means of controlling and channeling people's—sometimes noble, sometimes very ignoble—drives and aspirations. Realists say, "Present structures do an adequate job, so let's not tamper with them." There is bound to be some tension here between people who adhere to this concept and those who are constantly looking for something morally better. These latter span a whole spectrum, all the way from the reformists to very radical extremes. Understanding this distinction will help in understanding what is heard from Church people who cover a very wide spectrum in this regard.

EQUITY VERSUS EFFICIENCY

In the ideal order of academic disciplines, we talk about achieving goals of both equity and efficiency, taking on both the distributional questions of wealth and income and the efficiency questions of the proper use of the world's resources to maximize the output and growth. In modeling, the two are separated. In the real world, it is a big mish-mash; the two are not separated so neatly. Every allocative decision has distributional implications. Likewise, every redistribution changes the composition of markets, changes the composition of effective demand, and therefore changes the composition of future growth, production, and consumption. The circular flow of income is affected by both in an interactive way within the real world.

The Church has tended to focus on distributional issues, while the business world is concerned about growth, production, and efficiency. That is a polemical dead end—the battle will go on forever. We have to go back to the simple notions of the circular flow of income and the ways in which those two interact. Put in economic terms, the equilibrium positions of the static models is never achieved. The real world exists in those paths to equilibrium about which we know very little. Attempts to define these paths have not captured the components of human behavior. To find the way, it is necessary to think in terms of both equity and efficiency, of distribution and production.

Note, however, that the El Valle group chose to sidestep that issue. They chose an objective of full employment—as a direct goal rather than as a by-product.[7] Full employment, of course, has effects both in growth potential and in redistributional effects. Obviously, if you could reemploy all the people who are unemployed, it would change the mix of distribution; it would also change the size of the pie and its composition. That was a neat way to avoid the trap of academic debate such as that raised by the Simon-Novak preemptive response[8] to the first draft of the Catholic Bishop's Pastoral Letter.[9]

THE UNIVERSAL VERSUS THE SPECIFIC

There is a tension which arises between the universal outlook of the Church and the specificity of human activity—cultural and political specificity, sectoral specificity, class specificity, the private sector, the public sector, or the poor and the disinfranchasized versus those who have property and political clout. The Church message is for all people and must apply to each specific situation.

Take the example of private property. In Catholic social teaching, property has a social dimension. In the past, the teaching was "those who have should be nice in using it." They should be charitable, and they should be socially responsible. In our cultural setting, however, the John Locke approach prevailed. The private part came first and the social part came second. So, "those who had it" kept it, and it was hoped that if they also had religion, they would do some nice things with the benefits which they accrued. The strong social dimension of property that has been emphasized in Latin American theology since the 1950s and 1960s is much closer to the tradition of European Catholic social teaching than to nineteenth-century British secular thought.[10] Latin America has long been distinguished among regions of the world for its highly unequal distribution of land ownership. Consequently it is not surprising that the application of Catholic social thought to the Latin American pattern of land ownership has been perceived as a relatively radical threat to the economic status quo.

Differences in social teaching as it has evolved in different cultures help to explain how some of the religious people who work in the field with the poor in different cultural environments perceive the activity of multinationals and transnationals. The moral perceptions of religious people are colored by their understanding of the reality of the people with whom they live and work. These perceptions do not always mesh easily with the perceptions of the business person coming in from abroad. Consider, for example, the criticisms of certain imports or of some domestic production for local markets by multinational firms. The products are not deceptive; they are worthwhile and honest. From a local perception, however, they are often seen as the bearers of another culture, another ideology, another set of tastes — a set of tastes conditioned by a wholly different level of income and earning capability. For example, American cosmetics produced for the local market in Central Africa are seen by missionaries as a misallocation of local resources, even though the product is produced and distributed according to the highest Western standards. The distinction as it exists is particularly critical as the Latin American Church adopts and tries to implement its preferential option for the poor.

The tension between universal and specific also exists more impersonally between international markets and local production processes. Free trade and export promotion make sense in an ideal economic world, and even in the actual world for those who appreciate the interaction and somewhat automatic signals of the international marketplace. When one lives half-way up the Amazon, however, and has a small market for wood that is not part of the larger national market or the international markets, the poor can buy wood at very low prices. Most of the land is owned, of course, by absentee landowners of very large tracts, but the wood is available to the local people at the local-opportunity price. This price is not very high in the local market, and therefore, people can afford to build inexpensive wooden homes. On the other hand, with the arrival of economic infrastructure and capital, the owners of that land will want to maximize the possibilities of it. This means that the local price of wood will now rise toward its opportunity price on the larger national and international markets. Efficiency is maximized at the international level but the local poor can no longer purchase that wood. International profits are maximized, and some local workers get jobs cutting wood and helping to ship it, but there is an unfavorable tradeoff for local consumers of wood who can no longer afford wooden homes. Therefore, the local missionaries complain about the arrival of the large companies that deprive a local community of an important factor in its life without any compensatory local return from integration into the larger economy. Value is different when measured by basic human needs rather than by the norms of the international marketplace.

The Individual versus the Social

The contrast, tension, or paradox between the individual and the social is a very real one. Catholic social teaching stresses the fullest development of each individual human person and of all human people as a twin goal. In practice, however, those do not necessarily proceed in tandem.

The definition, for example, of the dignity of the human person that is used in the U.S. Bishops' letter, "Economic Justice for All," is the basis of the policy recommendations that the letter contains. The letter defines human dignity not individualistically but in relation to a social context and to human solidarity.

In the Simon-Novak "pastoral letter," the definition of the human person is different despite the use of the same vocabulary. Here the human person is defined principally as an individual and secondarily as a social person. Full dignity for the human person becomes almost synonymous with relatively unlimited individual liberty. There are significant policy implications that flow from this difference of emphasis. Both of them accept the dignity of the human person and the place of the human person in society, but from those initial definitions and distinctions flows a wholly different approach toward social programs.

The social emphasis of the U.S. Bishops' letter reflects the thrust of Catholic social encyclicals as well as the significant influence of the social thought of the Latin American Church. The letter is the first official document of the U.S. Bishops that substantially appropriates the modern universal social encyclicals of the Church to the U.S. economy. When Pope John XXIII's two encyclicals, *Mater et Magistra*[11] and *Pacem in Terris*,[12] and Pope Paul VI's *Populorum Progressio*[13] were written, they received considerable attention in the U.S. secular press, but there was little follow-up in the Church. Attempts by the official Church to apply those documents to U.S. situations are limited. Thus, the U.S. Bishops' letter on the economy is the first comprehensive official attempt to apply to the American economy the universal principles enunciated in the social encyclicals.

The evolution of Catholic social teaching in the Latin American Church with its incorporation of biblical theology and positive social analysis has been traced by McGrath and de Avila. The U.S. Bishops' letter has been substantially enriched by this development. It is unusual for a regional Bishops' conference in a "developed country" to draw explicitly, and with quotations, upon the documents of another regional conference of Bishops. The vocabulary about human solidarity in the U.S. letter drawn from the teaching of Latin American Bishops at Medellin and Puebla is a vocabulary that has not been a part of the

North American idiom. For readers unfamiliar with that vocabulary, it can be provocative.

There are other aspects of the U.S. Bishops' letter which deserve the attention of people concerned with the social effects of multinational corporations. Approximately 20 percent of that letter is devoted to the responsibilities of the United States, public and private sectors, in the international economy with an emphasis on the underdeveloped world. That is unusual in a country that ordinarily does not focus heavily on international concerns. Our own economics textbooks in the U.S. typically do not offer much about international economics.

RECONCILIATION VERSUS CONFRONTATION

There is also a tension between the reconciliation that we preach in our Gospel and confrontation. The word "confrontation" does not necessarily mean physical confrontation or violent confrontation, but confrontation of ideas, ideology, and analysis. Confrontation is difficult to handle, particularly for the magisterium of a universal Church. The magisterium teaches all the people in the Church, yet the call for a preferential option for the poor can easily assume a confrontative stance.

CONCLUSION

As Catholic social teaching is evolving universally, in Latin Ameica and in the United States, it offers sharper challenges to all of us. These comments have sought to highlight some of the tensions that arise in attempts to relate these religiously grounded, universal, ideal, equity-based, social notions to a secular world with specific economic values, both explicit and implicit. The fact that the diverse El Valle group could work through some of these tensions together is an indication that it can be done. For the rest of us, the task is not an easy one.

NOTES

1. *Hacia Una Economía Más Humana: Reflexiones Cristianas Para El Desarrollo De Panama Con Prioridad En Los Más Pobres* (Panama: Editorial Litografica, S.A., 1985).

2. See McGrath and de Avila, "Multinationals and Catholic Social Teaching in Latin America," in this volume.

3. U.S. Bishops' Pastoral Letter, "Economic Justice for All: Catholic Social Teaching and the U.S. Economy" (November 27, 1986), *Origins* 16 (no. 24) (Washington, D.C.: National Catholic News Service).

4. *Rerum Novarum* "On the Condition of Workers" (1891), encyclical letter of Pope Leo XIII (New York: Paulist Press, 1939).

5. *Quadragesimo Anno*, encyclical letter of Pope Pius XI, National Catholic Conference, 1942.

6. *Gaudium et Spes*, "Pastoral Constitution on the Church in the Modern World," *The Documents of Vatican II* (December 7, 1965) (New York: American Press, 1966).

7. Guillermo O. Chapman, Jr., "An Application of Doctrine to Economic, Political, and Social Policy," in this volume.

8. Michael Novak and William Simon, *Toward the Future: Catholic Social Thought and the Economy, A Lay Letter*, the Lay Committee on Catholic Social Teaching and the U.S. Economy, American Catholic Committee, 1984.

9. The first draft of the Catholic Bishops' Pastoral Letter, to which Simon-Novak addressed their preemptive response, was entitled "Capitalism and the U.S. Economy." The final draft of the letter was entitled, "Economic Justice for All."

10. For further discussion of the distinction between the U.S. and the Latin notion of "private property," see Trai Le's response to Rosenn's "A Comparison of Latin American and North American Legal Traditions," in this volume.

11. *Mater et Magestra* "Christianity and Social Progress" (May 15, 1961), encyclical letter of Pope John XXIII (Glen Rock, N.J.: Paulist Press, 1961).

12. *Pacem in Terris* "Peace on Earth" (April 11, 1963), encyclical letter of Pope John XXIII (New York: American Press, 1963).

13. *Populorum Progressio* "On the Development of Peoples" (March 26, 1967), encyclical letter of Pope Paul VI (Vatican Polyglot Press, 1967).

PART VI

Implications for Corporate Strategies

LEE A. TAVIS AND
WILLIAM P. GLADE*

After a lengthy period in which mistrust, sprinkled with occasional doses of outright hostility, generally characterized relations between multinational enterprises and host-country governments in the Third World, circumstances have increasingly drawn the two together and widened the area of mutual interest. No bonds of affection yet link the cohabiting partners, and there is still much wariness on both sides. Nevertheless, new understandings and modes of interaction have developed with sufficient force that a working relationship based on entirely practical considerations has come to overshadow the views once refracted chiefly through the prism of political ideology.

Consider the contrast between today and the 1950s and 1960s, when the animosity toward multinationals was reaching its zenith and sentiment was moving toward the increased regulation and codes of conduct that were instituted in the 1970s. New and resurgent nationalisms then colored the thinking of political leaders, sundry activists, and the Third-World intelligentsia, who were anxious to put an end to foreign domination and, in some cases, even to foreign in-

---

*Lee A. Tavis is C. R. Smith Professor of Business Administration and director of the Program on Multinational Corporations and Third World Development at the University of Notre Dame.

William P. Glade is a professor of economics and past director of the Institute of Latin American Studies at the University of Texas at Austin. A recognized authority on economic development, he is a member of Notre Dame's Helen Kellogg Institute for International Studies Advisory Council.

fluence. Partly just old-fashioned xenophobia, the animus against foreign investment was also fed by still fresh memories of how foreign concerns had often dealt with the local population in the days before the more enlightened and sensitive management of the 1950s was installed. For some, the ideology of the times served, as Harry Johnson has so astutely indicated, to anchor social and political privilege in the new order.[1] For others, the restriction, and sometimes even expulsion, of foreign companies was seen as prerequisite to carving out the economic space in which national firms, either private or public, could take root and flourish.[2] For still others, the overseas operations of the metropolitan economies were simply one of the many social pathogens with which they had to contend as they set about fashioning new institutional structures of their own.[3]

On the other side, foreign managers understandably looked askance at the rowdy political environment — and sometimes no less turbulent economic environment — of the less-developed countries. This scarcely diminished their misgivings about the new regulatory apparatus that was being built up in state after state. The growing resort to some type of national economic planning did little to allay the fears of multinational managers that policy was headed in the wrong direction so far as they were concerned — fears heightened by the feckless and inexperienced bureaucrats with whom they frequently had to deal. Having survived at home the dense regulatory burdens imposed by the New Deal and the wartime mobilizations, and not yet fully accustomed to operating in the traditionally more regulated arena of European business, American executives were often not only inexperienced in coping with the vagaries of underdevelopment but also were in no mood to complacently accept sets of controls and restrictions that, to them, appeared arbitrary if not downright capricious.

During what might be seen as the formative period of modern policy making, conditions were far from conducive to establishing a habit of dialogue between those who speak for the multinational interests and those in control of the policy machinery of the state. That there was a strong cultural preference in most developing countries for restricting candid communication to those sharing personal relations of family and friendship did not help matters, given the tendency of multinational managers (and local officials) to come and go. A variety of circumstances, then, put considerable social and political distance between the two.

In time, however, contextual changes have brought about an altered pattern of interaction, as well as an altered pattern of foreign investment. On the multinational side, the attraction of growing but protected national markets raised the commitment to establish production facilities abroad to serve those markets. Subsequently, the accumulation of managerial experience in less-developed countries' operating environments and the partial naturalization of multinational management in the overseas subsidiaries made for fewer unpleasant surprises and rather smoother, or at least more predictable, relations with the assorted local stakeholders. At the same time, the build-up of labor skills and the general elaboration of the business infrastructure was laying the basis for new export production when the global restructuring of industrial sourcing and marketing began to accelerate.

For its part, the organization of economic administration in the host countries was also becoming more experienced and technically competent, exhibiting more self-confidence in interactions with foreign professionals with whom the rising technocrats might even share university ties. As the limitations of the import-substituting-industrialization strategies made themselves felt and as the frontier of less-developed country industrialization pushed into organizationally and technically more complex branches of production, the need for more assured access to advanced technology and for facilitated entry into overseas markets grew increasingly apparent. In this respect, the joint ventures that have developed between multinational firms and local public and private enterprises have signaled the changed business climate, just as co-production and new licensing agreements have marked a radically different receptivity of multinational companies in several of the centrally planned economies.

Third World host country environments for the multinational corporation have, indeed, changed. This concluding paper begins with a discussion of the nature of Third World host government's developmental planning and how multinationals have and have not been a part of that process. Then, against the movement toward greater cooperation, alternative multinational strategies of interaction with host governments are analyzed. A consideration of the ethical dimension of multinational–Third World host government interactions forms the conclusion.

NATURE OF BUSINESS-GOVERNMENT INTERACTION

The astonishing expertise of multinationals in managing world-wide communication systems — for research, financing, production, and marketing — has come to be appreciated as the very process that host-country economic functionaries must master if the less-developed countries are to make sustainable advances beyond the initial stages of industrialization. The awareness has grown that the critical resource of contemporary development is information — along with the organizational capabilities for gathering, retrieving, processing, generating, and disseminating information that is technically and economically relevant. Without a way of tapping into the dense information system organized largely by multinational corporate networks, the potential for resource misallocation in the less-developed countries is vastly increased and the social opportunity costs of resource misuse are substantial. In the more remote corners of the world, even potentially useful off-the-shelf technologies may remain out of view unless they can be discovered through the kinds of information networks which multinational companies habitually use.

Although in principle the time horizon of governmental planners is more long-term than that of corporate planners, and their optimizing frameworks are different, in reality this distinction tends to break down. As a host of critical studies have revealed, the bureaucratic utility function may, for a variety of reasons, be much different from what is usually inferred from the term "public interest," and it is in any case constrained by (a) the knowledge that is available and (b) the cost of acquiring additional information. If the goals of multinational managers are narrower than the "national interest" of the host country, a similar disparity is ordinarily found between "national interest" and the objectives actually sought in various parts of the public-policy mechanism. Further, in practical terms the effective planning horizon of officials in a great many Third World countries may be rather shorter than that of their corporate counterparts if political conditions and actual implementation are taken into account.

In both public and private sectors, once the process moves beyond program design and planning into the implementation phase, circumstances in the operating environment may deflect the course of events in unanticipated ways. For both multinational managers and governmental officials, then, contingency planning and a high order of flexibility, even agility, in the execution of programs and project management are of the essence. Both must be keenly attuned to forecasts of future states of the world, given the force of balance-of-payments constraints and other exogenous variables on the outcomes of the policies undertaken.

Hitherto, interactions on the basis of the complementarity of interests between multinational managers on the one hand and functionaries in charge of macroeconomic management and sectoral planning on the other, have ranged from minimal to sporadic. Much of the contact between multinationals and host-country governments, in fact, has taken place in regulatory agencies that stand somewhat apart from the planning and policy-making organizations (e.g., in agencies regulating the entry of foreign capital, the transfer of technology, the repatriation of earnings, and so on). This has tended to be formal and event-centered rather than ongoing.

Indeed, the interactions that take place on the eve of entry into a Latin American market or as a preface to setting up shop for exporting constitute the largest body of experience since they antedate the institution of national planning and go all the way back to the early nineteenth century. The concessions for mining, for organizing and building railways, and for establishing public utilities and banks were all of this character. Thus it is perhaps not unexpected that negotiations over entry conditions prior to the onset of investment activity tend to go relatively smoothly, at least when no major policy change is implied that would, *de facto*, change the design of the development program. The recent IBM negotiations in Mexico show how sticky the interaction can become when a shift in development strategy is involved—and not only because the multinationals' point of contact is primarily an implementing rather than a policy-making or planning body.

What appears to take place in most countries is a kind of unilateral indicative planning in which the business community is, for all practical purposes, left out of the policy machinery except for ad hoc informal consultation and, occasionally, intermittent representation by trade and other interest-group associations. Over the years, however, this approach—which has often resulted in defective but largely unimplemented plans—has in some instances moved toward a more consultative form of planning. Planners and "plannees" have come together to share an enriched information base with resulting benefits for both program design and implementation. Where this has occurred, mostly at the industry level as in the complementation agreements of the Latin American Free Trade Association (LAFTA), the results have generally been more promising. Brazil has gone a step farther, beginning on a fairly ambitious scale in the Programa de Metas, and has established the framework for a collaborative planning in which there is a more-or-less ongoing dialogue between business and government in charting the course for industrial development. This includes in a good many instances the local affiliates of multinational corporations. Here, too, communication across these institutional boundaries has also been fostered by joint-venture projects linking public investment with both local and foreign private capital.

Although Brazil is the outstanding case of the collaborative mode of interaction, it is by no means the sole case, at least in certain policy areas. Along with Brazil, Colombia and Peru have both established working partnerships between the private and public sectors in labor-training programs. A variety of arrangements have been tested in technological development, such as the Instituto de Investigación Technológica Industrial y Normas Técnicas (ITINTEC) program of Peru in the 1970s, Venezuela's Instituto Venezolano de Investigaciones Científicas (IVIC) research contracts, and the technical information search services of Consejo Nacional de Ciencia y Tecnología (CONACYT) in Mexico. In contrast to the labor-training programs, the collaboration in these technological schemes has been chiefly between governmental organizations and local firms. While it may well be that the agreement negotiated recently between IBM and Mexico will turn out to be a landmark in initiating a new era of collaborative planning in research and development between multinationals and host country authorities, as yet there has been very little progress on this front, either in Mexico or elsewhere.

Consultative planning, much less collaborative planning, has been infrequent at best in a whole host of areas in which the capabilities of multinational corporations could be enlisted to the benefit of national development efforts: sectoral development programs (as in agro-industrial development), export promotion programs (though local private-governmental cooperation has paid off for Colombia and Brazil), local business development (apart from the impact of domestic content regulations), or even assistance on program design and implementation in social service areas (health delivery systems, education technology, family planning). Even where conscious decisions are taken to "delegate" planning to the market, there is room for more informed decisions to be generated through constructive dialogue.

Lest all this be thought to be an academic exercise in considering "second best" solutions (the "best case" being market-guided decisional processes), we would point to the experience of Korea and Japan, where the record provides a strong basis for believing in the efficacy of collaborative planning, and, contrariwise, for inferring the costs of the adversarial relation that has so often prevailed in Latin America. Although in both of these Asian countries national managers and investors enjoy a privileged access to the planning and policy-making process, and in Japan, especially, multinational interests are either relegated to the back seat or kept out, the growth experience demonstrates that the working partnership between the sectors can pay off handsomely, even if not in every field. For Latin America, Brazil's recent decisions in informatics notwithstanding, the promise of collaborative interaction would seem to be particularly great in agroindustry biotechnologies as well as in monitoring the external operating environment that affects the chances for success in export growth and diversification.

ALTERNATIVE MULTINATIONAL CORPORATE STRATEGIES

The drift in host government planning from unilateral indicative planning toward more consultative forms — with a promise of collaborative planning in some cases — must today be set against the economic realities of slowed growth and a heavy debt overhang for many countries. It is in this context that multinational corporations are reassessing their host government strategies. There are three broad strategies available to any firm.

1. Managing the subsidiary strictly to meet the objectives of the multinational organization. This is a power-based strategy. Host government controls would be respected but tested.

2. Managing the subsidiary to meet the objectives of both the multinational organization and the nation state. This is a participative strategy. With this strategy, the multinational would attempt to create or to fit the consultative mode of governmental control. In its purest form the multinational would participate, along with national firms,

in setting policy. In other forms, governmental objectives would be clarified through discussion and jointly implemented.

3. Selecting either a power-based or a participative strategy for different activities. This is a mixed strategy. A power strategy, for example, might be selected for profit remittances and a participative one for the transfer of technology.

Power-Based Strategies

Reliance on power is a component of any negotiation. If the multinational is staunchly to pursue its own objectives, however, the balance of power between the firm and the nation-state will be the sole determinant of the outcome. The general economic events of recent years have cycled the balance of power back toward the multinational.

With the anticipated role of multinational corporations in rekindling development, these firms are in a power position reminiscent of the 1950s and early 1960s. Foreign firms, especially those domiciled in the U.S., then controlled the main supplies of equity capital, dominated international marketing and access to advanced technology, and when dealing with Latin American authorities, could point to the attractiveness of competing investment opportunities in the Middle East, Canada, Asia, and above all in Western Europe. The preponderant control of the scarce supplies of managerial and technical talent was another element of no mean importance for the bargaining advantage held by foreign enterprises. At that time, many firms backed by such negotiating assets as these opted for defensive structuring as the principle basis of a power strategy. They relied on global sourcing as a defense against nationalization, while control of the access to global markets or the threat to withdraw were used effectively to gain local concessions.

The ability to exercise this corporate power declined in the late 1960s and 1970s as a result of several factors. Official aid had mounted, especially during the Alliance for Progress era, as an alternative source of external funding, at often concessionary interest rates, and additional loans were available on a considerable scale from the international lending institutions. During the mid-1960s, hopes were still high that regional integration schemes would enable the developing countries to do more under their own steam, and the propensity to regulate and limit the role of multinational corporations was given an intellectual rationale by the growing popularity of the *dependencia* school of thought. During the 1970s, commercial bank lending rose as well, and by that time yet another new factor had entered the picture: growing competition among multinational corporations with the rise of European-based multinationals and the spreading interest, however incipient, of Japanese firms.

Nowhere was this will to regulate multinational corporations more evident than in Latin America. By the 1970s, the impressive gains registered by Latin American higher education together with the growing number of Latin Americans who had studied abroad and/or had achieved valuable job experience as employees of foreign concerns produced a belief that the region was not nearly so dependent as it once had been on high-level labor resources from abroad—and a belief in growing regional readiness to get into industrial research and development. The combination of these factors, then, tended to shift negotiating power away from the multinational corporations.

In the 1970s, economic difficulties caused the power balance to swing back toward the multinationals. With the oil shocks and prices going up, up, and then down, the recession in the developed world, and the surge in interest rates, the borrowing that fueled the impressive real increases in gross national products turned into an oppressive burden as restructuring agreements were tied to austerity and structural adjustment. The international financial community has come to recognize the renewed importance of foreign equity capital (particularly as the awareness grows of how much capital flight has taken place) and the potential for multinationals to enhance productivity.

With the power pendulum now back more to the corporate side, the question returns as to how it should best be exercised. One fact must be kept in mind; the context is quite different in several important respects from the environment that prevailed before the mid-1960s. For all their problems, many less-developed countries, particularly those in Latin America, count on a vastly greater organizational capability than formerly, enjoy dramatically improved human resources, have evolved more sophistication and experience in supervision and control, and are keenly aware of the possibilities of playing multinational corporations against each other.

Using power to optimize the wealth of the multinational today does not mean that host laws or regulations can be ignored. Managers must optimize within these constraints, cognizant of the enhanced monitoring ability of many host governments. It does mean, however, that influence can be applied to relax those constraints where possible, and that constraints not enforced or clearly signaled may be tested to their limits. Given the nature of the regulatory interaction outlined in Part 4 of this volume and the market condition noted in Part 1, there is sufficient leeway in most host country systems and many opportunities for multinationals to enhance corporate wealth through the application of power-based strategies.

Ultimately, a power-based multinational strategy is dependent upon the ability of the multinational to apply positive or negative sanctions on the host government—a reward power or a coercive power.[4] This strategy will work only as long as the multinational can continue to deliver competitively attractive rewards or credible punishments.

For a reward strategy, the key is to convince the nation-state of the continuing value of the multinational presence. Since for specific rewards the influence tends to be short-lived, a reward strategy is necessarily based on the multinational's ability to continue to provide new rewards.

Dependency through the use of coercive power is also subject to deterioration over time. Moreover, coercive power is dangerous in that the dependent party is encouraged to disengage or to retaliate because of this negative tenor of the relationship.[5] We do not have to speculate on this, nor infer it from some theoretical basis. Historical experience during the twentieth century is replete with examples that show that if the terms of a bargain do not fall somewhere within an ill-defined but nevertheless deeply felt range of social acceptability, the situation is sure to invite, sooner or later, a reexamination of the issue of fairness and a redefinition of the terms of exchange wherever possible. The hostile climate that developed in Latin America during the 1950s and 1960s, so far as multinationals were concerned, was a clear reaction to what was widely perceived as a long history of unilateral exercise of power.

In spite of the desperate straits of so many Third World countries, power strategies cannot be expected to work the way they did years ago. Multinational power still erodes after entry. The regulatory sophistication of host government officials is, as noted, now far greater than in the past. As the field research in Korea and Mexico so clearly indicated, the concession granted today is not going to hold tomorrow and the determination to control on the part of governmental officials is still there in spite of their temporarily lessened clout.

Thus, in today's world, even though the multinational has greater power to wield, it is in all likelihood not a practical basis upon which to build long-term overall strategy. This is not to say that power will not be a key component in implementing any strategy. It will be, especially as a short-term tactic, when it can be reasonably calculated not to produce off-setting long-run costs. But a stubborn power-based determination to pursue narrow multinational objectives for the subsidiary in a host country is just not going to work as a basis for on-going operations.

Participative Strategies

In participative strategies, the objectives of the host government are identified and weighted along with the multinational objectives in the firm's decision models. Corporate objectives are not ignored, but neither are they given an absolute priority.

This strategy is based on extensive communication with host governmental officials as the ties between the multinational subsidiary and national objectives are identified and long-run versus short-run contributions ferreted out. Once national objectives are clarified, the impact of the subsidiary on the host society must be measured. A participative strategy places great demands, therefore, on the firm's information, planning, and control systems. New kinds of measures must be devised and transmitted through the firm's information networks. Host government national objectives must be considered along with the financially stated corporate objectives in the planning process.[6] Inevitably, the corporate planning horizon is lengthened.

While on the one hand this strategy places new information demands upon the corporate planning process and requires a broader monitoring of the operating environment, it also plays to the comparative advantage of the multinational corporation as an information gathering and processing system of global proportions. Much has been made in contemporary economic theory of externalities or neighborhood effects, and often enough such external economies and diseconomies are harvested willy-nilly. Yet there are certainly instances in which conscious action by some agent is required to tap into these externalities, which otherwise remain latent. A deliberate harnessing of the superior capability of the multinational corporation as an international information network is clearly one such instance. It is not at all inconceivable that in the cost-benefit calculations of a host government, the accessibility of these latent externalities (at low marginal costs, if any) may rank very nearly as valuable as the more direct effects of a foreign company's operations.

In the more distant past overtures from either party to the other to cultivate the possibilities of these neighborhood effects might well have been received with suspicion, save in exceptional instances. Increasingly, however, a combination of improved information-processing capacity (and higher information needs) on the part of host government policy organs and the circumstantially induced need of multinational corporations to look to a long-term salvaging of their sunk investments has brought government and corporate interests into a greater degree of partial convergence.

It is well to keep in mind that neighborhood effects can benefit the multinational as well as the host government. These arise from the heightened receptivity and understanding that foreign interests would enjoy in the policy circles of the host governments, thanks to the new insights the economic crunch has spawned. Inasmuch as these benefits, such as lower transaction costs in securing needed policies, and lowered risk levels can at least in principle be evaluated, they confer on the multinational corporations the reciprocal benefits for the externalities they, in turn, supply to host country authorities.

In recognizing the evolution of these more complex relationships, there is no need to fall into Pollyannaism. Frictions will surely remain, and few bargains fall into place automatically, without second thoughts by one or both of the parties to the transaction. Nevertheless, the probing of this seminar suggests that enough of a basis for mutual accommodation exists that it is well worthwhile, for all concerned, to assume the costs of negotiating with a realistic hope of striking an agreement serviceable enough to get both through the difficult years that lie ahead.

Mixed Strategies

For mixed strategies, the various activities of the firm that require interaction with the host government would be clustered at the power or at the participative ends of the spectrum. Separation of activities along the spectrum could be based on the classical game theory categories of negative sum, zero sum, or positive sum games.

For negative or zero sum games, a power strategy would be employed. In these circumstances the purpose is to minimize one's losses or to gain the maximum at the expense of the other party. While no rational player wants to participate in a negative sum game, it is sometimes impossible to avoid.

Nationalization can be an example of a negative sum game. Governmental officials can be pushed by the rush of political events to nationalize prematurely or to nationalize a facility they are unable to manage efficiently. If the compensation is inadequate, both sides can lose. Since nationalization usually concludes a relationship, the antagonism associated with the use of raw power will not endure to damage future negotiations, except insofar as it contaminates the environment within which deals are negotiated with other foreign interests.

Profit remittances are often approached as a zero sum game, particularly in times of acute foreign exchange shortage. With the debt overhang, foreign exchange has become the dominant concern of most newly industrializing countries. A zero sum view sees retained profits as saving foreign exchange for the nation-state while profits remitted as enhancing the wealth of the multinational. Seldom have host governments, particularly those in a crunch, been fully prepared to recognize that current profit repatriation may be part of the cost of securing future capital infusions. The same view would hold for importing and exporting components and finished products.

A positive sum game is one where both sides have an opportunity to gain, though in principle there is no need for the gains to be equal or even realized simultaneously. The transfer of technology, for example, can be a positive sum game. The nation-state needs the technology controlled by the multinational; the corporation also relies on its transfer for subsidiary productivity. There are differences in objectives, as indicated in the Korean field research. There may be disagreements also over the appropriateness of the technology for specific national conditions, as well as over price. However, with a mutual desire to transfer, concerns usually can be met and details worked out through negotiations which are satisficing if not maximizing.

Thus, positive sum situations are amenable to participative as opposed to power-based strategies. Power will surely be in evidence during these negotiations with the balance determined by the needs of each party, but power is not the exclusive determinant of the outcome. Since each specific negotiation is undertaken with the knowledge that other negotiations will take place subsequently, quite probably under different power relationships, participants will ordinarily be leery of making full use of the power that may be momentarily available. Hence, for positive sum games, power-based strategies should be avoided. For negative sum games, where the negotiation is the end of the game, they may be effective.

For zero sum games, the key may be to change the scope of the interaction and move the game to a positive sum. Raiffa has proposed a notion of "integrative bargaining" as a means of overcoming situations that are perceived as zero sum games.[7] After reviewing two-party/one-issue negotiations, Raiffa suggests that the domain of negotiation could be broadened.

> In the end, there may be no zone of agreement, or — because of stated commitments — there may be no way of achieving a solution even if there is one. But if the domain of negotiation is enlarged to include more complicated exchanges (for example, contingency arrangements) or to include additional issues, then a mutually profitable contract may be possible and desirable for both parties. Such bargaining — in which there are two parties and several issues to be negotiated — is called integrative bargaining. The parties are not strict competitors. It is no longer true that if one party gets more, the other necessarily has to get less: They both can get more. They can cooperate in order to enlarge the pie that they eventually will have to divide.[8]

As issues are added to a negotiation, the tradeoffs of objectives on the part of each negotiating party become more complex and, possibly, the net outcome more ambiguous. Costs may become more imponderable, while compensations are multiple — just as they often are in intra-organizational bargaining. For each party individually, the objectives as they apply to the separate issues may not even be strictly comparable, in which case the situation may afford more room for all concerned to define gains. A number of schemes have been proposed to assist the decision maker. In their conflict analysis model, Fraser and Hipel capture the players' value tradeoffs in a player "preference vector."[9] In a multinational setting, Tavis and Crum use both a subjective valuation matrix[10] and a vector of relative criterion weights in an optimization model to balance the subsidiary contribution to the multinational corporation and to the nation state.[11]

The IBM investment in Mexico is an example of integrative bargaining. The issues were the generation of foreign exchange through the export of components, ownership of the subsidiary, access to the local Mexican market, and technology. In the first place, the flexibility

of the Mexican direct investment law as exacerbated by its application
allowed this bundling of issues to occur and provided the needed flexibility for the governmental negotiators. Second, the deal worked because of the great differences in the preference vectors of the participants. The Mexican government assigned a very high utility to foreign
exchange earnings. IBM wanted one hundred percent ownership. There
were other considerations on each side of the multiple issues, as evidenced by the length (and implicit costs) of the negotiations, but
foreign exchange and ownership dominated the set. If these two issues
had been negotiated separately there would almost certainly have been
no agreement.

In most multinational — host government interactions, the factors of regulatory flexibility and difference in preference vectors can
be observed. Certainly this is the case in our Korean and Mexican field
reports. Thus, with a participative strategy, zero sum games can be
converted to positive sums. As for negative sum encounters, the key
is more how to stay away from them than how to get out of them.

It is very much to the point that all of the empirically derived
indicators in this volume suggest that the multinational manager should
pursue participative as opposed to power-based strategies wherever
possible in negotiations with host governments. Further, the increasingly rich endowment of externalities that we have posited as charac-
teristically associated with modern corporate enterprise works in the
same direction. A participative strategy is more amenable to widening the scope for the integrative bargaining and the conversion of
business-government encounters to a positive sum situation[12]

DIMENSIONS OF A PARTICIPATIVE STRATEGY

We have spent a good deal of space analyzing the environment
within which the cooperation between a multinational and host government takes place. As a firm approaches the implementation of a participative strategy within this environment, three considerations stand out.

Clarification of Signals

As demonstrated so clearly in the Korean and Mexican field interviews, the constraints on multinational activities are not nearly as
precise in the Third World as in the United States. Neither market

nor regulatory constraints are clearly signaled. Prices are not set in efficient markets; official preferences are difficult to assess. It can even
seem as if each action must be negotiated anew. In Mexico, the direct
investment law is flexible in its statement and more so in its application, and prices are themselves the subject of negotiations, although
this latter feature may vanish as Mexico implements its decision to enter
the General Agreement on Tariffs and Trade (GATT). In Korea, the
initial permission to invest, although a lengthy process, is only the
beginning of the interaction. The lack of clarity on the part of the
government bureaucrats has roots in cultural tradition; it definitely
leads to unsure relationships between the joint-venture partners. Further, as scrambled signals create uncertainty for the corporate decision maker and lead to a demand for higher yields, most decision
theorists would argue for environmental clarification as a means of narrowing the spread between reservation prices.

To our surprise, Mexican subsidiary managers seemed to get along
well in this kind of environment. They were able to cope with the uncertainty and the long delays in getting governmental response. As they
expressed it, their problem was in getting headquarters to accept the
Mexican reality, which includes, among other things, a calculated ambiguity on the part of government as a method of staving off political
criticism. In Korea, we sensed marginally greater frustration over the
mode of bureaucratic decision making. This is probably due to culturally
determined differences in negotiating techniques, a posture of cautious
reserve with foreigners as a defense, and to the complications introduced
by the existence of joint-venture intermediaries.

A successful participative strategy will require greater clarification demanded by the multinational and provided by the government.
Clarification will lead to more balanced solutions that meet the needs
of both parties which, with repeated interactions over the long run,
should identify and enhance their mutual benefits. Clarification also
means less reliance on relative power. In fact, environmental confusion enhances the effectiveness of a power-based strategy. Finally, confusion invites extortion and bribery.[13]

Information Sharing

Collaboration will also lead to information sharing. The multinational generally has access to more proprietary information than

does the nation-state. The ability of most firms to search for, collect, and process information is, as we have indicated, outstanding. The multinationals' global span puts them in close touch with sources of information not immediately available to the geographically bound nation-state, especially those in the Third World. With subsidiaries in numerous countries, multinationals have internal information on costs, productivity, and markets in these countries not available to others either within or outside of the country. For that matter, multinationals tend to access far more information of a general nature on overseas conditions, economic trends, policy trends, and even political developments than will public authorities in many of the countries in which they operate, information that may be important for improved policy formation in these states. In addition, advanced technology is predominately in private corporate hands, and multinational corporations will typically have a great deal more expertise on alternative technologies and their characteristics—over a broad range of fields in the case of conglomerates—than will most planning authorities in developing regions. Beyond information, and based on long experience in different contexts, multinationals have an impressive ability to apply knowledge to economic decision making: in feasibility studies, technology choices, forecasting, project evaluation, marketing, and financial planning.

This kind of information is especially important for governments that pursue an export strategy. In our IBM-Mexico example, the Mexican negotiators can push their exports through the IBM global linkages in return for meeting IBM's objectives of one hundred percent ownership. For the longer term, the Mexican government must also know how cost competitive their components are with alternative national locations and how those productivity levels are achieved, together with the economic trends that are needed for effective developmental planning.

There is an abundant literature indicating that bargaining outcomes are enhanced when they are based on improved information.[14] In some cases, as in United States labor negotiations, there is a legal requirement to share information.[15]

Still, there is a concern that, while sharing information might improve joint outcomes, it can lead to a shift of power away from the information provider. The potential loss of power through information sharing has been a consistent concern of multinational managers faced with a request or requirement to share information or information processing capabilities with host governments.

Information alone can be compared to the French and Raven "reward power" component of a power-based strategy where each individual source of information loses its influence once shared.[16] The power is in the promise of new data, the value of which is enhanced all the more when conditions are changing. When information is combined with expertise in its collection and application to decision making, it becomes what French and Raven refer to as "expert power."[17] Expert power has a greater initial impact than information alone and, of greater importance, is more enduring. This is particularly true where information processing capabilities are so badly needed by developmental authorities. Thus, in the French and Raven structure, when processing capability is transferred along with information as a component of a participative strategy, multinational managers need not be as concerned over the danger of an associated loss in power.

In a recent extension of their work on dependence, Bacharach and Lawler concluded that, "when bargaining relationships are ongoing, the sharing of benefits [again, such as information] can increase rather than decrease the power of the bargainer." In their general theory of bargaining power for ongoing relationships, Bacharach and Lawler conclude that the bargaining power of a party is based on the dependency of others on that party. "Within the dependency framework, the bargaining power of each party is determined on the OTHER'S dependence on them, not its own dependence on the other."[18]

Their conclusions support a strategy of collaboration. "The obvious implication of dependency theory is that to gain power you must make the other party depend on you. This is accomplished by providing benefits to the other (i.e., by giving the other something that he or she values)."[19]

Thus, Bacharach and Lawler link the provision of benefits such as information in a particular negotiation with a long-term relationship of the parties. This is the case with multinational–host government bargaining. With the exception of events such as nationalization, the relationship is an ongoing one, and the sharing of information and/or a continually improving technological capability of processing that information can increase the dependency of the host government on the multinational and thus the relative power of the firm.

In summary, the sharing of information as a component of a participative strategy is well supported in conflict and dependency theory as well as a natural outgrowth of multinational corporate collaboration with host governments.

A Proactive or Reactive Stance

A basic issue for participative strategies is whether the corporation should be proactive or reactive in its governmental interactions. A reactive policy is safe. The government takes the initiative, sets the agenda, and applies the relevant regulations. It is a matter of governmental control. The multinational enters into discussion with governmental officials when management believes the controls are unduly or unfairly constraining, discriminatory, or counter to economic development. Overall, however, the firm follows the lead of the government. From the government's point of view, a reactive policy is a negative imperative. The government can regulate to ensure that the multinational does not harm the society but is less able to force positive contributions.[20]

A proactive policy is a collaborative one in which the multinational participates in setting the agenda or takes the initiative in convincing the government of the appropriateness of some activity. Proactive policy, therefore, allows for socially beneficial actions to be initiated by the multinational and approved by the government.

At one point in our seminar discussions, participants were asked to address the question as to whether multinationals should pursue proactive or reactive policies. The reaction was that proactive stances are dangerous but necessary. There was full agreement that the most important proactivity is to set standards in local societies based on the broader, multi-country experience and organizational skills of the multinational. Common standards must be applied by the multinational in areas such as product quality and safety, conditions in the workplace, employee relations, or respect for the environment.

Proactivity in setting standards beyond the workplace met with some resistance. "The multinational is a guest in the host country. It is expert in business not necessarily in social issues." To stay out of political arenas was a unanimous constraint on proactivity. Nevertheless, aside from political and social issues on which unsolicited corporate advice might be interpreted as meddling, there is ample room for corporate managers to take the lead in alerting developmental policy makers to unnoticed issues and choices, and room also for influencing the social and political picture through the way in which the corporation conducts its own affairs.

The multinational attempts to dismantle apartheid in South Africa are an example of a corporate proactive stance, where in recent times, because of the special context, the actions of the multinationals have gone much beyond "setting a good example" and conducting one's own affairs in a defensible manner. Initially, corporations followed a participative strategy, and that approach was effective. More recently, however, the business-government interaction has moved to power-based strategies with far less effect.[21]

U.S. multinationals with investments in South Africa have struggled with apartheid for years.[22] Unequal treatment of employees according to their race is against U.S. corporate codes of conduct. Organized resistance began with the establishment of the Sullivan Principles, essentially a fair employment code, in 1978.[23]

By the early 1980s, the resistance had evolved into an odd form of business-government participation. The business community—multinational and local—quietly ignored the laws of apartheid in the workplace and the government quietly followed by repealing those laws. This process side-stepped the right-wing reaction of which the South African Botha government is so paranoid. Legal apartheid in the workplace has largely disappeared and discrimination has begun the long process of breaking down. The demands of the young but relatively sophisticated black unions have overtaken the fair-employment component of the Sullivan Principles.

Three years ago, however, the character of business resistance changed further and went well beyond the circumspect proactive policies on which our seminar participants would agree. In 1984, the Reverend Sullivan amplified his principles beyond fair employment and local community support to a requirement to "support the ending of all apartheid laws." Multinationals were directed to confront the basic tenets of apartheid, beyond the workplace. They were asked to resist the laws of the government beyond the shop floors and offices where the managers had control and beyond the local communities where they had direct contact through their employees. Multinationals were called upon to resist the heart of apartheid in influx controls, the pass laws, the group areas act, and the land act.[24] Resisting broad apartheid meant violating the firm's typical policies of political neutrality.

In other countries, multinational corporations that have become involved in political issues have paid dearly.

The strategy pursued by most firms in South Africa today is power-based, with businesses acting collectively to enhance their power. Strong public challenges to apartheid have been made by the American Chamber of Commerce, the Federal Chamber of Industries, and other business associations. This collective action, especially local business associations such as the Federal Chamber of Industries, mitigates the awkward position of the foreign investor in challenging host government laws.[25]

Confrontation and power-based strategies have not worked well although it is doubtful that participation would be effective either. For one thing, the task today is much greater as the South African government stubbornly resists the needed sharing of power with the black majority. At this point, the South African situation may be a unique set of social and political factors beyond any possible influence of multinationals.

Participation: A Demanding Strategy

Thus, in spite of the swing in the power balance toward multinational corporations and away from the nation-state associated with the current debt crisis, a return to corporate power-based strategies is not recommended. The evidence reported throughout this volume would argue against it. Moreover, the use of participative strategies when negotiations are ongoing is supported in conflict theory.

Effective participative strategies place great demands on the multinational organization. Information, planning, and control systems must be refurbished to include host government objectives and to measure the firm's full impact on host societies. In spite of the observed regulatory confusion in Korea and Mexico, a participative strategy seems possible, relying on a clarification of the regulatory environment. Information needs to be shared, and proactive risks taken.

THE ETHICAL CHALLENGE

In focusing on self-interest objectives, we have seen how experience counsels that multinationals pursue a participative strategy and seek to identify a mutuality of interests with the nation-state. This necessarily means that they must keep their own interests clearly in mind. Yet, given the extent and depth of poverty in Third World countries, the inefficient markets, the shortcomings of economic and social organizations, and the bargaining nature of the interaction between multinational corporations and host-country governments, it seems plain that there is a further, ethical dimension to the significant multinational corporate presence in the Third World. In what ways are these ethical issues and moral responsibilities different from those of the firms' operations in their parent, industrialized countries? And, what does this mean for the multinational–host government relationship?

At base, the difference lies in the large numbers of people in the Third World who are unable to represent themselves. While their needs are great, the ability of these people to do anything to meet those needs is severely limited.

A basic tenet of all major religions is to help the poor and those who cannot help themselves.[26] The ethical injunction to assist the vulnerable and the poor is also well established in the secular literature.[27] The needs of Third World peoples are stated in tables 1–3 of Part 1 of this volume. The depth and extent of their poverty is startling. Too often there is no mechanism through which the needs of these people can be represented. There are no efficient product or financial markets; they tend to be excluded from the political process; other organizations in the societies are unable or uninterested in supporting their needs. In face of such needs and the lack of self-initiated pathways out, the moral mandate for all those in a position to help is clear.

To what extent is a local multinational subsidiary in this position? In the seminar discussions, Joaquin Vallarino put it well, "You are surrounded by poverty, you cannot live with it, but you cannot solve all of it."

The multinational's potential to help depends on the linkages of the individual firm to the poor and disenfranchised. Producers of home health care products would have ties to consumers in need of those products. Manufacturing firms drawing employees from urban slums or rural poverty have close ties to employees that spread to families and communities. The same holds for local suppliers. When linkages are strong, these people are stakeholders in the firm and multinational managers have a specific responsibility to ensure that their needs are properly represented to the firm. This has been defined as a "developmental responsibility."[28] In this case, the manager takes over the role of an adoptive stakeholder. With developmental responsibility, however, the manager is on both sides of the interface, representing the disenfranchised stakeholder to the firm along with his or her responsibility to all other stakeholders — a tough spot.

The firm pursuing a participative strategy goes a long way toward meeting its developmental responsibility. Still, the exercise of developmental responsibility is beyond the optimization of long-term self-interest. The challenge is to go a step further, to seek out linkages and to represent the poor at the end of those linkages. In an experimental and sporadic fashion, managers are doing this all over the world.

Developmental responsibility applies to the operating decisions of the firm. There is another component of the call to help the needy — through personal and institutional philanthropy. While philanthropy is not the focus of developmental responsibility, multinational managers participate actively in Third World humanitarian projects, contributing their own talents and resources as well as the financial resources of the firm.

Preferential Option for the Poor

Nowhere has the call to help the poor been more clearly articulated, or the challenge more strongly put than in the Latin American Catholic Bishops' "Preferential Option for the Poor." McGrath and de Avila trace the evolution of the doctrine. In the conclusion of their paper, McGrath and de Avila pose the challenge well, "In an exaggerated, characterized sense of the word, ecclesiastics generally have the doctrine, and those working in the business community have the life."[29]

The articulation of this policy and the challenge are both helpful to the firm pursuing a participative strategy. These values will find their way into objectives in some, but not all, Latin American governments. Also, they could serve as the basis of integrated negotiations. How might a firm approach the preferential option for the poor as a component of a participative strategy and, beyond that, as an ethical responsibility?

The first step is probably to ensure that the firm is not inadvertently harming these groups. Here the notion of corporate constituents as stakeholders outlined in Part 1 would be extended to include those indirectly affected by the activities of the firm, such as the families and communities of employees and suppliers.

To ensure that activities do not injure local groups is a mandate in the First as well as the Third World. In less-developed countries, however, the multinational must be particularly alert to inadvertent damage. Cultural differences, poor local information flows, and lack of local organization may mask damaging side effects. These side effects can be social as well as physical. The rate of modernization can easily be too fast for traditional peoples; equal employment opportunities applied to women can be against some cultural norms; as people flock to multinational facilities seeking employment, communities become congested and polluted; attempts by Third World peoples to emulate First World consumption patterns can lead to unfortunate misallocation of resources.

A second approach would be a proactive stance — to transfer resources across local multinational linkages to the needy. Channeling resources to Third World poor means to reallocate resources globally from one group to another through the multinational organization. The links forged among countries by multinational corporations are links among specific stakeholders in those countries. To allocate resources to a group at one end of that linkage is to take them from the other end. Some of those groups have market power or effective organizations to enforce their demands. As noted in Part 1, the efficiency of markets and organization of stakeholders in the industrialized countries can dominate the less-powerful stakeholders in the Third World. To allocate resources to the unrepresented poor is to lean against that market and organizational power in the First World. Although multinational managers do this on a routine basis, it places them in the position of deciding what is best for someone else, and often for someone from a different culture. These kinds of non-market, organizational, or regulated tradeoffs are especially difficult decisions.[30]

For managers alert to their developmental responsibility, the well-being of the extended shareholder groups should be a component of discussions with host governments. As a component of a participative strategy, this can serve to integrate bargaining in Raiffa's model.[31] The primary responsibility to represent the disinfranchised lies with the government. In fact, however, governments are uneven in their desire or effort to represent many groups in their countries. We observed a number of differences between Korea and Mexico in this respect. When governments are not attentive to the circumstances of the unrepresented segments of their society, introducing an extended stakeholder notion is a matter of developmental responsibility beyond the firm's long-term self-interest.

The most valid long-term approach is to aid the poor in their ability to represent themselves to the firm and, for that matter, to the government. The goal is to make them effective consultative mechanisms.[32] In this way the firm works itself from an ethically based developmental responsibility to a participative strategy of optimizing its own long-term self-interest.

Universalism versus Cultural Relativism

Closely associated with the proactive/reactive component of a participative strategy is the extent to which multinational managers need to pursue a common set of policies versus modifying the activities of each subsidiary to fit local surroundings. Given the emphasis in this volume on the importance of the unique religious and legal traditions, economic structures, and national approaches to regulation, the balance clearly shifts toward modifying the activities of the firm to fit the specific circumstance of each country. Still, the participants agreed that in some areas multinationals should establish universal standards for their products and employees. There was, for instance, no dissent from the proposed uniform policy on extortion and bribery.

Is there guidance as to when to standardize and when to modify? To the extent that there are cross-cultural absolutes, shared values across cultures, universalization would seem to be appropriate. Alternatively, there is a moral principle of subsidiarity that favors delegating functions and responsibilities to the lowest organizational level possible, consistent with getting the job done.[33] Although the concept was originally framed around a notion of empowerment and to that extent validates the individual, it also recognizes the practical necessity of collective action in pursuit of group objectives. From the standpoint of our concern here, however, it is relevant to note that the decentralization implied in subsidiarity meshes neatly with the pragmatic need multinationals face to tailor operations to the widely varying conditions of the different countries in which they operate in moral no less than commercial matters.

Corporate managerial systems are based on policies that apply to the whole organization, that is, universal policies. Corporate codes of conduct are statements of where each firm places itself on the universalism-relativism spectrum. The Caterpillar Code of Conduct, for example, clearly states what Caterpillar management has defined as its absolutes. Although less specific, the Johnson & Johnson Code of Conduct is clearly a statement of that firm's ethical position.[34] Yet in Caterpillar and Johnson & Johnson as well as in other firms represented in this project, the expression of an ethically based developmental responsibility has been given different forms in different settings, in recognition that both needs and the possibilities for serving those needs vary from country to country.

Universalism and cultural relativism are not, then, competitive "goods" in the sense that it is either one or the other. Rather, as complementary insights into a complex reality, they work together to increase the effectiveness of developmental participation. And where they do tilt matters in favor of the dispossessed, the long-term interests of corporations and countries converge, for neither is well served by the kinds of upheaval that ensue when the people left out decide they want in.

Striking the Balance

The first five parts of this volume outline the structure of Third World economies, the richness of their cultures and the differences from our own, as well as the implications of these economic and social factors for the multinational corporation. The role of the multinational in these countries and how its presence is shaped by host governments has been treated conceptually and within the context of two countries, one Asian and the other from Latin America.

In this final part of the volume, we have turned to strategic options available to multinational managers, concluding that a strategy of participation with host governments is the most practical. Even though multinational corporations are presently in a position of economic power reminiscent of earlier years, host government officials are now far more capable of articulating and representing their national interest and, more importantly, more comfortable in their interactions with multinational managers as they jointly search for mutually beneficial courses of actions. While cultural differences continue to be reflected in unique institutional structures and behavior, as well as forming barriers to interpersonal communications, an improved understanding goes a long way toward mitigating their disruptive impact.

Participative strategies are demanding of the firm. Proactive risks must be taken, information needs to be shared on a continuing basis with weak guarantees (especially in the law) that it will not be used against the firm. Alternatively, in an ongoing relationship, power may well be enhanced through collaboration, and information may well increase the multinational's relative position of power.

A participative strategy leads naturally into an explicit ethical component, a component that is necessarily more a part of Third World strategies than for First World decisions. There are many unrepresented people in the Third World, some of whom are stakeholders or extended stakeholders of the firm. They can easily be run over by a maximizing manager. The constraints imposed on the corporation by markets, consumer groups, the law, local governments, or church activists, so apparent in the First World with their clearly stated and enforceable demands, are not present in less-developed countries.

The tradeoffs are powerful. If managers are to represent the poor and disenfranchised of the Third World, they must sometimes lean against the markets and powerful stakeholders of their home countries, striking a balance that, as often as not, will trade short-term earnings for longer-term viability. Still, considering the sizable portion of the world's resources contained in Third World countries and the magnitudes their economies will eventually reach, we cannot help believing that in due course a corporate policy sensitive to ethical factors will be vindicated even on a pragmatic level.

NOTES

1. See Harry Johnson, editor, *Economic Nationalism in Old and New States* (Chicago: University of Chicago Press, 1967). For a point of view that finds confirmation from a very different part of the political spectrum see James Petras, "State Capitalism and the Third World," *Development and Change* 8 (1977): pp. 1–17.

2. Of the many works exploring the political economy of import substituting industrialization, one good recent example is Dale Story, *Industry, the State and Public Policy in Mexico* (Austin, Texas: University of Texas Press, 1986) which brings up-to-

date the pioneering study by Sanford Mosk, *Industrial Revolution in Mexico* (Berkeley, Calif: University of California Press, 1950).

3. In an interpretation consistent with the cited insights of Harry Johnson and James Petras, John Johnson's classic study of the Latin American middle class — the middle sectors, as he calls them — shows that this group, which had come into its own, politically speaking, by the mid-twentieth century, hitched its fortunes to an unusual degree to policies expanding the state apparatus. Among other things, this widened the gulf between the perceived interest of the local political leadership and those of foreign enterprise. See John J. Johnson, *Political Change in Latin America: The Emergence of the Middle Sectors* (Stanford, Calif: Stanford University Press, 1958).

4. In their seminal work, "The Bases of Social Power," French and Raven identified five bases of social power. Identifying the agent exerting power as "O" and the agent being influenced as "P," they defined the bases of power as

> (1) reward power, based on P's perception that O has the ability to mediate rewards for him; (2) coercive power, based on P's perception that O has the ability to mediate punishments for him; (3) legitimate power, based on the perception by P that O has a legitimate right to prescribe behavior for him; (4) referent power, based on P's identification with O; (5) expert power, based on the perception that O has some special knowledge of expertness.

Since we are analyzing multinational strategies, we would designate the multinational as O and the host government as P. See John R. P. French, Jr., and Bertram Raven, "The Bases of Social Power" in *Studies in Social Power*, ed. Dorwin Cartwright, Research Center for Group Dynamics Institute for Social Research (Ann Arbor, Mich: University of Michigan, 1959), pp. 155–156.

5. Ibid., p. 158.

6. For a discussion of measuring host country impacts, see Lee A. Tavis and Roy L. Crum, "Performance-Based Strategies for MNC Portfolio Balancing," *Columbia Journal of World Business* 19 (no. 2, summer 1984): pp. 85–94.

7. See Howard Raiffa, *The Art and Science of Negotiation* (Cambridge, Mass.: The Belknap Press of Harvard University Press, 1982).

8. Ibid., p. 130–131.

9. Niall M. Fraser and Keith W. Hipel, *Conflict Analysis: Models and Resolutions*, ed. Andrew P. Sage, vol. 11 in North-Holland Series in System Science and Engineering (New York: Elsevier Science Publishing, 1984).

10. Tavis and Crum, "Performance-Based Strategies for MNC Portfolio Balancing."

11. Lee A. Tavis and Roy L. Crum, "Allocating Multinational Resources When Objectives Conflict" paper presented at the TIMS/ORSA Joint National Meetings, Boston, April 30, 1985.

12. This priority of participative strategies is also supported on a broader theoretical basis. John Murray addresses the distinction in negotiation theories between what he identifies as the proponents of "competitive theory" and those of "problem-solving theories,"

> Negotiation theorists appear to be deeply divided between proponents of competitive and problem-solving theories. Competitive theorists claim both a close

approximation to the actual experience of negotiators and a general superiority of outcomes. Problem-solving theorists assert the prescriptive superiority of their mode of conflict resolution in terms of outcomes, although some profess that competitive theorists describe reality more accurately. (John S. Murray, "Understanding Competing Theories of Negotiation," *Negotiation Journal* 2 [no. 2, April 1986]: p. 179)

We would expect a participative, as opposed to power-based strategy to be associated with a problem-solving as opposed to a competitive approach. Following a detailed comparison of the two competing theories (competitive versus problem-solving) in terms of recognizable patterns of negotiators, basic assumptions, and downside risk, Murray concluded:

> The analysis in this article suggests that the more proficient a negotiator becomes under either theory, the more his or her behavior will reflect the elements of problem-solving theory. The conclusion may be unavoidable that only the problem-solving theory satisfies all three quality standards for a general theory: It describes negotiation realities with reasonable accuracy, is useful in developing strategies, and provides consistent good outcomes for the competent negotiator. The recognizable competitive variant may just reflect different negotiator personality and style characteristics, and the quality and consistency of outcomes may depend partly on the relative levels of negotiator competence. (Ibid., p. 186).

13. On the other hand, confusion exists because it does serve its role in society. See William P. Glade, "Patterns of Similarity and Difference," in this volume. For an extended discussion of confusion as an active element in operating social structures and a reminder that clarification is not without its risks, see Wilbert G. Moore and Melvin M. Tumin, "Some Social Functions of Ignorance," *American Sociological Review* 14, (December 1949): pp. 787–795.

14. Two examples will make this point. Raiffa stresses the potential value of analysis in the mediation process.

> In problems of comparable complexity with a single decision maker, various analytical skills are frequently employed. But somehow when a problem has a tinge of competitiveness to it, attempts at joint analysis tend to be shunned. It is my belief that in a great number of such cases, joint gains could be realized if only the contending parties were willing to yield up enough sovereignty to allow a mediator to help them devise creative alternatives and to help them analyze their joint problem. (Raiffa, *Art and Science of Negotiation*, p. 219).

Straus supports the Raiffa conclusion, but suggests that analysis should precede the negotiation:

> Often our own self-interest would be better served by collaborating with our perceived opponent to seek a more complete understanding of the issues in the dispute *before* taking action or engaging in a contest to gain some advantage. (Donald B. Straus, "Collaborating to Understand—Without Being a 'Wimp'," *Negotiation Journal* 2 [no. 2, April 1986]: pp. 155–166)

15. The requirement evolved from the legal requirement to "bargain in good faith." The courts have interpreted this to mean that each participant must have sufficient information upon which to judge his or her position. In the United States this has generally resulted in businesses sharing information with labor. The provision of information on employees is commonplace. Sharing financial data is less common, generally required only when the business side ties its position to its costs. An intended result of the information requirement is a leveling of power between business and labor. See Leslie K. Shedlin, "Regulation and Disclosure of Economic and Financial Data and the Impact on the American System of Labor-Management Relations," *Ohio State Law Journal* 41 (1980): pp. 440–473, and Florian Bartosic and Robert C. Hartley, "The Employer's Duty To Supply Information to the Union—A Study of the Interplay of Administrative and Judicial Rationalization, *Cornell Law Review* 58 (1972–1973): pp. 23–50.

16. French and Raven, "The Bases of Social Power," pp. 156–157.

17. Ibid., pp. 163–164.

18. Samuel B. Bacharach and Edward J. Lawler, "Power Dependence and Power Paradoxes in Bargaining," *Negotiation Journal* 2 (no. 2, April 1986): p. 167.

19. Ibid., p. 168.

20. For an analysis of governments' inability to engender positive corporate contributions through regulation, see Christopher D. Stone, *Where the Law Ends: the Social Control of Corporate Behavior* (New York: Harper and Row, 1975).

21. The Notre Dame Program has been studying the South African situation as a part of its study on the multinational corporate interaction with religious activists. See Oliver F. Williams, *The Apartheid Crisis: How Can We Do Justice in a Land of Violence* (San Francisco: Harper & Row, 1986).

22. In the language of the Afrikaners who control the government of South Africa, apartheid means separate development. Through a complex set of laws, the different races—white, coloured, Asian, and black (often subcategorized by tribes)—are each directed to their separate development. As is now widely recognized, this legal separation of the races has led to legalized social injustice. Five million whites politically and economically dominate 22 million blacks and 3.5 million coloureds and Asians. While one can observe unjust treatment on the part of all governments, in the United States and elsewhere, these injustices are generally a side effect of programs directed toward some other, often socially acceptable end. With apartheid, the objective itself is unjust, yet it is codified in the law.

The result of political and legal apartheid is economic apartheid. The statistics within South Africa resemble those outlined for the four classes of countries in Part 1. The tenets of dependency theory, which is usually debated as it relates to the industrialized Northern Hemisphere and the poorer Southern, are clearly relevant within South Africa. In that country, without much doubt, the whites are rich because the blacks are poor.

23. The Reverend Leon Sullivan was a member of the General Motors board and proposed a set of principles which General Motors and other U.S. firms in South Africa were expected to follow. Though not presented as a preachment to local firms, the Sullivan Code supported indirectly the efforts of a number of South African firms that were opposing apartheid on economic grounds: namely, on the contention that

the exclusion of blacks from apprenticeships, from supervising white workers, and the reservation of jobs for whites was placing a cap on South African economic growth. While local business resistance was initiated in the English-speaking business community, it gradually spread to the smaller but growing Afrikaner-speaking business sector. This occurred without direct encouragement from U.S. corporations. Their example alone was sufficient to propel matters forward.

24. The Sullivan mandate to dismantle apartheid was supported by local events in the fall of 1984. In November, the Botha government arrested a number of black union leaders following a general strike. This led to more vocal and confrontational resistance on the part of the business community. During the resistance that followed the arrests, the business community came to the painful realization that the blacks did not see white business as their allies in the struggle. And business knows that the blacks eventually will come to power in South Africa. When that happens, they want the market system to survive.

25. In his response to the Korean and Mexican field findings, Suter makes the point that to "go it alone" is a dangerous policy for a firm in any of its host government interactions. See George Suter, "Patterns of Similarity and Differences," this volume.

26. In the Judeo-Christian tradition, there is the concept of stewardship. In Buddhism, Karuna is one of four principles of personality development. It calls for efficacious action to remove the cause of another's suffering. For Hindus, to help others is a form of prayer to God. In Islam, the idea to support the poor is one of the five pillars of the religion—the notion of Zakat, or "due to the poor."

The point here is that the moral commitment to aid the poor and helpless is a central component of all major religious traditions. Thus, a Western manager who accepts the Judeo-Christian obligation and attempts to ameliorate poverty in Third World countries, would not be imposing a principle from one culture unacceptably upon another.

27. Two recent works address this requirement particularly well. Onora O'Neill explicitly separates her arguments from religious beliefs:

> The road from theological conceptions of obligation—which at least were potentially accessible to all the faithful—to more abstract conceptions, which aspire to yet wider accessibility, has beckoned since the eighteenth century. Yet the journey still proves troublesome. (Onora O'Neill, *Faces of Hunger: An Essay on Poverty, Justice and Development* [London: Allen & Unwin, 1986] p. 130).

O'Neill develops a requirement to end hunger and poverty that applies to agencies as well as agents: "Ethical deliberations about problems of famine and hunger may then be possible not only for individual agents but for institutions and collectivities which deliberate in other ways about public affairs (p. 25). In our context, the requirement would apply to the multinational corporation as well as to the individual manager.

Robert Goodin extends the scope of the responsibility to protect the vulnerable to those "distant in time and space," beyond the duties toward our family and close associates. In his *Protecting the Vulnerable: A Reanalysis of Our Social Responsibilities* (Chicago: University of Chicago Press, 1985), he establishes two principles: the first applies to the multinational corporation, the second to the individual manager.

Principle of Group Responsibility: If A's interests are vulnerable to the actions and choices of a group of individuals, either disjunctively or conjunctively, then that group has a special responsibility to (a) organize (formally or informally) and (b) implement a scheme for coordinated action by members of the group such that A's interests will be protected as well as they can be by that group, consistently with the group's other responsibilities. (p. 136).

Second Principle of Individual Responsibility: If B is a member of a group that is responsible, under the Principle of Group Responsibility, for protecting A's interests, then B has a special responsibility:

a. to see to it, so far as he is able, that the group organizes a collective scheme of action such that it protects A's interests as well as it can, consistently with the group's other responsibilities; and

b. to discharge fully and effectively the responsibilities allocated to him under any such scheme that might be organized, insofar as doing so is consistent with his other moral responsibilities, provided the scheme protects A's interests better than none at all. (p. 139)

In considering how to balance the conflicting requirements placed by the numbers and kinds of vulnerable people to be protected, Goodin summarizes:

There I suggested that vulnerabilities and correlative responsibilities were greater the more strongly and directly they were affected by our actions and choices or the more limited their alternative sources of assistance. (p. 186)

Both Goodin and O'Neill stress the importance of changing the structures that create vulnerability and poverty. Nevertheless they each recognize the role of responding within existing structures. For a comment on the multinational manager's response within structures and changing structures, see McNeill and Tavis, "The Nature of the Debate," in the first volume, pp. 254–263.

Given the role of multinational subsidiaries in host countries and the vulnerability of local groups, those "distant in space" become much closer. The requirement to help the poor and the vulnerable would apply to the managers' individual relationships with those groups in the Third World through his or her attempts to influence the actions of their multinational organization and, finally, to influence governmental regulations and the broader structure of the international economic and political orders.

Finally, we should note that the line of reasoning pursued by both Goodin and O'Neill are based on Western thought even though both authors identify them as universal principles.

28. For a further discussion of developmental responsibility, see Lee A. Tavis, "Developmental Responsibility," in the first volume, pp. 127–139. For the ethical basis, see Lee A. Tavis, "Multinational Corporate Responsibility for Third World Development," *Review of Social Economy* 40 (no. 3, December 1982): pp. 427–437.

29. For an extended theoretical discussion of the preferential option for the poor and how it relates to the notions of the common good of earlier Catholic social doctrine, see Houck and Williams, editors, *The Common Good and U.S. Capitalism* (Washington, D.C.: University Press of America, forthcoming).

30. See Lee A. Tavis, "Stewardship Across National Borders," in *Stewardship: The Corporation and the Individual*, The ITT Key Issues Lecture Series, ed. T. R. Martin (New York: KCG Productions, Inc., 1983), pp. 74–88.

31. Raiffa, *Art and Science of Negotiation*.

32. Tavis, "Stewardship Across National Borders."

33. The principle of subsidiarity was a factor in the El Valle recommendations. See Guillermo O. Chapman "An Application of Doctrine to Economic, Political, and Social Policy," this volume.

34. Earl W. Doubet and Lee A. Tavis, "Managing the Social Response," in the first volume, pp. 157–168.

Participants

Ravi Singh Achrol	Marketing Department University of Notre Dame
Ricardo Arias	Law firm of Galindo, Arias, and López Panama, Republic of Panama
Fernando Bastos de Avila, S.J.	Latin American Episcopal Council Rio de Janeiro, Brazil
Werner Baer	Center for Latin American and Caribbean Studies Economics Department University of Illinois
Ernest J. Bartell, C.S.C.	Executive Director Helen Kellogg Institute for International Studies University of Notre Dame
Thomas A. Bausch	Dean College of Business Administration Marquette University
Ricardo Arias Calderón	President Christian Democratic Organization of the Americas Panama, Republic of Panama
Thomas P. Carney	President Metatech Corporation Northbrook, Illinois

John B. Caron

President
Caron International
Greenwich, Connecticut

Guillermo O. Chapman, Jr.

President
Investigación y Desarrollo, S.A.
Panama, Republic of Panama

John D. Collins

Partner
Peat, Marwick, Mitchell & Company
New York, New York

Roy L. Crum

Director
Center for International Economic
    and Business Studies
University of Florida
Gainesville, Florida

Paul J. Curran

Vice President and Director,
    Latin America
General Mills, Inc.
Minneapolis, Minnesota

William M. Dewey, III

Senior Vice President
Southeast Banking Corporation
Miami, Florida

Earl W. Doubet

President, Caterpillar Americas
Caterpillar Tractor Company
Peoria, Illinois

Rolando Duarte

President
Almacenes De Desarrollo
San Salvador, El Salvador

Roberto Eisenman

Chairman of the Board, La Prensa
Instituto Latino Americano De
    Estudios Avanzados
Panama, Republic of Panama

Raymundo E. Enríquez   Director
Grupo Cementos Mexicanos
Mexico City, Mexico

José Antonio Fernández-
    Arena   Centro Universitario De Ciencias
    Humanas A.C.
Mexico City, Mexico

Michael J. Francis   Chairman
Government Department
University of Notre Dame

A. Blake Friscia   Vice President, Economics Group
The Chase Manhattan Bank, N.A.
New York, New York

Yusaku Furuhashi   Ray W. and Kenneth G. Herrick
    Professor of International Business
Dean
College of Business Administration
University of Notre Dame

John J. Gilligan   Director, Institute for International
    Peace Studies
George N. Shuster University Professor
University of Notre Dame

William P. Glade   Economics Department
The University of Texas at Austin

José Luís González   Vice President and General Manager
Coca-Cola Latin America
Mexico City, Mexico

Denis A. Goulet   "Education for Justice" O'Neill Professor
University of Notre Dame

Msgr. Joseph Gremillion   Director, Institute for Pastoral and
    Social Ministry
University of Notre Dame

William J. Hank   Chairman and Chief Executive Officer
                              Moore Financial Corporation
                              Berwyn, Illinois

Chandra Hardy   Senior Economist
                              The World Bank
                              Washington, D.C.

James E. Hennessy   Executive Vice President
                              NYNEX Corporation
                              White Plains, New York

Peter J. Henriot, S.J.   Director
                              Center of Concern
                              Washington, D.C.

Theodore M. Hesburgh,   President
    C.S.C.   University of Notre Dame

John W. Houck   Management Department
                              University of Notre Dame

Federico Humbert   Chairman of the Board
                              Banco General
                              Panama, Republic of Panama

Kenneth P. Jameson   Economics Department
                              Helen Kellogg Institute for Interna-
                                  tional Studies
                              University of Notre Dame

Maryann O'Hagan Keating   Economics Department
                              Indiana University South Bend
                              South Bend, Indiana

Kwan S. Kim   Economics Department
                              Helen Kellogg Institute for Interna-
                                  tional Studies
                              University of Notre Dame

Douglas W. Kmiec	Director White Center on Law and Government University of Notre Dame
Robert F. Kohm	Manager, Environmental Planning and Analysis Aluminum Company of America Pittsburgh, Pennsylvania
Christopher M. Korth	International Business Department University of South Carolina Columbia, South Carolina
Jaime C. Laya	Managing Partner J. C. Laya & Co., Ltd. Manila, Philippines
Tang Thi Thanh Trai Le	Law School University of Notre Dame
David C. Leege	Government and International Studies Department University of Notre Dame
Ernesto G. Marcos	General Director Nacional Financiera, S.A. Mexico City, Mexico
Leonard Marks, Jr.	Independent Director and Consultant Redwood City, California
Dennis P. McCann	Religious Studies Department DePaul University Chicago, Illinois
The Most Reverend Marcos G. McGrath, C.S.C.	Archbishop of Panama Panama, Republic of Panama
Peter R. Moody	Director, Asian Studies Program Government and International Studies University of Notre Dame

John R. Mullen   Vice President of Corporate Relations
                               Johnson & Johnson
                               New Brunswick, New Jersey

John T. Noonan, Jr.   Judge, U.S. Court of Appeals for
                                  the 9th Circuit
                               School of Law, University of California
                               Berkeley, California

Joseph Ramos   Senior Economist
                               United Nations Economic Commission
                                  for Latin America
                               Santiago, Chile

Frank K. Reilly   Bernard J. Hank Professor of Business
                                  Administration
                               University of Notre Dame

Anthony G. de la Reza   President
                               Texaco Panama Inc.
                               Panama, Republic of Panama

John J. Ridyard, M.M   Executive Director, INTERAID
                               Washington, D.C.

Juan M. Rivera   Accounting Department
                               University of Notre Dame

Alfred M. Roman   Vice President
                               Johnson & Johnson International
                               New Brunswick, New Jersey

Keith S. Rosenn   Professor and Associate Dean of Law
                               University of Miami
                               Coral Gables, Florida

Norlin G. Rueschhoff   Accounting Department
                               University of Notre Dame

John T. Ryan, III	Executive Vice President Mine Safety Appliances Co. Pittsburgh, Pennsylvania
Leo V. Ryan, C.S.V.	Dean and Professor, College of Commerce DePaul University Chicago, Illinois
Michael E. Shannon	Executive Vice President Economics Lab Saint Paul, Minnesota
Henry J. Smith	Manager, Planning — Director Mobil South, Inc. New York, New York
David I. Steinberg	President Mansfield Center for Pacific Affairs San Francisco, California
Daniel J. Sullivan	Director, Manufacturing and Finance Johnson & Johnson Korea Ltd. Seoul, Korea
George Suter	Vice President Pfizer International Inc. New York, New York

Lee A. Tavis	C. R. Smith Professor of Business
	    Administration
	Director
	Program on Multinational Corporations
	    and Third World Development
	University of Notre Dame

Joaquín J. Vallarino, Jr.	President, Panamanian Chapter CICY Chairman of the Board and Chief Executive Officer

	Panama Coca-Cola Bottling Company Panama, Republic of Panama
Louis A. Van Houten	Vice President and Managing Director South and Central American Division Ralston Purina International Coral Gables, Florida
John A. Weber	Marketing Department University of Notre Dame
Mary Ann Welden	Director, Financial Controls Analysis Section General Motors Corporation Detroit, Michigan
Alexander W. Wilde	Associate Academic Director Helen Kellogg Institute for International Studies University of Notre Dame
Oliver F. Williams, C.S.C.	Management Department Associate Provost University of Notre Dame
Louis H. Wilking	Executive Assistant to Group Executive — Overseas Group General Motors Corporation Detroit, Michigan